Creating the American State

Creating the American State

*The Moral Reformers
and the
Modern Administrative World
They Made*

Richard J. Stillman II

The University of Alabama Press

Tuscaloosa and London

∞

The paper on which this book is printed
meets the minimum requirements of
American National Standard
for Information Science-Permanence of Paper
for Printed Library Materials,
ANSI Z39.48-1984.

Library of Congress Cataloging-in-Publication Data

Stillman, Richard Joseph, 1943–
    Creating the American state : the moral reformers and the modern
administrative world they made / Richard J. Stillman, II.
       p.   cm.
    Based on the 1994 Coleman B. Ransone, Jr. lecture series, given by
the author at Maxwell Air Force Base in Montgomery, Alabama, and
reworked into book form.
    Includes bibliographical references (p.   ) and index.
    ISBN 0-8173-0911-X (alk. paper)
    1. Administrative agencies—United States—History.
2. Bureaucracy—United States—History. 3. Public administration—
United States—History. 4. Social reformers—United States—
History. I. Title.
JK411.S75   1998
352.2'9'0973—dc21   97-35612
                                        CIP

British Library Cataloguing-in-Publication Data available

For my students, colleagues, and teachers of public administration, who have taught me during the past three decades more about this field than these pages can honestly acknowledge.

Where I belong and what I am living for, I first learned in the mirror of history.
—Karl Jaspers, *Origin and Goal of History*, 1953

Men can know more than their ancestors did if they start with a knowledge of what their ancestors had already learned.
—Walter Lippmann, *The Public Philosophy*, 1955

Contents

Preface

SCHOLARSHIP BUILDS ON PREVIOUS SCHOLARSHIP, and this book is no exception. In *Preface to Public Administration* (1991), I advanced the thesis that American public administration, as both a field of study and of practice, is different, very different, from that of the rest of the world, namely because we missed the European state experience. Indeed, the framers of the U.S. Constitution did just about everything to ensure that "the first new nation" would *not* create a European-style state. Instead, I argued, the United States had to "chink-in" or add an administrative state in bits and pieces more than a century afterward, in the late nineteenth and early twentieth centuries. This was well behind other industrial Western nation states, and, as a result of this unique "chinking process," our American administrative state continues to reflect an unusual cast and character compared with others.

In that book I sketched this "chinking process" only in the broadest fashion and left some questions unresolved: How did this "chinking" actually occur to form the American state? What factors caused state development to take place in this era? Who were its key leaders? Why did they devote themselves with such inordinate intensity and devotion to this particular cause of state building? How did they develop their ideas and work to put them into effect? By what means did the institutions they established shape our modern American governing processes—and our lives today?

Luckily my book's reviewers did not pick up on these general omissions or rather lack of specifics about such questions. Quite honestly, I had not figured out "answers" at the time. Nonetheless, these problems remained important issues, at least for me. Somehow and somewhere, I needed to try to sort them out, just for my own satisfaction, if nothing else.

By good fortune, I was invited to deliver the 1994 Ransone Lectures at Maxwell Air Force Base in Montgomery, Alabama, the site of the off-campus public administration doctoral program for the University of Alabama. The invitation provided a rare opportunity for me to try to deal with my "unfinished" academic interests. At least I had no more excuses *not* to try!

The Ransone Lectures are the oldest public administration and policy lecture series in the United States. For more than half a century these lectures have annually hosted some of the giants in our field: Luther Gulick, Leonard White, John Gaus, Marshall Dimock, Paul Appleby, and Dwight Waldo, to name only a few. Needless to say, I was humbled by this honor, but let me quickly add that the experience actually was far from humbling. To the contrary, it was most enjoyable, thanks to those who were my gracious hosts for five days in Montgomery, especially Professor William H. Stewart, chair of the political science department at the University of Alabama; Ms. Ann Riddle and Dr. Robert Bushon, who work in the program at Maxwell Air Force Base; and my hosts, General and Mrs. David Funk. They and the public administration students I addressed there were superb and helped immensely to sharpen my ideas through their thoughtful questions and remarks. I am also indebted to Malcolm M. MacDonald, the former director of the University of Alabama Press, and Nicole Mitchell, the current director, for encouraging me to prepare these lectures for publication, and I am grateful to the fine press staff, especially Kathy Swain, assistant managing editor, for their superb editorial efforts and to the anonymous reviewers for their helpful comments. I also thank my graduate assistant at the University of Colorado, Lynn Nestinger, for her invaluable research help and Ms. Barbra Ding for efficient typing services. In addition, the persons who provided the photographs used in this book were extremely gracious and helpful, and in that regard I want to thank especially Sylvia Goldstein from the American Society of Mechanical Engineers for her assistance.

Finally, I must concur with the accuracy of Dwight Waldo's prophetic observation after he delivered these lectures forty years ago. Permit me to repeat what he said in the preface of his now classic *Perspectives on Administration:* "To lecturers who in the future may be invited to participate in the lecture series, I wish to express regrets—my own selfish regret that I cannot be in your places. For my week . . . at the University of Alabama was one of the most pleasant experiences of my life."

Creating the American State

1

Introduction
From Whence the American State?

religion (ri lij'ən) *n.* [ME. *religioun* < OFr. or L.: OFr. *religion* < L. *religio*, reverence for the gods, holiness, in LL. (Ec.), a system of religious belief < ? *religare*, to bind back < *re-*, back + *ligare*, to bind, bind together. —*Webster's New World Dictionary*

ON FEBRUARY 14, 1996, THE Federal Aviation Administration's Aircraft Maintenance Division, known as AFS 300, filed a five-page, single-spaced memo to top FAA executives pointing out its concerns about a new start-up, low-fare airline, ValuJet. "Consideration should be given to immediately [regarding] . . . recertification of this airline," the memo began, and it went on to outline several reasons: "absence of engine field monitoring data"; "absence of adequate policies and procedures of maintenance personnel to follow"; concerns that ValuJet's "continuous airworthiness maintenance program may be inadequate"; and "critical surveillance activity [by the FAA] did not receive much attention from 1993 to 1995."[1]

Behind this ordinary bureaucratic communication was the basic message: enough problems were evident in ValuJet's current operations to warrant the airline's immediate, temporary shutdown so as to force the carrier to undergo the thorough, complicated process of relicensing.

Yet, the shutdown and relicensing review never took place. Instead, the FAA gave ValuJet a reprieve by launching a 120-day general review of its operations. That review was three-fourths completed when on May 11, 1996, only twelve minutes after takeoff, ValuJet Flight 592, on a seemingly routine trip from Miami International Airport to Atlanta, plunged into the Florida Everglades, killing all 110 passengers and crew aboard. As investigators pieced together clues from the wreckage of the McDonald Douglas DC-9, the cause of the crash increasingly pointed to dozens of used oxygen-generating chemical canisters (about the size of shaving cream cans) stowed in a cargo hold below the cockpit. They were accidentally triggered, produced intense heat, and started a fatal fire in the plane's cabin. The generators, which provide emergency oxygen for passengers by burning the chemical sodium chlorate, create high temperatures with choking smoke and poisonous cyanide gasses when activated. No fire detection or fire suppression systems were inside Flight 592 sealed cargo holds to extinguish the fire.

SabreTech, the Miami-based maintenance firm contracted by Valu-Jet, had, according to regulations, removed the spent canisters from another ValuJet MD 80 because the canisters' shelf life had expired and were told, according to company officials at ValuJet, to dispose of them. SabreTech, however, said they never received such an order, so they put the canisters into boxes that were mislabeled with the words "oxy canisters empty" and placed them aboard Flight 592 to be returned to Valu-Jet's Atlanta headquarters. ValuJet's president, Lewis Jordan, blamed SabreTech for mislabeling the canisters and for not packing them properly with safety caps, but the contractor said it was ValuJet's responsibility for loading them onto their own plane.

Was it the carrier's or the contractor's mistake that resulted in the crash of Flight 592? What caused the outdated oxygen canisters to be stowed under the cockpit of Flight 592? Who was at fault?

Certainly the immediate blame can be pinned on the combination of errors by the carrier and the contractor. In the broader sense, however, the Federal Aviation Administration, the key federal regulatory watchdog over airline safety, and its inspection system had failed to function properly, leading to 110 deaths in the hot, swampy Florida Everglades. For years, the National Transportation Safety Board had urged the FAA to require installation of smoke- and fire-detection devices in jet-cargo compartments. "This accident was unnecessary, absolutely unnecessary," said Bernard Loeb, chief of the NTSB's accident investigations. Not only had the FAA failed to act on the NTSB recommendations and on the February 14 memo from its own AFS 300, but also it had assigned only four of its twenty-six hundred inspectors to check on ValuJet's operations, although this carrier statistically had one of the worst safety records in commercial aviation. FAA line inspectors further claimed that they not only were overworked because of lack of personnel but also were given inadequate training, funding, and technology, even such basic items as computers, to perform their oversight roles properly. Worse, the FAA's multipurpose mandates, which included promoting *both* airline travel and aircraft safety, were often at odds, which, some suggest, accounted for lax enforcement.

Even more critical, the growth of "outsourcing," or the use of many contractors and subcontractors at various airports to service and maintain planes, during the 1990s led to increasingly distant, and often disconnected, complex chains of vendors, such as SabreTech, being responsible for vital components of airline operations. Before the 1978 federal deregulation of the airline industry, most of this work was accomplished in-house, in turn making it relatively straightforward for FAA regulators to examine the internal records and operating aircraft to determine whether safety procedures were followed. Today, by contrast, competitive pressures of the marketplace to save money and to make the bottom line look good in quarterly reports to shareholders force most airlines, such as ValuJet, to farm out more and more critical maintenance services to various low-bid contractors such as SabreTech. As outsourcing grows, knowing who is in charge and what is being done or not done—such as the details of returning oxygen canisters—becomes increasingly complicated, even problematic. The FAA's inspection system that was designed in the preparation era, some experts argue, simply failed to keep pace with the new realities of outsourcing, especially by start-up firms such as ValuJet.

As the ValuJet story demonstrates so vividly, our administrative state is very much a central factor, perhaps *the* central factor, influencing what happens in contemporary life. Our nation, its citizens, and even our future personal survival, just as it was for those aboard Flight 592, are dependent on vast, interconnecting webs of complicated administrative systems, regulatory procedures, and nameless bureaucrats. From the routine daily mail delivery to our homes to the exploration by NASA satellites into the far-flung reaches of outer space, and, yes, for those who fly on planes—for better or worse or better *and* worse—nearly every aspect of modern life is touched by the often invisible activities of public administration. Indeed, it is difficult to imagine how modern civilization would exist without the immense, complicated services and goods provided by the administrative state. This administrative state and the public administrators who work for it may be vehemently unwanted and unloved by Americans today, but to be certain, they are also essential for making modern civilization a reality. In the words of Dwight Waldo, "Public administration exists massively, centrally, and often decisively for our individual and collective lives."[2]

Ironically, while the ValuJet story is just one more poignant reminder of how all our lives are dependent on and intertwined with the workings of unseen administrative systems and what immense tragedy can result from their breakdown, a positive side to this story exists. The American administrative state in recent years has been asked to perform more and better services for the public, and many of its achievements have been remarkable by almost any standard. I will cite just a few examples: the 1991 Desert Storm Operation proved to be one of the most successful military campaigns in American history, carried out with the loss of few American lives, conducted in the glare of round-the-clock media attention, and waged halfway around the globe; the air we breathe and water we drink are by most measures cleaner today than a decade ago; the Social Security system operates smoothly and efficiently for the most part, especially given that in scale it is the largest income redistribution system in the world; significant medical and health research breakthroughs are routinely reported by the National Institutes of Health; and the government's responses to the Los Angeles earthquake of January 17, 1994, the 1995 Oklahoma City bombing, and even the ValuJet crash were swift and sympathetic.

In addition, these events do not begin to describe the routine work of the modern American administrative state such as educating forty-three million public school children from the most diverse cultural backgrounds in the world every year; maintaining 300,456 miles of interstate highways and another 4 million miles of public roads; running 172 veterans hospitals with nearly one million patients; awarding 4 percent of the U.S. population welfare assistance; handling 166 billion letters and packages annually; registering and licensing fourteen million autos; funding one-third of all the scientific research conducted in the United States; and much more.

Whether this work is conducted efficiently, wisely, or well—or even whether it should be performed at all—is open to argument. My point is, though, that by any standard, the modern American administrative state accomplishes a great deal every day for society, sometimes truly amazing accomplishments like no others in the world, within a culture where the depth and dimensions of hostility it faces are also without comparison. Yet, the ValuJet story also vividly describes the downside: namely, Americans live and work, indeed survive or at times die, because of the functions—or failings—of an administrative state. It is basic to making modern society tick—or not! Ironically, even though the administrative state may well be central to contemporary American life, no precise definition of it exists, at least none on which scholars today agree.

Seven Features of the Administrative State: A Working Definition

Despite the absence of any single definition of "administrative state," the ValuJet story does highlight seven of its essential features: (1)

unelected experts, such as the FAA officials, who (2) operate within formal hierarchical organizations, such as the organization of the FAA, which (3) use impersonal rules, procedures, and informal methods, such as airline relicensing, on the basis of formal legal authority vested by legislative, judicial, or executive action or, in this case, federal laws, to (4) carry out important government functions, such as airline industry regulation, to protect the health, safety, and general well-being of the public or, in that instance, specifically airline passengers (5) often through formal and informal networks of nonprofit or for-profit firms such as SabreTech, or even other governmental entities, such as the NTSB; to perform these activities, government agencies and public officials such as those at the FAA require (6) "soft" intangible technologies, such as managerial competency, methods of rational analysis, and even secrecy and ethical values of fairness and neutrality, as well as (7) applied "hard" or tangible technologies such as computers, records, and budgets to fulfill their legal mandates and public responsibilities.[3]

Of course, at times, as the ValuJet story also reveals so vividly, managerial competency, record keeping, rational analysis, ethical conduct, and even funding and other "hard" or "soft" technologies can fall far short of minimal requirements necessary to carry out agency activities. The mere existence of agencies and their activities, in other words, does not necessarily insure their sufficiency to tackle the tasks assigned. The effectiveness of the administrative state depends on the specific situation, the people, the people's support, and the kind of work involved. Nonetheless, these aforementioned seven features comprise a significant share of its key attributes: unelected officials, hierarchical organizations, application of rules and procedures, based on law, for carrying out government functions, often through administrative networks of providers, to promote the public welfare, using a variety of "soft" and "hard" tools.

As a means of gaining a clearer understanding of the administrative state and its current activities, we must answer the following: From where did this administrative state, which is so vital to our lives and all-encompassing within our society, come? What were its origins? What were its historic sources? The answers will provide a basis for helping us gain a better understanding of its decisive role in modern American life.

Perspectives on the Administrative State

Today, popular discussions, particularly political rhetoric, frequently choose to ignore the administrative state. Candidates on the stump "damn the bureaucracy" for short-run political advantages without connecting their rhetoric to reality, namely, how do we then operate modern society without public administrators? Even people who should know better avoid the seemingly obvious, namely, the American administrative state. Authors of basic American government textbooks frequently give the major share of coverage to issues of the presidency, Congress, and the judiciary, with scant attention to public administration or the administrative state. Beverly A. Cigler and Heidi L. Neiswender, after a careful content analysis of eighteen current American government texts used at the college level, concluded, "Significant omissions or inaccurate information may contribute to a general public uninformed about the role of the public service in governance."[4] Using statistics they cite that less than 6 percent of a typical text contains *any* references to administrative topics.

If popular discussions and current textbooks tend to misinform, how do serious scholars in recent years deal with the American state and its sources of development and growth in modern society? What "answers" have been put forward by major theorists or schools of theorists about the origins of the American state? What are their perspectives and their assumptions? What are the roots and motivations for the rise of the administrative state, according to modern scholarship? In brief, what created the administrative state in its present form that governs the United States and so decidedly influences our public and personal lives? Or, from whence the American state?

To be sure, there are no settled answers, yet the last decade or two of the twentieth century has witnessed an amazing outpouring of ideas purporting to examine, wholly or in part, this issue. Following are some thumbnail sketches of how leading contemporary scholars from three major schools view the sources of the American state and its development. Certainly these sketches are by no means meant to be comprehensive, but rather a sampling of recent historic perspectives.

The Bring-the-State-Back-In Movement

Of all contemporary scholarship, the "Bring the State Back In" movement,[5] made up largely of political scientists and political sociologists, stimulated the most intensive and largest volume of research today on such issues as, Where did the state come from? What were its origins? How did it grow and evolve into the dominant—and disliked—structures we confront in the 1990s? Why does it exist in its present form, and how do American institutions compare and contrast with various nations? Generally the thrust of these studies during the last decade or so has been to move the social sciences in general away from the behavioralist "society-centered" to "state-centered" theories of political development. So pervasive has been the influence of these return-to-state scholars that one leading student of political interest groups wrote, "In the 1990s, we are all neo-institutionalists."[6] The "state" now matters; maybe it is the only common theme that matters throughout social science, thanks largely to the work of these authors.

Yet, ironically, by the late 1990s, despite the flurry of research interest in institutional development, the "Bring the State Back In" movement shows little consensus about the origins of the American state, let alone solutions to the broader intellectual issues of the role and operation of modern state today. Even what the state is and how it should be defined remain problematic within these writings. For example, three of the most impressive books associated with this movement during the last decade or so come to different conclusions about the beginnings of the American state. All three accept the state as central to shaping what happens in modern society and reject the notion that it (the developed modern American state) began with the ratification of the American Constitution, but they pinpoint its origins differently. Richard F. Bensel's *Yankee Leviathan: The Origins of Central State Authority in America, 1859–1877* (1990)[7] argues that the Civil War was the most important state-making event in American history. The Civil War not only prevented the southern secession, but also, of more importance, stimulated the growth of the American national government by creating market-oriented economic policies for the federal government to direct. That in turn, argues Bensel, strengthened a financial class in the North, who gained control of the federal government and who subsequently opposed the Republican-led Reconstruction in the South. To further their own economic plans, they eventually not only halted Reconstruction but also created political and economic coalitions that served to limit the subsequent expansion of the American welfare state until the post–World War II era.

This economic, class-based interpretation of American state formation, centering around a single event, the Civil War, stands in marked contrast to Stephen Skowronek's *Building a New American State: The Expansion of National Administrative Capacities, 1877–1920* (1982),[8] which views the American state as a product of the late nineteenth and early twentieth centuries or, more precisely as the book's subtitle indicates, of the years between 1877 and 1920. The story begins in 1877 with a highly developed party democracy and ends in 1920 with a strong national central authority in place as a result of a transformation that "occurred through political struggles rooted in and mediated by pre-established institutional arrangements."[9] This detailed Namier-like, historical-political analysis describes a two-stage institutional evolution, first by "patching" and then by "reconstituting" institutional arrangements during this forty-three-year period. For Skowronek, state building was a result of the convergence of tensions provoked by crisis, class conflict, and complexity (i.e., the dislocations caused by industry) and mediated by existing institutions and electoral politics. Crises in this era revealed weaknesses in the state order that were first patched up and later reconstituted permanently. In the words of the author: "The new American State emerged with a powerful administrative apparatus but authoritarian controls over its powers were locked in a constitutional stalemate . . . a hapless administrative giant, a state that could spawn bureaucratic goods and services but that defied authoritative control and direction."[10]

Theda Skocpol's *Protecting Soldiers and Mothers: The Political Origins of Social Policy in the United States* (1992),[11] a third significant contribution from the "return to state" literature, dates the American state from the growth of generous veterans benefits after the Civil War, as well as the "social spending, labor regulations and health education to help American mothers and children."[12] Political support was garnered through extensive networks of women's federations, clubs, and volunteers, and, as a result, the United States "would have fashioned an internationally distinctive maternalist welfare state."[13] Largely administered by female professionals, this emerging state system between 1910 and 1920 attempted to ensure public protection for mothers and children regardless of their ties to male wage earners. The nascent maternal welfare state, according to Skocpol, who draws on extensive comparative and gender studies to support her thesis, "might have gradually extended to all families," but "it was clipped off by Supreme Court and Congress during the 1920s."[14] By contrast, the New Deal established the Social Security Act of 1935, with a male-dominated agency to administer compulsory insurance programs in which the requirements of families, women, and children "were subordinated and often pushed to the side."[15]

These all-too-brief sketches of the central themes of three recent major "bring back the state" pieces of scholarship perhaps do not do adequate justice to their immensely rich and complicated arguments. Nevertheless, despite their intensive research and pervasive intellectual impacts overall on the social sciences, these works do not by any means reach a common consensus on the origins of the American state, how it evolved, when it began, or even what "it" is or why it exists today in the form it does and now presents so many profoundly challenging dilemmas. Especially problematical in these writings, collectively and individually, is the omission of the *administrative* foundations of the modern American state. Budgeting, management, organizational issues—the basics of the modern administrative state—are, for the most part, given scant attention, or are overlooked entirely, by scholars associated with "return-to-state" thinking. Nor do ideas *and ideals* that framed the founding of the administrative state matter much, or at all, to these authors.

The Internationalists

From the earliest theorists of international relations such as Aquinas, Machiavelli, Bodin, Grotius, Hobbes, Leibniz, Hegel, Rousseau, Bentham, and Marx to contemporary twentieth-century theorists such as Lenin, Morgenthau, Carr, Waltz, Kennan, Niebuhr, Kissinger, and Fukuyama, "state," in the words of one scholar of this subject, has been "the primary object of discussion."[16] Unlike American social sciences in general that abandoned state-centered approaches in the postwar era, international relations theorists, especially those associated with realist and neo-realist schools of international relations scholarship, never lost sight of the state and its interrelationships as integral to their analyses of world affairs. Global, post–cold war, geo-strategic issues involving nationalism, ethnic tensions, power vacuums, territorial expansion, terrorism, nuclear threats, alliance management, and national security affairs in the 1990s, in one way or another, relate to the problems of the state, including its definition, goal(s), role(s), and influence. Hardly a serious book on international affairs finds its way into print today without some mention of state issues (although few agree precisely on what the content of "state" actually includes, let alone whether even such a thing as the "administrative state" exists).

One example of a treatise from recent international relations scholarship pertaining to American state development is Bruce D. Porter's *War and the Rise of the State: The Military Foundations of Modern Politics* (1994).[17] His sweeping five-hundred-year history of war in the West begins by flatly asserting that "states make war, but war makes states."[18] Throughout his analysis, Porter emphasizes how the two—states and war—have been *and* are interdependent. Even for the United States, a nation that scholars often cite as an exception to that thesis, Porter concludes: "Throughout the history of the United States, war has been the primary impetus behind the growth and development of the central state. It has been the lever by which presidents and other national officials have bolstered the power of the state in the face of tenacious popular resistance. It has been a wellspring of American nationalism and a spur to political and social change. . . . It is difficult to deny that its [American] government was reared during war."[19]

Given the waning of external threats in the post–cold war era, Porter raises some provocative questions about the future of the American state: "If war built the American State, is it possible that the absence of war will unleash forces that could threaten to unravel it? The end of the Cold War, after all, places the United States in the same position it faced after the war of 1812, the War with Mexico, the Civil War, and World War I. Suddenly, it has no serious enemies and faces no military threat from abroad. In similar situations in the past, American unity has deteriorated and the power of the state waned. Will the same happen again?"[20]

Like Porter, other international relations scholars, such as Kenneth Waltz,[21] conceive of the state as the principal unit of analysis in international affairs and more often than not define the state and its role in society from the standpoint of realistic "power relationships." These scholars challenge readers by their bold, provocative conclusions. Their globalist points of view, however, often tend to overlook the fine points of state development, particularly in the American context, which was and is unique in important ways compared with Western Europe.

Was the American state primarily a product of war, as Porter argues? Possibly war contributed to state growth at the federal level in this century, but did it stimulate state formation at local levels as well? And what accounts for many scholars of this topic dating its origins from the late nineteenth and early twentieth centuries, well before the United States assumed the role of global leadership after World War II? Did the elements of the administrative state (i.e., budgets, civil service, planning, and the like) emerge from war? Or, in fact, were their beginnings a product of relatively peaceful eras in the late nineteenth and early twentieth centuries (for example, 1883 marks the passage of the Civil Service Act)? Certainly European states were products of warfare, often bloody warfare, but was war the most significant factor in form-

ing the American state? Or were other more important causalities at
work?

Perspectives from Public Administration

Academic experts in public administration have also been busy during the last decade or so examining the roots of the administrative state,
especially as related to its legitimacy within American government.
More than any other scholarly work in recent years within public administration, John Rohr's *To Run a Constitution: The Legitimacy of the Administrative State* (1986) is the most serious and thorough attempt to uncover the origins and development of the modern administrative state.
The U.S. Constitution, Rohr finds, is the principal source of state legitimacy. His argument thus begins by grounding the American state in
a constitution's framework, and his thesis is elaborate and carefully
crafted. In part one, Rohr emphasizes that although the framers constructed the Constitution on the principle of separation of powers, the
U.S. Senate was established not merely as the upper house of the legislature but also as an institution that combined all three powers: executive, legislative, and judicial. Rohr reasons that the founders' conception of the Senate has striking similarities to the role of the higher civil
service today. As he writes, "The closest approximation to such an institution (the U.S. Senate) today is the career civil service, especially its
higher reaches."[22] Just as the Senate serves to act as a balance wheel for
overcoming some of the defects in the U.S. Constitution imposed by the
separation of powers, so too "the administrative state heals important
defects in the Constitution."[23] One key defect Rohr sees is the inade-
quacy of representation. The number of people that the Constitution
allocates to the House and Senate are too few to govern a large, complex
society. "Thus the administrative state has the capacity to increase and
multiply public spiritedness, and thereby infuse the regime with active citizens."[24] He sees the Constitution legitimizing the administrative institutions as a means of "releasing the energies of high civic purpose latent in Public Administration."[25]

Rohr carries his argument further in part two, "Founding the Administrative State in Word, 1887–1900." He shows how Woodrow Wilson's and Frank Goodnow's writings, although credited as being some
of the earliest works, were decidedly contradictory to "the principles of
the Founding of the Republic."[26] Whereas they were "elegant, cogent
and logical, they did not conform to constitutional structures and in-

deed they were fundamentally at odds with the founding of the Republic,"[27] writes Rohr. Instead, as described in part three, "Founding the Administrative State in Deed: The New Deal," Rohr sees the American administrative state's origins as actually rooted in the New Deal era. "The New Dealers," Rohr says, "perhaps more from necessity than from conviction, worked within Publius's structure to bring about changes that were intended to safeguard the purpose of the Constitution in an industrial age."[28] New Dealers, in Rohr's view, were committed to creating an administrative state in order to adapt the United States to the harsh modern economic realities imposed by the Great Depression in the 1930s by establishing a strong centralized national government, making the federal government supreme over the economy, and making the executive supreme over the Congress and courts. They also sought to curb the excesses of the administrative state by means of their unswerving commitment to protecting individual rights. The New Dealers thus were "founders in deed" because they made "a serious effort to square their administrative innovation with the founding principles of the Republic."[29]

Rohr's view of the origins of the administrative state as rooted within the American Constitution is ambitious in the depth of its scope and detailed arguments, although his constitutional perspective is not without problems. First, the Constitution, as Rohr readily admits at the outset, says nothing about civil service, budgets, the executive branch, or anything that smacks of public administration. Although some, such as Hamilton, valued good administration, collectively the founders forged a Constitution that did everything to *prevent* creating a European-style state through erecting such roadblocks to state-building as federalism, separation of powers, periodic elections, and the like. In reality, the entire thrust of the Constitution was to reject, or certainly thwart, the development of an administrative state.

Moreover, Rohr's argument seems to try too hard to read back into the constitutional debates more than what actually was agreed on or what Madison called these "tedious and reiterated" debates that "did not in fact lead to any coherent or conclusive theory" of administrative power.[30] Harvey C. Mansfield, Jr., recently characterized the founders' perspective as "the ambivalence of executive power."[31] Or, as Jack N. Rakove points out, "The first sentence of Article II of the Constitution did little to dissolve this ambiguity when it boldly stated that 'the executive power shall be vested in the president of the United States of America' without explaining what executive power is."[32] One is especially hard-pressed to find a significant (or minor) commitment by any of the framers to vest broad administrative authority in the higher civil service modeled along the lines of the U.S. Senate, as Rohr suggests.

Nevertheless, can the New Deal be credited with origins "in deed" of the modern administrative state? Rohr certainly is correct that the New Dealers went to great lengths to expand administrative activities and centralized authority of the national government in many sectors, but most historians and political scientists, such as Bensel, Skowronek, and Skocpol, as cited previously, look to earlier eras of American history, to roughly the late nineteenth and early twentieth centuries, for the sources of the administrative state's development in the United States. That period saw the establishment of the first national regulatory commission, modern executive budget, civil service system, and so forth. In short, the New Dealers may have refined and advanced administrative innovation, but they hardly can claim to be its originators or its founders "in deed."

Much like Rohr's work, a second important scholarly book published in public administration, James Stever's *The End of Public Administration: Problems of the Profession in the Post-Progressive Era* (1988), addresses the legitimacy problem of the modern administrative state but suggests a different source of its origins. His text begins not with the Constitution but with what he views as a fundamental "contradiction within American Culture," namely, a fear of bureaucracy on the one hand and "an affinity for the programs and goals that generate increasing amounts of public administration" on the other.[33] At the outset Stever outlines three alternatives to resolve this contradiction: (1) allow the contradiction to continue, which he believes would be "risky"; (2) reduce the dependency on government, which Stever says is "infeasible and somewhat romantic"; and (3) "embark on the arduous task of enhancing the status of public administration in American Culture," which Stever views as the best alternative.[34]

Essentially this last alternative is the objective of the book, that is, to propose a strategy for positively legitimizing public administration by developing it as "a polity profession." Stever sees that "visible, legible authority is vital for positive legitimation of public administration."[35] Without going into the details of his ambitious agenda, we can say that the bulk of his book is a historical review of how we got to where we are. For Stever, the modern administrative state is equated with the rise of professionalism before the dawn of the twentieth century. As he argues, "The roots of America's professional organizations extend back to a restless middle class in the latter part of the nineteenth century."[36] The striving for status, combined with cultivating the "idea that knowledge bestowed or signified special powers beyond those of a commoner," significantly influenced the origins and growth of an administrative state in the United States. Stever, nonetheless, identifies "three contributing failures" in the twentieth century that fostered the administrative state's current legitimacy problems. One failure occurred after World War One, an era Stever labels the "post-progressive era," in which public administration greatly expanded in size and complexity, with the resulting loss of integrity and increased intellectual fragmentation. A second failure involved the rise during this period of entrepreneurial values that substituted for neutral expertise and that led to the infiltration of "alien business values into the public sector." A third was the inability of public administration and the administrative state to develop institutional integrity and institutional vitality, which left the public sector to become diffuse, sprawling, and blurred with private sector roles.[37]

Stever's work presents a stimulating argument that addresses, like John Rohr's book, a central—perhaps *the* central—dilemma for the field today, namely, its very legitimacy, although he parts company with Rohr, who finds the U.S. Constitution as the origin and "answer" to the legitimacy issue. For Stever, the background of the administrative state is rooted in the rise of professionalism as well as in its historic failures in this century to find legitimacy.

Nonetheless, Stever's thesis that interprets the origins of the administrative state from a professionalism perspective—or lack thereof—is open to question. Can, for example, professional organizations, as well as the professionals who inhabit their ranks, their rise, and their influence, be viewed as the primary source of the founding of the modern administrative state in the United States? To be sure, they are a part, perhaps a big part, but can—should?—they be seen as the whole? Can professionalization, which is a highly nebulous and contentious construct (one on which few scholars can even agree regarding what "it" is), become the model for comprehending the origins, development—and even the future—of the entire state enterprise?

Camilla Stivers's *Gender Images in Public Administration: Legitimacy and the Administrative State* (1993) is a third important book published recently in public administration literature addressing the issue of the origins and legitimacy of the administrative state. It ranks with Rohr's and Stever's in its scholarly significance for the field. Stivers's focus, in contrast to Rohr's constitutionalism and Stever's professionalism, draws explicitly on gender theories to examine the origins and critical dilemmas of, as its subtitle indicates, "legitimacy and the administrative state." Her thesis is as follows: "The images of expertise, leadership and virtue that mark the defense of administrative power contain dilemmas of gender. They not only have masculine power features but help to keep in place or bestow political and economic privilege on the bearers of culturally masculine qualities at the expense of those who display culturally feminine ones. . . . The characteristic of masculinity of public administration is systemic: it contributes and sustains power relationships in society."[38]

The heart of Stivers's book is a careful examination of the ideas and ideals that undergird the intellectual development of the modern administrative state, specifically expertise, leadership, and virtue, and she concludes that the very language the field used to found the administrative state was "gender-bound," or rather bound to one gender, implicitly or explicitly excluding another. Therefore, a new legitimacy for the administrative state, she contends, can only be discovered via creating a more inclusive language and involvement for many, specifically women and minorities, within public administration. As she writes, "If we keep seeing Public Administration as genderless, we risk either continuing masculinization of administration or marginalizing 'others.' "[39]

The solution that Stivers presses for is thus found through broadening the inclusiveness of the field to restore its legitimacy. Nonetheless, are the origins of the administrative state as well as its present legitimacy flawed because of problems primarily stemming from gender or inclusivity? Or are there other aspects of this problem that transcend that issue, such as moral, ethical, and value concerns? Or are there dimensions of historical, legal, social, institutional, and even cultural realities that move well beyond the dilemmas of gender and inclusiveness? Does feminist theory, though impressively pointing up a serious flaw in the past and present inequities of representation within the administrative state, miss the wider scope of the historic formation of the American state because of various sociopolitical and economic complexities?

Sources of the Modern American State: A Hall of Mirrors?

Certainly the aforementioned three clusters of scholars from the "return to state," internationalist, and public administration schools of thought who write about the origins of the American state do not exhaust the variety of ideas currently attempting to address—and debate—this issue. Others could be added from management theory, political history, economics, and even ethics and theology. Yet, the books discussed in this chapter represent a good sampling of some of the more prominent recent scholarly studies. What emerges from these possibly far-too-brief sketches is an absence of an agreed consensus about the birth of the modern American state: Where did it came from? What were its origins and evolution within the context of American history? What were the causes for its creation? What is "it"?

It is ironic that such an important subject, namely, from whence the American state, should find so little agreement among experts today. The present plethora of ideas offered by leading scholars or schools of theorists to answer such questions indeed may strike one as akin to a hall of mirrors in a funhouse where images are reflected and refracted in so many different distorting angles that one is not sure what the "correct" historic perspective is. "It"—the source of the American state—is seen in many ways, from many perspectives: An economic class struggle? A political problem? Forged by war? A constitutional issue? A professional question? Or a gender dilemma? In the case of American state formation, different disciplinary perspectives seem only to add up to confusing, contradictory portraits of the state and its origins, role, purpose, and influence in the United States today. Each perspective seems to read "the problem" from a unique vantage point, with different normative and historic starting points and value prescriptions, sharing little common ground with each other, leaving readers in a quandary over what is the answer or even what is the problem— or worse, how do you begin to describe what the problem is?

Looking Backward at Individual Biographies as a Means of Seeing Forward?

The past may well be the best route for Americans to begin to see their way forward to understanding this "problem" and perhaps even offering some "answers" to it. By gaining a better comprehension of the origins of the administrative state, possibly we can better define it and its role in modern society today. How did the state originate? Who were its key founders? What were their motivations? Visions? How did they conceive of their ideas and bring them into fruition? What factors served to advance their agendas? How did their ideas and ideals ultimately evolve into our present complex administrative state that governs the United States today—and in turn, engenders so much deep-seated public scorn and hostility?

American history places a major emphasis on the study of great political leaders from the founding fathers onward, often bordering on hero worship, but frequently forgets, or neglects entirely, those who were instrumental in developing the modern American state. Perhaps our selective national memory of the past is symbolic only of our contemporary popular hostility toward the administrative state. We prefer to overlook what we dislike. Whatever the cause of our collective amnesia, the following chapters are meant, in part, to remedy this apparent historical imbalance and offer better, more realistic perspectives on the sources of the rise of the modern state and its role in contemporary American society.

Each of the following chapters presents critical biographical portraits of individuals whom I consider to be among the leading founders of the twentieth-century American administrative state. Admittedly, the choices for biographical examination were based on the assumption that the modern American state is an *administrative* state. Hence, I selected those state founders who most decisively influenced the formation of the seven features of the modern administrative state cited earlier in this chapter. Sometimes the creation of these essential administrative elements are viewed by scholars as caused from a single event, a collective product of several minds, broad impersonal forces of history, or multiple socioeconomic-political factors, but in fact, a careful look at history reveals that indeed institutional innovations, like many technological inventions, are the handiwork of relatively few individuals who "invented" these administrative elements and whose creative achievements have been largely neglected by history.

Who were the men and women whose ideas and work served to originate and develop so significantly the various features of the administrative state? The next chapter, for example, reviews the achievements of George William Curtis (1824–1892). Curtis was one of the most important individuals for putting into practice the merit system as a basis for creating the modern civil service system. This system is the main vehicle today that recruits, selects, promotes, and sustains various unelected experts to run the modern American state. The next biography, in chapter 3, analyzes the work of Charles Francis Adams, Jr. (1835–1915). He was chiefly responsible for initiating the first regulatory agency in the United States, a formal government organization charged with critical legal authority to protect public health, safety, and welfare. The third biography, in chapter 4, focuses on Emory Upton, (1839–1881). A person unknown to most contemporary historians, political scientists, and public administration scholars, Upton was in fact a key state founder who introduced public professionalism and its various institutional practices, ideas, and ethical elements into American government for the first time. In chapter 5, we witness the life and work of a remarkable woman, Jane Addams (1860–1935). Addams was one of America's great social welfare reformers, and who, as a by-product of her welfare innovations, invented formal and informal networks of government officials and private citizens that became important governing mechanisms for setting policies and carrying them out in various government arenas. Frederick W. Taylor (1856–1915) is the subject of the next biography in chapter 6. As the father of scientific management, Taylor, more than any other individual, can be credited with inventing the "hard" and "soft" technologies that run the modern administrative state. In chapter 7, Richard S. Childs (1882–1978) is described as a person who developed key institutional state structures and successfully introduced grassroots administrative reforms throughout the United States. Chapter 8, the last featured biography, that of Louis Brownlow (1879–1963), tells the story of how Brownlow brought administrative state reforms to the top levels of government, the executive office of the president. Individually and collectively, these "inventors" fashioned and implemented many, though certainly not all, of the vital elements that add up today to what we know as the modern administrative state.[40]

The following chapters, it must be quickly added, however, are by no means meant to be complete or definitive biographies of the American state founders. Rather, they only describe and analyze aspects of their lives that chiefly touch on their intellectual and political leadership and their motivations and achievements that significantly contributed to the development of the modern state. Certainly some of their handiwork was not entirely their own doing. They at times relied on others, or worked with and through others, to achieve their purposes, and even then, frequently what they thought they had accomplished, or in some cases believed they *failed* to achieve, in fact turned into something different over the course of events that followed. Administrative ideas and institutional inventions have a strange habit of working themselves out in unusual ways in history, even surprising their inventors (who in some cases did not even realize that they were in fact administrative state inventors—nor would even have *wanted* such a label attached to themselves).

The focus of this book will therefore be on those few key leaders and particularly on the seminal ideas and the strategies they used to implement those concepts that were crucial to the formation of the modern American state. So, another assumption of this book is that state formation in the United States cannot be seen *only* as a product of broad, impersonal economic, political, or social forces or single historic events; it also sprang from the intellectual handiwork and concrete leadership of a gifted few. Just as with any technological invention, administrative inventions are likewise as much a product of ideas and leadership of flesh-and-blood individuals. Again, however, this book is not meant to praise or paint in roseate colors their personal achievements, but rather to try to understand and analyze critically the sources of their motivations and aspects of their careers that led them to play such significant roles in the development of the modern American state and then, in turn, how their accomplishments played out in ways that they did not often anticipate.

But why, asks a reader, should a biographical approach be used to attempt to come to grips with the central issues of the American state? Why not use some other methodology, such as any of those already outlined by previous books cited in this chapter? Why select biographies for comprehending the origins and evolution of the modern American state?

Ultimately, the thesis that will emerge from these biographical sketches that follow argues that the American state was created by adding bits and pieces of administrative inventions incrementally during the late nineteenth and early twentieth centuries by men and women motivated profoundly by moral idealism. All were products of intensely Protestant, small-town cultures. As youth, they were raised in homes where belief in God, sin, guilt, atonement, resurrection, salvation, damnation, and other Protestant values were very real theological beliefs that gave meaning and shape to their communities and to their personal lives.

Protestantism, in the words of historian Page Smith, "placed Christ once more at the center of history." It "revived the millennial expectation and insisted that God's grace ruled the world of man and that man unassisted by God's grace was radically deficient in goodness."[41] This gulf—between what is and ought to be—spurred the individual conscience to strive continuously for ethical perfectionism and moral reform in daily life. Believers felt a pressing and persistent urge to "do good." Protestantism looked to the future because the world was seen, in Augustinian terms, as "the progressive revelation of God's will" and "brought all areas of life of the faithful once again under the scheme of Christian dogma." As Smith says, "The thrust was clearly prophetic; this life must be mastered as a preliminary to the life of the world to come."[42] It also must be mastered directly by the individual, without intervention by popes, bishops, or a church hierarchy. Yet, Protestantism looked backward as well, to restoring ideals of early Christianity. "Luther and Calvin referred everything back to the primitive Christian Church. Here was the model of the perfect Christian commonwealth."[43] And it would be this "perfect Christian commonwealth" that the American state inventors attempted to re-create on these shores in the late nineteenth and early twentieth centuries, again piecemeal, though under the guise of "public administration."

These individual state inventors not only grew up in families and communities that inculcated deeply profound moral, especially Protestant norms but also, as young adults, encountered rapid, unsettling changes in society, rates of change so quick that they were unlike any before or since in American history. The changing world they confronted, or had to confront, forced them to respond by inventing new administrative institutions and practices to cope with immense societal transformations. These state inventors not only foresaw and understood the necessity to cope with what was happening around them but had the intelligence and creativity, in addition to leadership skills, to deal with these events in new ways that brought about the birth and development of the modern American state apparatus. The administrative institutions that they ultimately forged did come out of thin air, but the solutions that they reached for were very much patterned by and motivated by the fundamental religious beliefs in which they were raised. From their own deeply held religious convictions the substance and contours of the American state emerged. In other words, the new American state grew up out of highly personal religious experiences forged from a collective Protestant vision of "the perfect Christian commonwealth."

Fortunately for them, the nineteenth-century American state builders began largely from a clean slate. As the Harvard sociologist Theda Skocpol reminds us, just as Prussia at one time in the seventeenth century was less of a state with an army than an army with a state, the nineteenth century saw the United States "not so much a country with a post office, as a post office that gave popular reality to a fledgling nation."[44] During the 1830s and 1840s, more than three-fourths of all federal employees were postal workers, and until the Civil War, 85 percent of the growth in the American bureaucracy came from that single department. In short, the American state in the mid-nineteenth century consisted of post offices and little else. As Alexis de Tocqueville, the most astute foreign observer of the United States, described, "Nothing is more striking to a European traveler in the United States than the absence of what we term the government, or the Administration."[45]

By looking carefully through the lenses of individual biographies of these administrative state founders, particularly at the moral heritage in which they were reared and how it compelled each of them in different ways to respond to the significant forces of societal change engulfing this comparatively clean slate, we can begin to comprehend the unique origins and evolution of the modern American state. Understanding the lives and work of these moral reformers who crafted key elements of the American state, what beliefs they held so deeply, and why these moral values so fundamentally motivated them to reshape the world they knew can give us ultimately a better, perhaps even a more balanced, perspective on the American administrative state that so decisively shapes our own lives and destinies today.

2

George William Curtis
Leading Missionary for Merit

George William Curtis, 1824–1892
(from *Orations and Addresses of George William Curtis,* vol. 3, ed. Charles Eliot Norton [New York: Harper and Brothers, 1894])

We have laid our hands on the barbaric palace of patronage and have written "Mene, mene," upon its walls, nor will it be long, as I believe, until they are laid in the dust.
—George William Curtis
   Presidential Address to the National Civil Service League

FOR A QUARTER OF A CENTURY George William Curtis was the acknowledged leader of a small but extraordinarily capable and highly effective group of civil service reformers that included Richard Dana, Dorman B. Eaton, Thomas A. Jenckes, Carl L. Schurz, Charles T. Bonaparte, Daniel Gilman, and William D. Foulkes, among others. Paul P. Van Riper, who wrote the definitive history of the U.S. Civil Service, called

Curtis "the central figure from 1865 to 1890" in civil service reform.[1] During this period he worked tirelessly for this cause, without financial remuneration or hope for any reward, often enduring vilification heaped on him and other reformers by opponents.

A typical taunt by party regulars directed at Indiana civil service reformers was as follows: "The Indiana Civil Service Reform Association composed (if such a clique exists at all) of Republican moral lepers, who if capable of distinguishing between truth and lie, always chose the lie just as a buzzard prefers a carrion to fresh meat. The representation of this aggregation of Republican ulcers, warts, tumors, sties and fistulas pretended to investigate affairs at the [Indiana State] Insane Asylum. Their purpose was to manufacture and publish a lying report. They constituted the dregs of partisan malice. Each one of them was a moving, crawling, breathing pestilence."[2]

Faced frequently with such opposition, Curtis and his followers were armed with few resources other than the power of the pen, their oratorical eloquence, their organizational talents, and an unswerving belief in the moral justice of civil service reform. Curtis led his intrepid band not only because of the prodigious time and energies he devoted to "the cause" but also because he was one of the best speakers and writers of that day. He was able to articulate forcefully and convincingly the depth of the reformer's moral arguments. Curtis was a highly regarded lecturer on the popular lyceum circuit of the late nineteenth century, and his *Orations and Addresses* fill three thick volumes. He was a prolific writer as well. Like a modern-day newspaper pundit, Curtis held forth on numerous literary, social, and political topics from his "Editor's Easy Chair" column of the leading American highbrow magazine of the nineteenth century, *Harper's Weekly*.

As a young political reformer prior to the Civil War, Curtis was rabidly antislavery, proabolitionist, and therefore involved in the founding of the Republican party in the 1850s. He remained a devoted and well-connected Republican throughout his life, though he was never a political candidate and never held any elective office. Always more of a political reformer than party regular, Curtis after the Civil War devoted himself while working full time as *Harper's* senior political editor to what was first his part-time hobby, civil service reform. Then, through extensive reading and investigation, Curtis became one of the foremost respected authorities on the topic of civil service reform, so much so that President Grant named him head of the first U.S. Civil Service Commission, 1871–75. In that unpaid position, Curtis set up the first commission, undertook the major studies, wrote its annual reports, and created the first regulations to establish and administer a civil service system in this country. His unique handiwork in fashioning the first commission eventually became the model for the Civil Service Act of 1883 (the Pendleton Act) at the federal level, which many state and local governments follow to this day. Of equal importance, he founded and was president for many years of the National Civil Service Reform League (the chief lobbyist organization on behalf of the civil service) and the New York Civil Service Association.

In addition to working for civil service reform, Curtis maintained a remarkably broad range of civic interests, such as women's rights and welfare reform, throughout his life. Curtis also actively promoted educational reform by serving on the board of regents of New York University. He eventually became its chancellor (an especially remarkable feat for a man who never went to college) and held the position until 1892, when he died. As his close friend Carl Schurz, himself no small contributor to civic reform causes, said of Curtis, "Without injustice to others whose work cannot be overlooked, it may be well said that Curtis, by his wide knowledge, authority and experience, his ripe and calm judgment, his gentle temper and his scarcely asserted but easily acknowledged authority, was most perfectly fitted for that essential task of leadership in such a cause. . . . He was to the day of his death, more than any other person, the intellectual head, the guiding force and the constant moral inspiration of the civil service reform."[3]

What knitted the reformers together so tightly, and perhaps what Curtis succeeded in articulating better than any other reformer, was the clear and compelling case for the moral necessity of civil service reform. To him and his followers, it was a cause akin to a religious crusade, with all the fervor and frenzy of saving souls, but for Curtis it was the soul of the nation, the whole society, that he sought to save from what was perceived as the villainy and vileness of the spoils system and machine politics. The language he used was the sort of Manichaeanistic extreme contrasts in black and white, evil and good intertwined within religious morality that contained few "grays" or qualifications. Spoils was painted as "the devil"; civil service was "the way, the truth, the light." Over and over again, Curtis's speeches and writings repeated ringing moral refrains of the degradation of public service that must be rooted out by the "cure" of a higher ethical standard imposed through civil service reform. As he emphasized:

Civil Service is not merely the observance of certain rules of examination. It is the correction of corruption in politics. . . . What we affirm is that the theory which regards places in the public service as prizes to be distributed after the election like the plunder after the battle, the theory that perverts public trusts into party spoils, making public employment dependent upon personal favor and not on proven merit, necessarily ruins the self-respect of public employees, destroys the function of political parties in a republic, prostitutes elections into desperate strife for personal profit and degrades the national character by lowering the moral tone and standards of the country.[4]

At times, Curtis used vivid personal examples to drive home his point:

The perversion of the Civil Service to mere party machine is pitilessly cruel. Lately there was an officer in one of the departments, faithful, industrious, valuable. Misfortune fell upon his home, and from his lean salary he scraped a shred to buy a comfort for a sick daughter. One day he was politically assessed, but honestly stated his utter inability to pay. He was reported and condemned. To remove him was impracticable because of the influence that appointed him—so he was "cut down." Against this inhuman blow he struggled as he could, seeking extra work at night, fighting to keep himself and his family honestly alive. The struggle was too severe . . . and he died.[5]

At other times Curtis's graphic rhetoric stressed the dangers of moral decline in general society because of spoils: "In a country like ours the evil consequences of such an organization [of the spoils system] of the public service cannot be limited to it. Such a system deprecates the moral standard of the country."[6] More often, though, Curtis's speeches attacked spoils as morally evil for fostering simply bad government:

The evil results of the [spoils] practice may be seen, first, in its perversion of the nature of the election itself. In a free country an election is intended to be, and of right should be, of differing policies of administration by people at the polls. It is properly the judgment of the popular intelligence upon the case which has been submitted to it during the canvass by the ablest and most eloquent advocates. But the evil system under which the country suffers tends to change the election from a choice of policies into a contest for personal advantage. It is becoming a desperate conflict to obtain all the offices, with all their lawful salaries and all their unlawful chances.[7]

Yet, Curtis always provided a message of hope that indeed a better alternative was near at hand: "The Civil Service Reform therefore begins with the assertion that there is no reason in the nature of things or of our form of government that the United States should not manage its affairs with [the] same economy, ability, and honesty that the best private business is managed; and that to do this, it must take the most obvious means not incompatible with the Constitution, with a popular government, with experience and common-sense. It therefore proposes a system of examinations and probations open to all citizens; the appointments to subordinate offices to be made from those proved to be the best qualified."[8]

The moral rightness of civil service reform was erected in part on a declinist view of history. For reformers such as Curtis, the federal personnel system was envisioned as one long descent from the Federalist era of Washington, Adams, and Jefferson. Curtis especially blamed the introduction of the four-year rule in 1820, which required the resignation of all public officials after each presidential election, for facilitating the growth of spoils. "The year 1820," said Curtis, "marks the distinct epoch in the progress of the spoils system." The passage of the four-year rule had "as its real purpose to secure the influence of all the incumbents in office upon the peril of displacement, and of five or ten times as many ravenous office-seekers eager to supplant them."[9]

It was the perversion of democracy that most worried reformers, however. The chief villains in the reformers' view were Andrew Jackson and Martin van Buren, whose presidencies, they believed, firmly established and extended "spoils" throughout all facets of the federal government. Reformers such as Curtis were appalled by the irresponsibility and immorality the spoils system brought to government. The custom of using public offices openly and continuously as ammunition in party warfare, as well as the easy acceptance of rotation in office or the notion that the party in power should rotate in its own men, seemed a steep descent from the high ideals of "the fitness of character doctrine" that had served as a chief criterion for selection to public office in the Federalist and Jeffersonian eras. "To the victors belong the spoils," Senator W. L. Marcy's reputed phrase, summed up for reformers everything that was wrong with spoils.

For President Jackson, though, rotation in office was plausible because it brought not only more equality and opportunity for the common man but also more vitality to government by continual turnover. As he said in his first annual message to Congress: "The duties of all public offices are, or at least admit of being made so plain and simple, that men of intelligence may readily qualify themselves for performance; and I cannot but believe that more is lost by the long continuance of men in office than is generally gained by their experience."[10]

In reality, the practice of spoils that grew up after 1829 worked because of the relatively small scale of government operations. By the end of the Civil War, the U.S. federal bureaucracy contained only seven departments with 53,000 employees, more than half of whom worked in the post office. The post office and, to some extent, the Department of the Treasury, especially its customs houses in major port cities, and parts of the Department of the Interior, particularly patent offices and the Indian Affairs Bureau, became the chief patronage plums. In these areas spoils grew rampant, but it was also true these jobs demanded relatively little skills or training. In the words of Leonard D. White, "The system could work only because it was a vast, repetitive, fixed, generally routine operation."[11] Furthermore, in a largely rural, isolated, and agricultural-based society, citizens demanded little in the way of the vast range of goods and services that modern twentieth-century society expects from government. Large-scale defense programs, welfare assistance, social services, and the like require highly trained, competent professionals to deliver government services. Without requirements for such huge, technologically complex organizations, nineteenth-century government could operate tolerably well, for the most part, staffed with untrained patronage personnel.

Even during Jackson's presidency, with its drive for egalitarianism in personnel appointments, competence, however, was not entirely neglected. Indeed, there were surprising continuities with the Federalist-Jeffersonian eras, as Frederick Mosher notes:

Jackson's appointments reflected no less concern about ability and competence than did those of his predecessors. While . . . a somewhat smaller proportion of his appointees were drawn from established upper class families, he depended equally upon educated and capable men. His efforts to democratize the public service—to make it more representative of the entire population—were only moderately successful because the pool of qualified potential appointees was still limited. Actually, the percentage of office-holders whom he removed following John Quincy Adams was very nearly the same as that of Jefferson's removals following Adams' father. Clearly, Jackson did not always follow what he preached.[12]

As Ari Hoogenboom notes, however, ability received less and less emphasis as time went on. By 1865, capacity was an unnecessary prerequisite for most offices. "Professionalism was almost nonexistent in the civil service, and politics permeated into its core."[13] Tenure for most civilian offices was short and uncertain, though a few long-term occupants of public positions could be pointed to; these individuals provided consistency and direction of policies and administration within government agencies. Overall, no system of personnel or rules of employment existed as we know today, aside from fixed working hours and rudimentary classifications of clerks. Also, no recruitment, promotion, training, or retirement processes existed. By the 1860s patronage and nepotism were commonplace; for example, in 1867, 219 of the 282 employees in the Treasury Department had been appointed within the previous four years. It is estimated that during the Civil War President Lincoln spent more time dealing with patronage problems than military issues, a situation that began to alarm some—but only some—politicians to initiate reforms to curb the excesses of spoils. Again to cite Leonard White, "To a young man becoming aware of public life after the Civil War, patronage must have seemed the national order. It generally prevailed in governments of the states and cities as well as Washington, D.C."[14]

The exigencies of the Civil War, however, only highlighted the glaring weaknesses of a spoils-based government and accelerated the pressures for reform. Some sporadic attempts to reform federal personnel practices occurred prior to the Civil War. In 1853, for example, seven hundred clerk positions in Washington, D.C., were classified into four categories, and a basic "pass" examination system was established (though it was poorly administered and operated only briefly). During the Civil War, Secretary of State William Seward set up competitive examinations for entrance into the diplomatic service, but Seward's changes were also ineffectively administered and put into practice only for a short period. In 1864, during the Civil War, Senator Charles Sumner (R., Mass.) introduced the first civil service legislation, which required that federal appointments be made by open, competitive examinations and that promotions be based on the criteria of four-fifths determined by a candidate's seniority and one-fifth determined by his or her ability. Removal from the federal service was to be made only for "good cause." Sumner's bill was tabled, and he turned his attention instead to the problems of post–Civil War Reconstruction and bitter controversies involving Andrew Johnson's presidency.

In 1863 Rhode Island elected Republican Thomas Allen Jenckes to the House of Representatives. A wealthy patent attorney, Jenckes devoted most of his nine years in the House to studying civil service systems abroad and promoting civil service reform at home. He carried on extensive correspondence with British civil service reformers Sir Charles E. Trevelyan and Sir Stafford H. Northcote, authors of an 1853 paper on British civil service reform, the Northcote-Trevelyan report.

In 1865 Jenckes sponsored the first House bill for civil service reform. Like the Sumner legislation the year before, Jenckes's initiative was tabled without debate. Jenckes was undeterred, however. He went on to become a prominent leader on the Joint Select Committee on Retrenchment, the chief congressional committee in the post–Civil War era devoted to reducing the cost of government, improving its efficiency, and withdrawing the public service from use as an institution for political and party patronage. This committee in the postwar era became, under Jenckes's leadership, a primary source for collecting materials on civil service reform, investigating federal personnel problems, and publicizing the waste and abuse caused by patronage and spoils.

Almost every year until he was defeated for reelection in 1873, Jenckes introduced civil service legislation in the House that was routinely tabled. Jenckes, like Sumner (though the former in much more detail), proposed to, in the words of Paul Van Riper, "attack the problem in the manner of the English reformers through a refined limitation on the power of appointment."[15] Jenckes, like the English reformers, preferred what is called "front door screening" (i.e., open competitive exams and merit-based appointments) as opposed to "back door closing" (i.e., permanent tenure to prevent patronage abuses). Novel for the times, Jenckes's proposals sought to shift the personnel processes entirely to the executive branch.

The civil service reformers faced immense impediments in the post–Civil War era. Again, to cite Paul Van Riper, "In fact the spoils system and its mate, machine politics, developed a sort of massive inertia. . . . It was this dead weight or custom, practice, machine maneuver, tacit alliance of politics and economics, personal political selfishness, and sheer practical partisan advantage which any post–Civil War reform movement had to counteract. Even if it had been the only object of public concern in the eighteen sixties, reform of the public service would have been a considerable task."[16] The dominant beliefs of the era, aptly labeled the Gilded Age, the Great Barbecue, the Era of Robber Barons, and the Period of Laissez-Faireism, made public service idealism, in general, and civil service reform, in particular, hardly fashionable. Certainly the reformers' beliefs were out of fashion—by a long shot!

Enter George William Curtis. Curtis was born on February 24, 1824, in Providence, Rhode Island, with Puritan ancestors on both sides of his family (Ephraim Curtis on his father's side was the first settler of Worcester, Massachusetts). "In every fiber I am a child of the Pilgrims,"[17] Curtis once said of himself, though by the time he was born his family had considerably softened its Calvinistic Puritanism and lived, thanks to his father's substantial business interests, a comfortable, middle-class lifestyle of that day. Curtis had little formal education other than briefly attending a private school in Jamaica Plains, Massachusetts. In his words, he "was practically self-taught." He tried apprenticing as an accountant in an "accounting room" of the Bank of Commerce on Wall Street in New York City when he was fifteen, but he did not like it and saw himself as largely unsuccessful in business.[18]

What he became deeply involved with between ages eighteen and twenty, with his older brother Burrill, was the Brook Farm Transcendental Experiment in West Roxbury, Massachusetts. The eighteen months beginning in the spring of 1842, as one biographer recounts, "was a variegated and extremely important episode in Curtis' life."[19] As Curtis himself testified: "I was attracted to this place by a general restlessness and the promise of an Arcadian and beneficent life. During the year and a half that I remained, it was the most unique episode of my life. . . . It was the purely pastoral chapter in most of our lives. I was there during the golden age. I was young, I saw none of the cracks, I heard none of the creaking, and I confess that my residence there is entirely idyllic in my memory."[20]

Transcendentalism, the philosophy on which Brook Farm was founded, was rooted in a New England spiritual revolt against the formal, organized religion of Calvinism. As Odell Shepard writes, "Transcendentalism was in essence a philosophy and religion of reform."[21] Donald Kostner adds, "The Transcendentalists were, almost to a man, the direct descendants of those who had come to New England in pursuit of the impossible dream of establishing the Kingdom of God on Earth."[22] Reform, specifically spiritual reform, was very much in the blood of these individuals who set up Brook Farm. "They," in the words of Octavius Frothingham, a participant and chronologist of Brook Farm, "asserted the veracity of consciousness, and demanded an absolute acknowledgment of that veracity." As he suggested, "His [the Brook Farm participant] prime duty consisted in deference to the integrity of his own mind. The laws of his intellectual and moral nature were inviolable."[23] Or, as another close student of transcendentalism, Van Wyck Brooks, wrote: "They had no interest in size, numbers and dollars. They had begun to explore the inner life, the depths of thought and sentiment. They had returned to another level to the mental habits of their Pilgrim fore-bearers."[24] In many ways transcendentalism can be viewed properly as the direct descendent—and logical advancement—of the Pilgrim's faith in spiritual revolt and individual quest for a new (or a renewed) genuine faith.

Curtis became an active participant in this heady group of young New England thinkers that included Margaret Fuller, John S. Dwight, George and Sophia Ripley, George Bradford, Issac Hecker, and Louisa Alcott. In this cooperativist community experiment, George and Burrill joined with others "to establish a community where work was to be shared among all, selfishness eliminated, and a practical Christianity established." They all shared in the chores of the farm, took turns at cooking, waiting on tables, doing the wash "in the spirit of unselfish cooperation, which the Association wished to engender."[25]

Here both Curtises had their first taste of formal schooling, along with learning what the Brook Farm residents termed "functional association" at Brook Farm, or a sort of applied community work experience. George Ripley taught philosophy and mathematics; George P. Bradford, literature; John S. Dwight, Latin and music; Charles Dana, Greek and German; and John S. Brown, theoretical and practical agriculture. Emerson, Hawthorne, and Thoreau were regular visitors and lecturers at Brook Farm. Often the Brook Farm residents went into nearby Boston to hear the great theologians of that era, William Henry Channing and Theodore Parker, preach. Yet, it was not all seriousness, as Curtis's biographer notes. "Burrill and George entered gaily into the 'play' of this cheerful community, participating in the masquerades, the balls, and the concerts. . . . George enjoyed singing as well as dancing and often rendered duets with his brother Burrill."[26]

At first George Curtis said that he had been skeptical of the transcendentalists when he had first been introduced to them in Emerson's library. They had all seemed so dignified and erect "as if to ask, who will now proceed to say the finest thing that has ever been said," but as time went on and he participated in their community, he grew to have great affection for them and their ideals.[27] Indeed, he maintained a lifelong friendship with many at Brook Farm, and above all, as one writer noted, "Curtis never escaped its [transcendentalism's] influence."[28] With his lofty idealism, Curtis was imbued, like the others, with a commitment to social progress through practical good works, the shunning of materialism for the enhancement of spirituality, and the belief in the importance of following one's individual conscience. As his biographer writes: "From Brook Farm Curtis . . . drew a moral enthusiasm which never deserted him. The courage of the Associationists, their belief that it was possible to found an early Paradise on a New England farm and [that] the truculent competition of the world could be replaced by a realm of serene cooperation struck a responsive chord in George Curtis and he shared their desire to implant in society a sounder moral standard."[29]

The collapse of the Brook Farm experiment must have had a heart-rending effect on the young, idealistic Curtis. By his own account, he traveled—wandered—"trying to find himself" for several years in Europe and the Middle East, much like the German youth of the *Wandervogel* movement in the 1920s. He spent a year in Italy, then another at Berlin University, where he witnessed firsthand the tumultuous revolution of 1848. Next he spent two more years in Egypt and Syria. On the basis of these foreign travels, Curtis published two novels shortly after returning to the United States in 1850: *Nile Notes of a Howadji* (1851) and *The Howadji in Syria* (1852). He also produced a collection of his travel letters written for the *New York Tribune,* titled *Lotus-Eating* (1852). The first two books were a curious mix of his travel observations with his personal transcendentalist spiritualism in fictionalized form. These books marked Curtis as a promising young author, although he never tried writing another novel. Increasingly Curtis turned to journalism. He wrote prolifically for thirty-seven years, penning weekly or monthly columns on social and political commentary for the *New York Tribune, Putnam's Monthly Magazine,* and *Harper's Weekly,* where he rose to become its senior political editor in 1863 with his own regular "The Editor's Easy Chair" column.

By the 1860s Curtis was recognized as one of the most popular journalists of his day, his columns reaching an estimated two million readers monthly. Charles Eliot Norton, Curtis's close friend, said that his success stemmed from his barometric sense "of the atmospheric currents of popular opinion. . . . The rise or fall of his mercury indicates coming changes. His principles are as firm and clear as the glass table, but his feelings and his opinions as to the modes of action and course of policy vary with the popular weather. This makes him an excellent and useful political writer."[30]

Curtis gained considerable fame nationally as well from his lyceum lectures, which, as noted earlier, were a popular form of nineteenth-century oratory. Curtis excelled at lyceum lectures, speaking across the country in town meeting halls, large and small, on various contemporary topics. As one observer remarked of his style, "Mr. Curtis' manner as a speaker was peculiarly attractive. He was not fiery and not impassioned; he was rather more graceful and winning. His voice was musical and had a rare charm of fluency, and he was always dignified in bearing before an audience."[31] His oratorical style and grace commanded such national respect that his speeches were frequently published and quoted—although some also suspect that Curtis labored so hard on the lyceum circuit because he had no choice. He assumed the debt of *Putnam's Monthly Magazine* when it collapsed. Although he was not legally responsible for it, he felt personally obligated to repay the debt, which he succeeded in doing fully by 1873.

During the 1850s and 1860s Curtis gravitated increasingly toward Republican politics, drawn by the idealism of its antislavery and abolitionist platform. He involved himself in the party's founding and was a delegate in 1860 and 1864 to the Republican conventions. He also was active in Lincoln's election and reelection campaigns. In the fall of 1866 E. L. Godkin, publisher of *The Nation,* and Curtis's friend Charles Eliot Norton worked to launch Curtis in a campaign for Republican senator from New York. It failed. Roscoe Conkling, the "boss" of the New York Republican machine, blocked the attempt and secured the position for himself. Curtis recognized anyway that he was more of a reformer than a politician. As he wrote to his friend Charles Eliot Norton, "I am not enough of a politician for the purposes of men who make senators."[32] Although he remained active in Republican party politics and was even offered a counsel generalship in Egypt by President Lincoln and later posts as minister to England and Germany by President Hayes, he turned down these political appointments. Curtis also never sought another elective public office.

Some speculate that perhaps the beating he received at the hands of the New York Republican machine encouraged Curtis to support the Jenckes civil service bill, then expiring in the Thirty-ninth Congress, and eventually take up with a vengeance the cause of civil service reform. Certainly his defeat by "Boss" Conkling accelerated and sustained his interest in the subject. More and more frequently in his *Harper's* "Easy Chair" column and in his speeches on the lyceum circuit, Curtis focused on the civil service issue with all the moralistic fervor he could muster: "The perversion of the Civil Service to a mere party machine is pitilessly cruel"; "It is the crime of the system"; "It is an unspeakable cruelty"; "Such a system deprecates the moral standards of the country."[33]

While such fiery rhetoric turned into a single-minded devotion toward the moral crusade for this cause, Curtis also diligently went about collecting facts to bolster his case for reform. He corresponded with Charles Trevelyan, Stafford Northcote, John Stuart Mill, and other leaders in the British civil service reform movement, in addition to the Americans who had done work on the topic, namely, Senator Sumner and Representative Jenckes. Many of the early reformers, like Curtis, looked to the British for a role model, and his writings, as those of other reformers', are salted with glowing references to the virtues of the British reform experiences. As Trevelyan summed up the British experience in a one-page letter to Curtis, "This is our experience. It is for you and those who are acting with you to judge how far it is applicable to the circumstances of the United States."[34]

Agitation by Curtis and his followers led President Grant, in his first inaugural address in March 1869, to declare himself in favor of civil service reform. Grant's statement was the first presidential backing the reformers received (ironic for a presidency renowned for its lax moral standards). Grant followed up his open support with a call for legislation in his second message to Congress in December 1870. Congress discussed the proposal but did nothing. Finally, in a last-minute effort on the last day of the 1870–71 session, Senator Lyman Trumbull (R., Ill.) attached a rider to a civilian appropriations bill that, with some difficulty, was passed by both houses. The rider, all of one sentence, read:

> Sec. 9. The President of the United States be, and he is hereby, authorized to prescribe such rules and regulations for the admission of persons into the civil service of the United States as will best promote the efficiency thereof, and ascertain the fitness of each candidate in respect to age, health, character, knowledge, and ability for the branch of service into which he seeks to enter; and for this purpose the President is authorized to employ suitable persons to conduct said inquires, to prescribe their duties, and to establish regula-

tions for the conduct of persons who receive appointments in the civil service.[35]

Even though the rider was not mandatory in requiring that the president must take action, Grant immediately appointed a seven-member civil service board, comprising three members from within government, three from the outside, and Curtis as chair. Curtis began working immediately after his appointment to organize the commission and to persuade the committee's other members to put civil service reform into practice. The committee received no salary, had no offices, held no daily meetings, was assigned only one full-time assistant, and furthermore had no precedents by which to guide its direction. Much of the work, therefore, fell on Curtis. To Curtis's credit, armed with so few resources and only brief and general enabling legislation, a rider to an appropriations bill, he accomplished a great deal during his relatively short two-year tenure. Lionel Murphy, the foremost student of the work of the first civil service commission, summed up its achievements as follows:

> Much of the terminology and many of the concepts employed in the proceedings, reports, and other recorded activities of the Commission still prevail. . . .
> Most significant of all is the fact that the principle of competitive examination was adopted in a form the nature of which was very closely analogous to the British application and administration. . . .
> The first Civil Service Commission attempted to solve other personnel problems . . . such as position classification, efficiency ratings, and super annuation. It undertook to administer competitive promotions, to determine positions for inclusion in, or exclusion from, the competitive system based upon their duties and responsibilities. . . .
> In their efforts these civil service reformers sought to place the responsibility for administration upon the President and the heads of departments. In the evolution of administrative management their work becomes most significant as marking the beginning of the President's rise to the actual leadership of administration in the federal government.[36]

In the broadest sense as well, Murphy underscores that the Curtis committee was a landmark commission because for the first time the federal government established a central personnel agency to deal with oversight of civilian personnel issues. Murphy rightly dates modern government personnel administration and administrative reform to the rider of 1871 and to the work of George Curtis and his fellow commissioners. It was accomplished, again in Murphy's words, by "a small group of men, without a popular following but skillful in speech and phrase in behalf of a new political morality, [who] forced a trial in administrative reform upon a hostile Congress and an unenthusiastic President."[37]

Specifically, when the Civil Service Act of 1883 that created the civil service system for the federal government is compared with the rules and regulations devised in 1873 by Curtis's commission, it is clear how the handiwork of Curtis eventually became the framing model for the civil service system a decade later. The commission established the following: (1) an independent commission to administer the civil service; (2) the criteria of merit to guide selection and promotion to the public service; (3) open, competitive exams to test the fitness of applicants to the public service; (4) a classification of positions; (5) a probationary period for candidates; (6) a "rule of three," or the certification of the three highest candidates for possible appointment to a position; (7) prohibitions against political activity and other forms of influence on the civil service; (8) methods for internal procedures and for examination practices by the civil service commission; (9) enforcement mechanisms by the commission; and (10) procedures for noncompetitive exams and temporary appointments.

Later, after the 1883 act was passed, other features of Curtis's rules found their way into the civil service, such as qualifications for employment that required citizenship, loyalty, and satisfactory health. Even the terminology used by Curtis's commission was eventually used by the American civil service system, at all levels of government, to run activities, that is, terms such as "test," "grade," "eligible," "ineligible," "register," "military preference," "superannuation," "political assessments," "rule of three," "boards of examiners," and "certificate," among others.

Certainly, as Richard Titlow observes, "Reformers such as Curtis supported their recommendations with examples from the experience of Great Britain."[38] They drew many ideas and ideals from there. As Curtis liked to remind his audiences, in England "not a single officeholder was assessed to sustain it [the Tory Party then in power] or remove or strengthen it" except in the top policy positions such as the governor-general of India. "On the other hand, every government em-

ployee in the United States fears removal while others struggle to replace them as a result of the election upon which we are entering."[39]

Curtis's leadership was critical for adapting and modifying the English experience in five important ways. First, while the reformers accepted some of the fundamentals of the British system, such as the concept of competitive exams and neutrality of the public service, they
rejected others as being impractical. Curtis and his commission did not
(nor did the 1883 act) divide the civil service into a series of four classes
with entrance open only at the bottom level of each class, as did the
British system. Clearly such a system would have been thought elitist
and was never seriously considered. Indeed, still today, as Curtis first
envisioned it, anyone can apply to openings at any level of the civil
service in the United States. Likewise, American reformers rejected the
British academic exam format, instead requiring that examinations be
"of a practical, job-related" nature (which is still true today). Third, no
special ties were created between American universities and the civil
service, as was the case of the Oxbridge connections with the British
civil service. Only in the 1930s did the federal government actively begin recruiting college graduates for public service, but even then—and
today—civil service recruiters focus on finding particular skills required for government jobs, which are not monopolized by any one
or few universities. Functional needs, not class backgrounds related to
higher education, drive, for the most part, American civil service patterns of recruitment and promotions. Fourth, Curtis and his commission (as did the 1883 act) rejected the British system's class of neutral
permanent undersecretaries near the top of government. Policy direction, it was thought then, and today as well, should rest with the president and his political appointees not protected by civil service regulations. Civil service coverage during the course of the twentieth century
gradually was pushed upward throughout federal, state, and local governments, but top policy leadership posts remain in the hands of the
elected chief executive.

Finally, unlike the British group, the reformers such as Curtis viewed
civil service reform—and pushed their reforms—ultimately as a moral
crusade of good versus evil or "the right" versus "the wrong." They
connected it in their minds with an extension of human liberty, democracy, and popular freedom over tyranny, or, in Curtis's words, "Civil
service reform, therefore, is but another successive step in the development of liberty under law. It is not eccentric or revolutionary. It is a

logical measure of political progress."[40] Whereas the Northcote-Treve-lyan reforms sought to make British institutions simply more effective, Curtis and other reformers wanted to purify the public service by re-moving spoils. The connection of civil service to morality in the minds of the reformers led to their arguing for sharp distinctions between politics and administration to advance their cause.

On one hand, the politics-administration dichotomy, as it later came to be called, gave a legitimacy to creating a separate academic field of public administration, one concerned with analysis, "facts," and even "science," as opposed to values or "mere politics." On the other hand, such a hard-and-fast separation between politics and administration came to be viewed by succeeding generations of scholars as both unre-alistic theoretically and unworkable practically. In some ways the situ-ation was ironic because Curtis and most civil service reformers were well connected with the politics of their era. Indeed, they believed it their duty to be actively engaged public citizens in party affairs throughout their lives. Again, they were not opposed to parties; their view was that civil service reform was the chief route by which to im-prove politics, especially party politics. By eliminating the desire for spoils, which they thought subverted parties into special inter-ests merely out for personal gain, parties would better serve the pub-lic interest as a whole. To quote a thoughtful scholar of this era, Stow Persons: "The security of liberty under law . . . required that public-spirited citizens actively engage in party politics. This was the only alternative to control by selfish, venal and ignorant politicians; edu-cated men must shoulder duties that were often wearisome and dis-tressful—attendance at caucuses and committee meetings, the assump-tion of duties and expenses, and the willingness to stand for public office. Practicing what he preached, Curtis engaged himself actively in politics."[41]

Stow Persons's insight helps explain why Curtis, despite his heavy schedule of writing and speaking engagements from which he earned his living, accepted the onerous, unpaid chairmanship of the commis-sion; commuted regularly to Washington, D.C.; engaged in all the myr-iad details of establishing the commission; worked out the detailed compromises between the other commissioners; wrote much of the civil service regulations and rules; dealt with the endless complaints and requests from various agencies; fended off the harsh attacks of the "spoilsmen"; initiated investigations; drafted the major annual reports to the president and Congress; and oversaw the general progress of the establishment of the first civil service system (without even a secretary and only one paid assistant, let alone the modern personal computer, fax machine, or photocopier).

It also explains why he resigned suddenly on March 23, 1873. Legally and morally, he argued, Grant violated "both the spirit and letter of the [civil service] rule" when he made a certain political appointment in the New York Customs House. As a result of this patronage appointment, Curtis could no longer work under such conditions because of his principles, or felt he could no longer do so, and immediately so tendered his resignation. Grant appointed Dorman Eaton, Curtis's close friend, as his successor to the chairmanship, but the commission had a short life afterward. The following year the House voted to repeal the rider of March 3, 1871, that created the commission, while the Senate voted for $15,000 to continue the commission's work. The two houses failed to concur, leaving the law on the books but no appropriations to fund it. Grant announced simply in his annual message in December 1874: "I will regard such action as a disapproval of the system and will abandon it." With that statement the commission ceased to exist.[42]

Out of this apparent defeat, how was the Civil Service Act of 1883, largely modeled on the work of Curtis's commission, eventually enacted? Why did the reformers ultimately succeed in the end? Here again, much of the credit belongs to the astute leadership by Curtis of his small, yet highly effective, group of reformers.

First, Curtis took the lead through his own personal and considerable backroom political maneuvering. In 1876 Curtis was a delegate to the Republican national convention and drafted the plank in the platform calling for civil service legislation. He also was the only delegate from New York to vote for Rutherford B. Hayes and against New York State's "native son," Roscoe B. Conkling. Thus, when Hayes won the presidency after a close and complicated election against the Democrat, Samuel Tilden, Hayes remained indebted to Curtis for the support. As stated earlier, the president offered Curtis ministerial posts to England and then to Germany, both of which he declined. Curtis chose instead to stay home and work for civil service reform. The effect of Curtis's informal influence on the Hayes presidency is shown in the annual presidential addresses to Congress. All four speeches supported civil service reform. In the first message, Hayes merely advocated impersonal appointment and security of tenure, but by the third address he devoted nearly a quarter of the speech to this single reform initiative.

Hayes's appointments also reflected Curtis's invisible influence, which can be seen particularly in the selection of Carl Schurz as secretary of the Department of the Interior. Urged on Hayes by Curtis, Schurz placed the entire department under Curtis's 1871 and 1872 civil service rules and enforced those rules rigidly—and with success—during his term. The New York Customs House was long riddled with patronage and corruption. Hayes, with Curtis's active involvement (Curtis served as an unpaid assistant to the investigating commission), appointed new men who rigorously enforced merit rules throughout the entire New York City Customs Service. In 1877, with Hayes's approval and Curtis's backing, Dorman Eaton went to England to study the English system of examinations and appointments (at his own expense). Hayes submitted the Eaton report to Congress. It was later published in book form, titled *The Civil Service in Great Britain* (1880), with an introduction by Curtis.[43] The book received considerable praise and notoriety for the cause of civil service reform.

Second, Curtis was able to use his political connections effectively not only inside the Hayes administration but also outside. In the late 1870s, Curtis, along with other civil service reformers, organized a movement that led to the creation of the National Civil Service League (NCSL). Until it closed down its operations in 1970, the NCSL was chief lobbyist on behalf of establishing federal, state, and local civil service systems. At the NCSL's first meeting in Newport, Rhode Island, on July 29, 1881, Curtis was elected the league's chair, a position he retained until his death in 1892. He devoted enormous energies to the details of its agenda and organizational activities and took particular care when crafting his lengthy annual addresses to the national conference to make sure he charted the areas of progress as well as NCSL priorities for the following year. Under Curtis's leadership, the NCSL evolved into one of America's first successful nationwide good government groups, with an elaborate set of committees, regional and local chapters, and annual national conferences aimed at enacting national, state, and local civil service legislation. It effectively supported open, competitive examinations and appointments to the public service based on merit and vigorously opposed arbitrary removals from office as well as all interference by members of Congress. The NCSL backed state, local, and federal candidates for public offices who supported their agenda and campaigned against those who favored spoils. Their membership grew quickly in the 1880s. By 1883, only three years after its founding, the NCSL claimed fourteen hundred members in fifty-nine states and territories.

Third, Curtis's leadership effectively forged the NCSL into a potent national public relations force on behalf of civil service reform. As A. Bower Sageser describes, the NCSL was skillful in its propagandist activities:

The League came to play the role of the agitator in history. Although it was organized after the [civil service] reform movement was well under way, it became an effectual agent for promotion of the cause, especially from the standpoint of molding public opinion. Its membership was made up of men who were highly educated, men of literary talents who could write and speak effectively. An educational campaign was vigorously conducted. Public addresses were made by the reformers, and thousands of pamphlets were printed and circulated to all parts of the country. Articles were written for the newspapers and magazines. Prizes were offered to the schools presenting the best essays on reform. Candidates were canvassed regarding their stand on reform and their replies printed and circulated. Reformers petitioned Congress, and attempts were made to prosecute violators of the law on political assessments. In order to send out news more effectively, in 1881 the Massachusetts Civil Service Reform Association began to publish its own magazine, the *Civil Service Record*. Every available form of propaganda was used to shape a sympathetic public opinion.[44]

The immense volume of literature at the state and regional levels became especially significant. The New York Association of the National Civil Service League (which Curtis also headed) alone circulated nearly 30,000 pamphlets and documents in 1880, 230,000 in 1881, and 330,000 in 1882. The national committee even set up a special committee to let fly a barrage of news editorials, political cartoons, and press stories after President Garfield's assassination, linking his death to "a disappointed office seeker" (a phrase that has stuck throughout history). The committee also circulated Garfield's own favorable expression about civil service reform and put up large placards eulogizing the dead president in all post offices throughout the country. "This sad occurrence," as Frank Stewart suggests, "furnished the opportunity for the greatest single example of successful League propaganda."[45]

Above all, Curtis spurred on the actual written legislation for congressional enactment after the terrible national tragedy of Garfield's death. Curtis was one of the vocal proponents of the Pendleton bill (named for its chief Senate sponsor, George H. Pendleton, a Republican from Ohio). Modeled essentially on Curtis's own work as head of the first civil service commission a decade earlier, the bill became law on January 16, 1883, only months after Garfield's death. This act, the Civil Service Act of 1883, was, and remains, the most important statutory element creating the modern American state. It is difficult to conceive of the U.S. government operating today without the innumerable and invaluable experts recruited on the basis of merit. Curtis, by means of his insider political connections, his NCSL organization and its potent publicity campaign for merit, and his format of the rules framed in 1871 and 1872, did more than any other individual to bring the act into fruition.

Yet, why should Curtis have hungered for and worked so hard on behalf of this particular reform? Why not some other one? What drove Curtis to lead the fight against spoils and for merit? Was it his beating at the hands of Boss Conkling in 1868 that made him turn on the machine with a special vengeance? Or, as he frequently professed, was it his great desire to stamp out the corrupting force of spoils in government and promote wider opportunities for freedom of expression and popular participation? Or was his prime motivation to turn back the clock to a lost "golden age of politics," to the Federalist-Jeffersonian era, an era that Curtis and his reformers so much admired, when people were appointed on the basis of fitness of character, not party loyalty? Or was it more simply his desire to be a "public man," to participate actively in the public life of his day and to take on the leadership of a cause involving what was then one of the major issues of the times?

Possibly all these factors weighed into the complex amalgam of his own personal choices and motivations. We will never know for sure which one was most critical, though we cannot help but suspect that, for Curtis, championing civil service was a uniquely fulfilling reform effort to devote himself to with such single-mindedness throughout the second half of his life. More than any other cause during that period of rampant materialism, civil service represented the idealistic hope that the best, another Protestant elect chosen by merit and moral worth, might once again rule, possibly ushering into existence a better world, another reverential golden age. For Curtis, just as for the select Brook Farm participants, the flame of Emersonian idealism continued to burn and to hold out spiritual hopes for a better tomorrow.

Curtis never strayed far from this transcendental faith of youth in which idealism was valued, human progress was deemed essential, a renewed reform faith was sought, materialism was rejected, and, above all, the "good" was respected for its intrinsic worth to rule. So too, by being the leading missionary for merit, Curtis discovered—or did he rediscover?—the strong sense of moral purpose that he missed since Brook Farm. Here he would find an avenue for moral fulfillment through active political participation in civil service reform during his adult life. Here was a way—maybe the only way for his times—he and his followers could realize the Emersonian faith. "They are always called visionaries who hold that morality is stronger than a majority," Curtis once exclaimed proudly, but he added, with typical Emersonian certainty, "whether visionaries or not, they were correct!"[46]

In 1870, almost a quarter century after he left Brook Farm, Curtis headed a committee to bring Emerson to speak with what he regarded as "true and high eloquence" to a local club in New York City. "We can have him once in three or four seasons," Curtis is reported to have told the committee. "But really," Curtis added, "they had him all the time without knowing it. He was the philosopher of Proteus, and spoke through all the more popular mouths."[47]

Perhaps Curtis was only joking, or was he?

3

Charles Francis Adams, Jr.

The Conscience of the Sunshine Commission

Charles Francis Adams, Jr., 1835–1915
(courtesy of the Library of Congress)

Born in Boston, May 27, 1835
Died in Washington, May 20, 1915
Known to his Time in many Paths
Soldier, Civilian, Administrator, Historian
His Character, Courage and Abilities
Were Doubted in None
After Eighty Years of Active Life
In a Restless and Often Troubled Age
He Left to His Descendants an Honorable Name
Worthy of Those Which Had Before Him
Shone in the Annals of the State
—Words on the Gravestone of Charles Francis Adams, Jr.

THE ABOVE EPITAPH OF Charles Francis Adams, Jr., written by his
brother Henry, not only captures the essence of the multiple, distinctive
contributions of Adams during his lifetime but also depicts the com-

pelling family legacy into which he was born. "Worthy of Those Which Had Before Him Shone in the Annals of the State" was not idle commentary added to his gravestone. After all, his great-grandfather, John Adams, was the second president of the United States and one of the truly great founding figures of the Republic. His grandfather, John Quincy Adams, was the sixth U.S. president and an equally formidable scholar and diplomat and later an abolitionist congressman. His father, Charles Francis Adams, Sr., had also served in Congress and, as President Lincoln's Civil War ambassador to Great Britain, had successfully dealt with one of the most difficult and challenging diplomatic assignments during the war. Few families in that era—or to this day—have provided the nation with such illustrious leaders over several generations.

So, for Charles Adams, Jr., simply being born into this family tradition proved an immense problem: how can one follow, let alone keep up with, such namesakes? As biographer Thomas K. McCraw writes of Charles Francis, Jr., "For any Adams of his generation, life by definition meant a continual struggle with one's conscience; a fateful quest to fulfill one's responsibilities to stern ancestors and to God."[1] Adams inherited the family's keen sense of civic responsibility derived from a strict Puritan conscience to "do one's duty." As he wrote in his posthumously published autobiography, "They [his ancestors] were . . . afflicted with an everlasting sense of what is to be accomplished—so much to do, so little done! The terrible New England Conscience implanted in men, who inheriting its traditions, had largely outgrown Calvinistic Theology. They were, in a word, by inheritance ingrained Puritans and no Puritan by nature probably ever was really companionable."[2]

Adams may very well have been talking about himself, not just his ancestors. He was through and through a Puritan without Puritanism. Although he was no longer a believer in the Calvinist God of his forefathers, their Puritan conscience nonetheless pressed hard on him throughout his life to find "a calling," to act "responsibly," to shun personal glory for "the public good," and to think and work diligently. Being so self-driven or, in contemporary social science terminology, being "an inner-directed man," Adams himself, like his forebears, was hardly likable; he was respected, yes, but even he admitted, as noted above, that by nature he was not "really companionable."

Each of his three brothers followed different careers: John Quincy II, the eldest, went into law and became involved in local civic affairs.

Henry, the second oldest, pursued teaching and writing history and eventually became well-known for his famous *The Education of Henry Adams*. Brooks, the youngest, turned to history and social commentary. All led remarkable lives, yet all believed the family was in "sharp decline." As Charles Francis, Jr., mused in his mid-fifties, "Why is [it] that the tendency in the family is toward the development of elements of weakness and deterioration; while in the mass a distinct improvement is perceptible?"[3]

Charles Francis, Jr., may have viewed himself as a failure like his brothers, yet his lifetime achievements do not justify such harsh self-criticism. At first he studied law and tried a writing career briefly but was drawn to prove himself in public service in the difficult, inhospitable Gilded Age that followed the Civil War. In the process of pioneering the field of public regulation, Adams forged a new institutional framework, the regulatory commission, which later became the model at the national level for the first federal regulatory commission, the Interstate Commerce Commission (1887). Throughout the 1870s, Adams labored at the local level, creating the first effective state regulatory agency that in turn became the pattern for other federal and state regulatory agencies. This institutional innovation, invented largely from the ideas and leadership of Adams's efforts in Massachusetts, remains to this day the chief public instrument in the United States for governing various private economic markets.

In many ways this administrative innovation, the regulatory commission that Adams forged, was as significant a contribution to the development of the United States government as any of the remarkable achievements of his illustrious ancestors—for it extended public power to supervise directly the private marketplace for the first time in the United States. The U.S. Constitution, as framed in 1787, largely focused *internally* on controlling the abuses of public power through its elaborate arrangement of checks and balances. Although the Constitution's founding fathers may have talked about limiting the excesses of private interests or, more precisely, groups adverse to the common good ("factions," as Madison called them in *Federalist* 10), they were more fearful of potential public rather than private misdeeds and therefore established complicated constitutional checks to serve largely those ends.

Adams's handiwork a century later immeasurably extended and broadened the original founders' Constitution by creating effective institutions to control the abuses of private power that were contrary to the public interest. He not only developed a new administrative structure but also added another new institutional dimension to the Constitution that combined government powers of two or three branches in novel and fundamental ways. Yet, at the end of his life, Adams believed that he had actually done little compared with previous Adams generations—nor did the general public credit him with accomplishing a great deal in his lifetime. Like his brother Henry, he became increasingly withdrawn, believing that his regulatory ideas were being neglected. He even felt embittered toward what he viewed as the excesses of democracy and a belief in what he sarcastically called "the peepul" [sic].[4]

Charles Francis Adams, Jr., was raised in a demanding New England household that he remembered as being hardly pleasurable. As he wrote of his father, "In plain language, I do not like my own Father, . . . strong, not generous, kindly or sympathetic, self-contained, introspective, Puritanic in the English and virtuous in the Roman sense. . . . I thought in all my life I had never seen but one other face as cross as his." His view of Boston Public Latin School that he attended was little better: "a dull, traditional, lifeless day-academy in which conventional, commonplace, platoon-front educational drill was carried on." His entire boyhood, he remembered, "wasn't very attractive anyhow." He viewed with equal unkindness the home where he was raised: "It was 46 years ago that we moved into that house, and I have not one pleasant association connected with it. I went out of it today with a sense of relief." Nor were his four years spent at Harvard College much of an improvement: "No instructor produced, or endeavored to produce, the slightest impression on me, no spark of enthusiasm was sought to be infused into me."[5]

It is difficult to believe that the Adams family, who lived in comparative comfort for that time, could have raised a son with such a degree of discomfort toward his upbringing. Possibly, however, life was extremely regimented from the start: Charles Francis was probably not given much choice of where to live or what school to attend; even the choice of which college to attend was inevitable. John Adams had graduated from Harvard in 1755; John Quincy Adams had graduated in 1787 (later becoming the first Boylston Professor of Rhetoric and Oratory); Charles Francis, Sr., was graduated in 1825 (later becoming president of the board of overseers), and all of his sons were graduated from Harvard (two eventually becoming professors there, Henry and Brooks).

For an Adams, therefore, going to Harvard or, for that matter, experiencing anything else that concerned childhood development, followed family tradition. It was hardly a dull environment in which to be reared, however, at least in the way that Charles Francis recalled. In the small world of Boston society of that era, a remarkable circle of intellectuals were family friends, such as Ralph Waldo Emerson, Henry Wadsworth Longfellow, and James Russell Lowell. Charles's own family likewise included several of America's ablest scholars, especially diarists, from whom Charles claimed later in life that he inherited an ink-stained thumb. Indeed, John Quincy Adams took a lively interest in his grandchildren's academic preparation from their earliest days: "The grandchildren often tumbled about the old man's house in Quincy. He gave each an inscribed Bible. He tried to teach Louisa her alphabet, but had not the patience for it. One day in Quincy, when Henry Adams refused to go to school and stood arguing with his mother, the former president strode out of his study, took the six-year-old by the hand, and walked him not just to the school, but right to his desk. Adams was rather formal with his grandchildren; he was never called 'Gramps' or even 'Granddad' but 'the President.' . . . But he was tolerant of them and fond of them all."[6]

Moreover, the Adams household was always a center of animated political discussions. Charles Francis's grandfather was one of the leading abolitionist congressmen in the 1830s and 1840s, and his father was active in politics, taking Charles, Jr., on campaign swings. The election of 1848 was especially important in the Adams household: "Northern splinter groups from eighteen states met in Buffalo, New York—a cross section of disgruntled Whigs, Democrats, Barnburners and abolitionist Liberty Party members. They nominated Martin Van Buren for president, and Charles Francis Adams for vice-president. Their slogan was 'Free soil, free speech, free labor and free men,' and these Free-Soilers went out to topple Whigs and Democrats. In fact, they beat no one in any state. But the Van Buren–Adams ticket did manage to gather enough votes to swing New York, and the election of the Whigs."[7]

Despite his harsh verdict of his father, Charles, Jr., learned firsthand at his father's and grandfather's knees, often in the heat of abolitionist and Free-Soil third-party politics, how important it was *not* to compromise virtue, integrity, and honesty. Just before he died, John Quincy Adams faced down the taunts of his own party for being one of the few members in the House of Representatives not to vote in favor of the popular Mexican War. Likewise, Charles, Sr., worked hard for Free-Soilers, even though it doomed his chances for future elective offices.

After Harvard, Charles, Jr., tried reading for the law and, as was then the custom, prepared for the profession in the offices of Francis E. Parker, a family friend. Charles, Jr., admired Parker, along with his partner, Richard Henry Dana, who had written the literary masterpiece *Two Years Before the Mast*. Although he was admitted to the bar, Adams found law boring and seldom practiced it. He later said that he lacked the attention to detail, but perhaps the difficulty arose more from the fact that relationships with his client were rarely attentive or smooth. As he confessed, "I was a good deal of a prig"[8] (at least too much so to be prosperous and successful at the bar).

Nevertheless, larger events unfolded to change the direction of his life and the lives of many others of his generation. At age twenty-six, Adams witnessed the outbreak of the Civil War. While his father was advising him to keep out of the conflict because "no man who dips his hands in this blood will remember it with satisfaction,"[9] Charles, Jr.'s Harvard friends were enlisting. In addition, Charles, Jr., was bored with the law. Possibly war could be an escape from the tedium? From his first brief exposure to garrison duty at Fort Independence in Boston Harbor, Charles, Jr., discovered how much he enjoyed military life. Just after Christmas 1861, he applied for and received (through family connections) a first lieutenant's commission in the First Regiment of the Massachusetts Cavalry Volunteers from which he was assigned to Hilton Head and Beaufort, North Carolina. He wrote: "God! What an escape! I was swept off my feet, out of my office and into the army. Educationally and every other way, it was the most fortunate experience of my life. . . . I can't think of my life without that experience!"[10]

After drifting for some years without ambition or direction, he found a youthful calling in which he could focus his restless energies. Now he could devote himself to a higher cause, the abolition of slavery that he and his family so staunchly opposed and at the same time save the Union that his ancestors had fought to found. The war could not have come at a more propitious time, nor could it have been better suited to Adams's immediate personal needs and values. It gave him a moral purpose for which to live. Above all, it fostered in him a sense of independence.

The cavalry for which he volunteered for the duration of the war was an elite organization, made up from his own social class from his home state. It was therefore not an inhospitable unit for an Adams to join. His regiment saw its share of intense, front-line action at Bull Run, Gettysburg, and the Wilderness campaign, though not without the normal boredom, fatigue, and monotony of military life. On the whole, he recalled his service fondly: "During my service—and it was very active service—I did my duty as well as I knew how and to the best of my ability. I never shirked."[11]

The words Adams used, such as "did my duty," "to the best of my ability," and "never shirked," only underscore how his own deep-seated Puritan conscientiousness, in the words of William G. McLoughlin, "succeeded in carrying the nation through its most serious national crisis. The Union was preserved because God willed it."[12] The war, for Adams and for many in his generation, was fought for a mixture of motives, but particularly for New Englanders, its morality carried a significant Christian, militaristic, and millennialistic symbolism as illustrated by "The Battle Hymn of the Republic," written by Julia Ward Howe:

> In the beauty of the lilies Christ was
>   born across the sea,
> With the glory in His bosom that
>   transfigures you and me;
> As He died to make men holy, let us
>   die to make men free,
> His Truth is marching on.

"His Truth is marching on" meant a moral imperative to most of those who, like Adams, came from upper-class New England homes and risked their lives for the Union cause. Many of his comrades in arms had lost their lives or were severely scarred by battles—emotionally, physically, or both—in pursuit of that moral mission. Adams himself on several occasions came close to losing his life for the cause. When he resigned his commission in August 1865, as brevetted brigadier general, he had been reduced to a mere 130 pounds as a result of the dysentery, jaundice, and malaria that he contracted while in service. Recovery was not easy. He did experience some happiness during his long recuperation, however; he met, proposed to, and married Mary Ogden. They went on a long European honeymoon where he reflected on his future. Once again, as before the war, old issues came back to haunt him: Where do I go? What should I do with my life? or, in Protestant vocabulary, What is my 'calling'? My life's 'mission'?

Now thirty years old, Adams no longer saw law as his lodestar—a feeling he had experienced in the legal profession even before the war. Again, greater events unfolded to rechart the direction of his life. The coming of the railroads in the nineteenth century decisively changed the United States as no other technology had done before. Just as radio, television, and the automobile would transform twentieth-century life, so too no other invention in the nineteenth century would more profoundly recast the United States as the railroad. In 1825 John Stevens constructed a track on his Hoboken, New Jersey, estate, where the first American steam-powered vehicle ran for less than a mile. Thereafter the "iron horse" rapidly expanded across the United States. The railroad system grew so quickly that by 1860, as historian Jack Shepherd writes, it had "30,626 miles of railroad track east of Mississippi, 1,264 of them in Massachusetts alone. Between 1865 and 1873, the number more than doubled, to 70,000; 1887, it would then double again to 157,000. By 1900, the amount of track in the United States would exceed that of Europe. Railroad expansion begun in the 1840s reached across the continent by 1869 and touched the life of every American, from Wall Street to the mineral mines of the Far West. The railroads were fast-growing, big, rich and corrupt—an ideal field for a reform-minded Adams."[13]

Aside from agriculture, no other industry in the United States—even the federal government, which then employed only about 50,000 workers—hired as many people as the railroad industry in the 1870s. By 1875, the 62 railroads operating in Massachusetts alone employed 20,000 people, moved 46 million people, and annually grossed $22 million. The railroads therefore unleashed the most potent economic, political, and technological forces that drove industrial change throughout the United States in the nineteenth century. As historian Edward Kirkland points out correctly, the rapidity of these changes made the times ripe for railroad reform: "There was a need for reform. Railroads were a business experiment; correct principles of construction and, more important, administration had neither been formulated nor understood. Furthermore, railroads had not always fulfilled their promises nor had they brought benefits. Security holders had not received dividends and, in some cases, interest; the rate structures, by its general level and by departure from it in discrimination, perplexed and outraged shippers and travelers. In short, communities, which had largely looked upon railroad corporations as agencies to achieve public purposes, failed to perceive gains from their existence."[14]

Nevertheless, the lure of railroads and their continued growth relentlessly pushed on in the nineteenth century because, as business historian Alfred D. Chandler, Jr., writes: "The railroad's fundamental advantage . . . was its ability to provide a shipper with dependable, precisely scheduled, all-weather transportation of goods. Railroads were far less affected by droughts and floods than were waterways. They were not shut down by freshets in the spring or dry spells in the summer and fall. Most important of all, they remained open during the winter months."[15]

Into the role of railroad reformer stepped Adams. As he described in his autobiography, "I endeavored to strike out a new path for myself, not, as Mr. Emerson recommends, to a star but to a locomotive-engine. I made for myself what might be called a specialty in connection with the development of the railroad system."[16] Much as his forebears had agitated against King George III to create a federal union and later battled against slavery and the succession of the South to preserve the Union, Charles, Jr., would at last find his own calling by wielding his pen and leadership talents on behalf of railroad reform and the maintenance of the constitutional union in the face of an incredible industrial revolution sparked by a new and unrelenting technological force, the railroad. First it was a part-time hobby, and then it developed into a full-time vocation.

Between 1866 and 1871, Adams wrote a series of important essays in which he educated himself and the general public about railroad issues. "I want a war with the [railroad] rings," he wrote to his friends.[17] His mind became increasingly fixated on what he saw as the "monstrous evils" perpetrated by these rings. His investigations riveted on exposure of the corruption caused by private interests' desire for selfish, swift profits. Just as the Puritan divines of the seventeenth century attacked with vigor and realism the sinful, corrupt nature in man's soul, so too Adams and his writings that appeared in the *Nation,* the *North American Review,* the *Journal of Social Science,* and the *American Law Review* exhibited an intense preoccupation with realistically uncovering the human corruption that seemed to him to be spawned in abundance by this new technology. Adams sought to uncover the men and their motives and methods behind railroad corruption to reveal its scope and impacts and thereby to root it out. His research technique included closely studying primary sources. "My pen was always busy," he later reflected.[18] More than any other individual in his day, he came to comprehend the profound influence of the railroad. As he wrote, "The application of steam to locomotion is the most tremendous and far-reaching engine of social revolution which has either blessed or cursed the earth."[19]

Second, like the Puritan divines who interpreted the entire course of human history through the lens of a progressive triumph of Christianity, especially the reformed faith, so too Adams viewed the United States as a "child of steam" and believed that "it was useless for Americans to stand in the way of steam engines."[20] Just as God was seen by the Puritans as working throughout history, for Adams rail technology also was an unstoppable, irreversible historic force that was remaking the United States. Therefore it had to be understood, accepted, and, where possible, reformed to achieve the public good. Yet, the economics of this industry, unlike any other up to that time, required huge investments that made railroads highly capital intensive. Railroads, as a result, tended to evolve into natural monopolies. Unlike other industries, this business was not open to the laws of simple competition where laissez-faire and supply and demand freely operated to set prices; new rail lines could not easily be built, nor could overbuilt lines be eliminated without enormous costs incurred by the industry. Thus, railroading economics, as Adams studied it, naturally impelled the industry toward monopolistic structures. This apparent trend posed a fundamental dilemma for Americans who, for the most part, had been opposed to any sort of business regulation up to that day: how could railroads exist as private corporations and serve the public good while adhering to the then-dominant laissez-faire principles? Outright government ownership of the railroads was not the answer to the problem, as Adams saw it, because government would not necessarily operate them any better. Indeed, government ownership, in his view, would only turn railroads into another bureaucracy and perhaps into far less efficient and innovative entities. Nor was enforced competition conceivable, given the peculiar economics of this industry. The attempt to legislate strict profit limitations of, say, 10 percent, as some states tried to impose at the time, did not work either. To Adams, profit ceilings would only reduce incentives for innovation and business growth, which in turn would harm not only customers but also the whole industry. "The chief tendency of a clause limiting profits," wrote Adams, "would . . . bring into direct antagonism the interests of community and cooperation—to put an end to the instinct of growth of the latter."[21]

Again, like seventeenth-century Puritans—and this third important parallel characteristic between his regulatory philosophy and the theology of his Puritan forebears is important—Adams had no problem calculating the dollars-and-cents costs to the various parties. Like Calvin, Adams approved of returning a fair profit for a fair day's work. He also recognized that returning a fair profit to any capitalist would not be all that bad for society as a whole. Indeed, the act could, if properly calculated, turn into a positive good for the community by motivating railroad corporations to reinvest their profits so as to improve equipment, goods, and services, thereby potentially reducing costs and enhancing benefits to shippers and passengers alike. The common good would result when individuals were allowed to pursue their own private gains—although only if wisely "channelled" (Adams's favorite term).

In an era where economics and the social sciences were in their infancy, one cannot help but be impressed with Adams's mastery of complex, regulatory economics and his comprehension of the broad impacts of this new railroad technology on the United States in his day. He accomplished this research and understanding largely on his own and communicated the results in clear, vivid prose, which was free of specialized or confusing terminology, to a general reading audience. Adams's forceful writing style made his essays popular. Today, even though they are now more than a century old, his essays still speak cogently to modern readers about regulatory issues.

Fourth, there remained always a strong strain of Puritanism infusing the ultimate purpose behind his ideas, especially his insistent emphasis on finding the "right" reform solution to the railroad problem, as if his investigations could uncover "God's plan." Like Job, a man wrestling with divine destiny, Adams tried his best to come to grips—honestly, truthfully, and openly—with the central social and moral dilemmas confronting his age, at least as he viewed them. He rejected the easy solutions, the popular ones that some state legislators were using at the time, such as putting legislative ceilings on corporate profits (i.e., limitations on railroad earnings). On the other hand, he could not find much to recommend letting these railroad natural monopolies operate unrestrained, given their enormous economic impacts and social costs to society as a whole. Some realistic, midway solution must be found— but what?

The reform solution that Adams eventually arrived at and then pushed for with uncompromising conviction for the rest of his life was the creation of a railroad regulatory commission composed of nonpartisan specialists who would identify, analyze, and publicize problems in the industry. This "sunshine commission," as Adams coined it, would bring to light the heretofore concealed public issues of railroads and by doing so foster, in his view, mass public pressures for reform. He distrusted leaving the task to the legislature because, as he wrote,

"Knowledge cannot possibly creep into the legislature, because no one remains in the legislature long enough to learn."[22] Adams understood the importance of the application of long-term expertise to public issues, particularly when one confronts complicated, powerful special interest groups. The legislature was no match for railroad pressure groups. Nonetheless, he distrusted giving too much authority to a permanent set of government officials who could, in the long run, abuse their power by operating beyond the boundaries of community control or accountability. Adams advocated permanent structures in government, outside the legislature, with an independent, analytical capacity to investigate, expose, recommend, and advise the legislature but without direct rate-setting or other regulatory authority. In his words, "Commissions—advisory bureaus—might scientifically study and disclose to an astonished community the shallows and eddies, and the currents of business: the why and the wherefore, the shoaling of channels; the remedies, no less than the causes of the obstructions."[23]

Throughout his writings he placed great faith in public exposure as a remedy to the defects of the railroads: "The indisputable fact was recognized that those corporations [the railroads] are so large and so far removed from the owners of their securities, and the community is so deeply concerned in their doings and condition, that the law-making power both has a right and is duty bound to insist on that publicity as respects to their affairs without which abuses cannot be guarded against."[24]

And so here was the fifth important parallel between Adams's evolving regulatory philosophy and Puritanism: a sunshine commission, like an elite body of the Puritan elect of Calvinism, the consistory, would serve to guide "those corporations" to a new enlightened way through "publicity as respects to their affairs." Or, as Adams put it in other words, "the financially loose, corrupt and dishonest" were "to be kept under immediate and constant supervision."[25] In this manner, both the sin and the sinful could be exposed and made to serve the public good by the threat of revealing their misdeeds to society. The commission replaced the consistory as the superego for society, with Adams serving as its chief elder.

His philosophy toward railroads evolved into one based on corporate volunteerism with control by the threat of public disclosure and potential legislative or judicial intervention. Its assumptions were the inevitability of technological progress; the essential beliefs of capitalism; and the voluntary guidance by an appointed, nonpartisan elite, the sunshine commission, to moderate, through analysis, the more damaging side effects of change. Adams's regulatory ideas emerged from the series of thoughtful essays he published between 1866 and 1871 "and in that way identified my name with railroads; but it was a discouraging process. I never seemed to get anywhere, the outlook did not brighten."[26]

One essay published in 1869, however, did make a difference and brought him the instant name recognition he sought. Titled "A Chapter of Erie," this lengthy exposé, written in Adams's straightforward, gripping prose style, told the amazing story of how Commodore Vanderbilt, president of the New York Central Railroad and then reputedly one of the richest men in the nation, sought to take control of the Erie Railroad, his cross-state rival. Erie was managed by an unsavory crew—Daniel Drew, Jay Gould, and Jim Fiske—who were not about to let the commodore snatch their railroad. The story starts on Wall Street where Vanderbilt went to buy controlling interest in Erie's stock but was repeatedly foiled by the Erie nefarious ne'er-do-wells who manufactured new stock so rapidly that even the wealthy commodore could not keep up with buying such massive amounts of "stock watering." The contest moved on to the courts, where each side bribed its own crooked judges with their own crooked lawyers, then to Albany, the state capital, where each side went to gain favorable legislation from an equally villainous crowd of legislators. Although the story is told in a detached, almost Olympian manner, it takes on a Keystone Cops comic quality: "At ten o'clock the astonished police saw a throng of panic-stricken railway directors—looking more like a frightened gang of thieves, disturbed in the division of their plunder, than like the wealthy representatives of a great corporation—rush headlong from the doors of the Erie office, and dash off in the direction of the Jersey ferry. In their hands were packages and files of papers, and their pockets were crammed with assets and securities. One individual bore away with him in a hackney-coach bales containing six millions of dollars in greenbacks."[27]

Here was Adams's journalistic talent at its best: ironic, muckraking, and exposing all the human foibles, vanities, and corruption in this comedy. Here one could see "men as nature made them with every affection cast aside," as he wrote.[28] The moral was clear also for anyone to read; if it could happen in New York, it could happen anywhere, even Boston! The tale was a not-so-veiled public warning that reform was needed—now.

In large part due to Adams's sensational investigations and public revelations, Massachusetts established the Massachusetts Board of Railroad Commissioners. Actually, it was not the first state regulatory board; other states had enacted rudimentary legislation before. In 1839 Rhode Island created a board to set rate schedules; in 1844 New Hampshire established one to deal with problems of eminent domain; and in 1853 Connecticut created one for railroad safety. Massachusetts, however, developed the first general regulatory body that, through Adams's leadership, became the model for other states and, in 1887, for the federal government. As Adams explained in military-like metaphors his role in creating it:

> Up to that time [1869], Massachusetts had no department of government specially connected with its growing but still wholly unregulated railroad system. I fixed my mind on the great probability of such a department being soon created, and determined to try for a place in it. In this, I succeeded; nor, as things go in life, did I have long to wait.
>
> It was in October 1866, that I began operations, in July 1869, my purpose was accomplished. An act creating a State Board of Commissioners was passed by the Legislature, in the Spring of 1869 largely through my instrumentality, and, making a strike for the position, I was appointed the third member of it. I had worked my problem successfully out in two years and nine months; a very creditable consummation.[29]

The new board on which Adams served had considerable status, with each member receiving $4,000 (a large salary for that day). The charter called for three nonpartisan appointments with overlapping terms and contained broad, unspecified powers. The enabling legislation simply read: "The Commission shall have the general supervision of all railroads in the Commonwealth" and shall make an annual report "containing such facts, statements, and explanations as will disclose the actual workings of the system of railroad transportation."[30]

On July 4, 1869, Charles Francis Adams, Jr., was sworn in as one of the three commissioners, along with James Converse, its chair, and Edward Appleton. By 1872 Adams had assumed the chair, largely because he willingly took over most of the work. He volunteered to draft all the annual reports; undertook field investigations; recommended reforms and new legislation to the governor and legislature; and even handpicked replacement commissioners when Converse and Appleton resigned. From the board's early years onward, Adams chose to stress a general policy-making role for the board rather than one of issuing specific legal opinions. In addition, he worked closely with the legislature throughout his tenure to insure adequate support for the commissioners' decisions. Overall, his reports were models of well-reasoned, detailed, and well-researched analysis. Generally, the reports focused on establishing clear operational standards to promote the public interest and safety, the efficiency of railroad corporations, and fair pricing practices without entering into specific details of case law or regulations.

What Adams basically put into practice during his ten-year tenure on the commission was his own sunshine regulatory philosophy that he had devised from nearly five years of journalistic investigations. "The board of commissioners was set up as a sort of lens by means of which the scattered rays of public opinion could be concentrated to a focus and brought to bear upon a given point."[31] Again, this point of view was a product of his own fundamental assumption that if only enough publicity could be focused on corrupt practices, the general public could be educated about the problem and in the process the public interest would be well served by means of voluntary compliance. The threat of public sanctions would be enough to force conformance on the parties involved. Adams stamped the board's work irrevocably with this philosophical approach. As William A. Craft, who served with Adams on the board throughout much of the 1870s, said, "He gave direction to the inquiries and shaped the action of the Commission on all questions."[32]

A case in point of Adams's bent to use voluntary compliance came in the Revere disaster of 1871. A violent rear-end collision of two train locomotives occurred on a heavily traveled rail line to a popular beach resort in Massachusetts. For ten consecutive days the commissioners went out to survey the wreckage, question witnesses, and meet with railroad executives, citizens, and community groups, many of whom were enraged at the loss of twenty-nine lives, destruction of property, and neglect of public safety by railroads. The investigatory report, written by Adams promptly after the accident, exposed the failures of the system that caused the disaster, such as improper signaling, inadequate brakes, overcrowded rail lines, poor scheduling, and cars not constructed well enough to prevent telescoping (i.e., the accordion-like compression of railcars in an accident). The report attempted to educate the public on the reforms needed in the system as a whole to improve its general operating safety, and the investigators resisted the heated public pressures at the time to find villains or blame someone. A model of restraint, the report earned the respect of all parties and ultimately helped achieve the desired goal of improved rail safety because most of the reforms that the report recommended were eventually instituted by the railroads. It also established a prototype of crisis-response investigations that regulatory commissions follow to this day.

Just as in the Revere case, public pressures on the commissioners were also intense in other situations, particularly those involving rate-making issues. The rate charged by railroads for shippers and passengers was, and still is, the most complex and controversial problem confronting regulatory bodies because it represents the key to profits and losses for railroads and for the customers they serve. Here, as usual, Adams relied on "the eventual supremacy of enlightened public opinion" to curb excessive rate charges. "The Commissioners had to listen, and they might investigate and report—they could do little more," said Adams.[33] This method contrasted sharply with regulatory commissions in western states at the time. As Adams wrote, "In the West, the fundamental idea behind every railroad act was force—the Commission represented the Constable. In the Massachusetts Act the fundamental idea was publicity—the Commission represented public opinion." Yet, there was always the not-so-hidden iron fist in that velvet glove of commissioners "merely" representing "public opinion." As Adams went on to say, "Without remedial or corrective power themselves, behind them stood the legislative and judiciary ready to be brought into play should any corporation evince an unreasonable spirit of persistence."[34]

Similarly, in other areas such as labor disputes, Adams argued, "the appeal in industrial difficulties was to an enlightened public opinion, based on facts elicited by a fair-minded public investigation." Increasingly, however, he believed that he was "a voice crying in the wilderness. Our people as a community do not share in my faith in publicity, but, all the same, public opinion and patience are the best possible agents for solving industrial, social and economical problems. . . . Were there in this country a great many more investigations into alleged railroad abuses, and not so many repressive laws, the conditions of affairs would be greatly improved."[35]

In the end he perhaps placed too much faith in enlightened public opinion and the capacity of the commission to guide it, but he had only a few regrets about his own service on the commission: "As for myself, looking back, I think, all things considered I did well. I made some mistakes of judgment, and bad mistakes in applications. Frequently, I proved unequal to the occasion. More than once, I now see, I was lacking in firmness, and even courage."[36] The Adams conscience made him his own best critic.

In 1879, after a decade of service, Adams resigned from the commission, hoping next to help formulate a national policy in the field of railroad regulation. Adams went on to chair the Eastern Trunkline Association, an experiment by several eastern railroads to cooperate voluntarily to set rates and other practices, or to "pool," as it was then called. Once again, volunteerism guided his working beliefs. The association was short-lived, however. As Adams would later admit, too many self-interested parties were involved. He ended his career in the railroad industry, serving for five and one-half years as president of Union Pacific, and eventually became comparatively wealthy through his various private investments. He did regret that he never directly shaped national policy; he had hoped to serve on the Interstate Commerce Commission, the first federal regulatory commission, which, as noted earlier, was established by Congress in 1887. In addition, he increasingly believed that he and his ideas were being neglected.

His last years in business, even as the president of one of the most powerful railroads in the United States, were not happy ones. He admitted that "he had stayed too long" and viewed the people he worked with negatively: "They were a coarse, realistic, bargaining crowd."[37] He retired and returned to his family home in Quincy, Massachusetts, where he wrote history; engaged in various local civic projects, including serving on the town library board and on Harvard's Board of Overseers; and occasionally issued invectives toward the regulatory policies promulgated by the Interstate Commerce Commission. "What asses officials [of the ICC] of the second class are!" he wrote.[38] They strayed far, too far, from voluntarily serving as the guiding independent moral conscience of a community, the Puritan elect, as he had envisioned.

Nevertheless, history has a strange way of fooling even the most perceptive participant observers such as Charles Francis Adams, Jr. State after state framed their regulatory commissions along the lines Adams had first established in Massachusetts. His model decisively influenced Shelby Cullom, whose Senate committee in 1887 wrote the Act to Regulate Interstate Commerce. That act set up a commission that was to be headed by "five wise, able experienced men of reputation, commanding confidence and clothed with a limited discretion." Cullom wanted "legislation which could not possibly harm the railroads and other business interests."[39] In the end, the resulting federal legislation came to look very much like the sunshine commission that Adams had first developed in his home state, that is, an autonomous structure headed by independent, nonpartisan commissioners with overlapping terms, free of vested interests in the businesses they were regulating, charged with "the authority to inquire into the management of the business of common carriers," with the right "to obtain full and complete information," and with requirements to "issue annual reports on all aspects of internal business operations and establish uniform system of accounts."[40] Nevertheless, those who filled the ICC posts could never measure up to Adams's elitist standards. Also, the excessive legislative meddling and the commission's increasing use of legalistic powers and overreliance on case law were an anathema to Adams, but his fundamental ideas molded the basic form and structure not only of the ICC but also of other independent federal and state regulatory commissions that were subsequently established.[41]

In addition, in the applied practice of regulatory administration, his Massachusetts model, with its innovations of disclosure, uniform system of accounting, voluntary compliance, neutral "factual" analysis, crisis-response investigations, and the like, set much of the future administrative pattern for public regulation in the United States. Indeed, since the late 1970s, when deregulation of many phases of American industry began, Adams's philosophy stressing industrial volunteerism and minimal government intervention, combined with the constant threat of public exposure and legal sanctions, looks remarkably up-to-date.

In the broadest sense as well, Adams's handiwork in Massachusetts fundamentally served to alter the U.S. Constitution—not through any formal amendment to it but through the informal, unwritten processes and institutions that were essential to govern the nation in the twentieth century. In the late nineteenth century, through a novel public instrument, the regulatory commission, Adams created an "unwritten" constitutional method for the U.S. government to use to cope with the sudden growth of unrestrained private power.

More than his father, Charles Francis, Sr., and even more than either his grandfather, John Quincy, or great-grandfather, John, both illustrious early founders of the Republic, Charles, Jr., established a significant extra-constitutional method by which Americans in the twentieth century would be governed via innovative administrative arrangements. He originated and developed a new administrative device of modern governance that permitted the old American constitutional order to survive—and thrive—in the modern era. Certainly it would be hard to imagine how the United States today could operate without Adams's unique administrative institution, the regulatory commission, especially given the complex capitalistic, industrialized, and technological society within which Americans now live.

Yet, ironically, in the end he could never let go of the tendency to see himself as second-rate, at least compared with his ancestors. Even on the last pages of his autobiography, written shortly before his death, Adams engages in "what-ifs." Curiously, he concludes that if he could live his life over again, he would prefer not to be a president of the United States, a victorious general, or a captain of industry. Instead, he said he would prefer to be simply someone who made a lot of money, a "real-money bags," in his words, but not for selfish gain. Rather, he would donate all of it to his first genuine affection, that ancient bastion of Puritan learning, the university that John Harvard founded in 1636.

4
Emory Upton
Prophet for Public Professionalism

Emory Upton, 1839–1881
(courtesy of the Library of Congress)

Let us strive to show ourselves worthy of the kingdom of heaven.
—Emory Upton, in a letter from West Point, May 1, 1859

A YOUNG SOLDIER UNDER HIS COMMAND once described Emory Upton as "a young looking man with a thin mustache, high cheek bones, square jaw. . . . He had a small mouth, and thin, usually tightly closed lips. . . . His blue, deep-set eyes seemed to be searching all the time. . . . He had dark brown hair, a dark complexion, and an intensely serious look, emphasizing his moral rigidity—a well worn Bible was always on his desk."[1]

Photos of Upton taken throughout his life depict that same image of inner moral intensity, a righteous self-driven man, akin to a nineteenth-century Old Testament prophet in a young man's body. Although Upton was virtually unknown outside the military, his army career is the backdrop of good legend. Even before he finished West

Point in 1861, he was well-known in military circles for his frequent fistfights with southern cadets who opposed his open abolitionist beliefs. Serving as a Union officer throughout the Civil War in some of the bloodiest engagements, Upton displayed genuine heroic leadership in battle and rose to the rank of major general by age twenty-six.

Upton made his most remarkable contributions in his post–Civil War military career, however. His ideas have been of enormous lasting value not only to the armed services but also to public service in the United States. Upton's postwar writings, drawn heavily from his demanding wartime experiences, conceptualized a new professional ideal and the institutions to support professionalism inside the military. His ideas ultimately became critical for the professional advancement of civilian agencies throughout the U.S. government. Without his inventions of the general staff concept, advanced military training for officers, rotation of staff-line cadre, the use of "regulars" as the core of the military, and other ideas, World War I, World War II, and even the cold war would have been in all likelihood impossible for the United States to win. At least, it is difficult to conceive of the United States as a twentieth-century global superpower based solely on the founding fathers' notions of citizen-soldiers!

Yet, for all his brilliance in battle and foresight in theory, Emory Upton, at age forty-one, took his own life. He was deeply distressed about his career prospects in the military and the apparent failure of his thinking to gain acceptance from his superiors or the general public. He died tragically, too young, feeling too misunderstood, too ignored, and mourned by too few, but, in the apt words of Isaiah Berlin, ideas often flit about "like butterflies." We often do not know when, how, or where they will land and thereby influence the direction of history.

This insight proved true in Upton's case because within two decades or so after his death, many, if not most, of his ideas found their way into application. At the dawn of the twentieth century, Secretary of War Elihu Root drew greatly on Upton's writings to create major institutional reforms in the military, and still later the Taft Commission Report on Economy and Efficiency (1911–1912), the Brownlow Report of the President's Committee on Administrative Management (1937), and the Hoover Report of the Commission on Organization of the Executive Branch of Government (1949) brought these essentially military institutional reforms into fruition within civilian units of the executive branch. The reach and depth of Uptonian professional concepts thus turned out to be far more pervasive than he thought—or could have hoped—were possible.

Emory Upton was born to devout Methodist parents in Bastavia, New York, on August 27, 1839, the tenth of thirteen children. Upstate New York at the time was on the edge of what historians refer to as "the burnt over district," where moral reformism, such as temperance and abolition, flourished; where "the great awakening" of the early nineteenth century began; and from where the seeds of new religious faiths such as Mormonism sprang. As Stephen Ambrose, Upton's biographer, points out:

> While Emory was a youth, Dorthea L. Dix toured the region to advocate kinder, more intelligent treatment of the insane. William Miller
> . . . convinced thousands in the area that the Second Coming of Christ would take place on October 22, 1843. The Millerites sold all their goods and, to be closer to heaven, awaited the Second Coming on roofs, hilltops and haystacks. Mother Ann Lee and Jemima Wilkinson of New York State founded "Universal Friend" communities on the basis of celibacy. . . . Elizabeth C. Stanton and Lucretia Mott launched at Seneca Falls a woman's suffrage movement. That same year, 1848, the Fox sisters' spirit rappings and table turnings induced an outpouring of spiritualism.[2]

Emory himself was raised in the strict Methodist faith. "His parents taught him to love and respect God, to do his duty, and always to try to improve the world."[3] There was little time for fun or foolishness. Farming was a hard life for the Uptons, with many mouths to feed in a family of thirteen. In addition Emory was goaded by his parents to work hard to improve himself and a world badly in need of Christian enlightenment. As Upton wrote later of his home life with his father, "Many times he took advantage of my weakness to chastise me for acts which to a juvenile mind appeared perfectly proper."[4]

Methodists describe their church as "a company of men having the form and seeking the power of godliness, united in order to pray together, to receive the word of exhortation, and to watch over one another in love, that they may help each other to work out their salvation."[5] On the rural frontier where Upton was raised, however, Methodists belonged to one of the most demanding denominations, often tending toward unyielding moral perfectionism. As one frontier Methodist circuit-riding preacher at the time wrote of his work: "I traversed the mountains and valleys, frequently on foot, with my knapsack on my back, guided by Indian paths in the wilderness, when it was not expedient to take a horse. I had often to wade through morasses, half-leg deep in mud and water; frequently satisfying my hunger with a piece of bread and pork from my knapsack, quenching my thirst from a brook, and resting my weary limbs on the leaves of the trees. Thanks be to God! He compensated me for all my toil; for many precious souls were awakened and converted to God."[6]

In many ways Wesleyite Methodism turned into a far more severe, almost militaristic doctrine after it came to the United States. And as one writer has noted, Methodism's arrival in the United States resulted in "the most successful of a number of eighteenth century spiritual movements which challenged the moral and spiritual indifference. . . . If prior to the American Revolution, it was said 'a corncrib will hold all of them [Methodists],' by 1820 they had surpassed the Baptists as the largest Protestant denomination in the United States."[7] The frontier where Methodism flourished in the early nineteenth century was hardly a place of moral and spiritual indifference, however. To the contrary, in that day the frontier was a rough-and-ready, highly immoral or amoral world, full of gambling, hard drinking, swearing, violence, and sexual looseness. Therefore, the frontier Methodist minister—as well as the Methodist faithful—lived an especially hard, demanding, if not isolated, life in order to be true to God's word, at least as they interpreted its meaning.

Indeed, the severity of a Methodist life was not all that far removed from a soldier's doing "battle for the Lord," particularly in that time and place. Therefore, when Emory Upton announced at age fourteen that he wanted to be a soldier and began reading books such as the *Life of Napoleon*, it was not very surprising, given the characteristics of the faith he and his family professed with such intense conviction. Much like a minister of the gospel, as one admiring writer observed, "Upton's life was pure and unselfish in the highest degree, and it was controlled by an ardent love for the profession of arms, which from the earliest dawn filled him with resolve to acquire fighting fame."[8] He would become a seventeenth-century Cromwell in nineteenth-century America.

At age fourteen, Upton made up his mind that he wanted to go to West Point, but the local congressman, who controlled academy appointments for the locale (as congressional representatives still do), suggested he acquire more education. His father, Daniel, who was a poor, illiterate farmer but who respected education, sent him off to Oberlin on a scholarship. Since the 1830s, Oberlin College had been primarily a training school for evangelical ministers and a hotbed of abolitionism. The curriculum at the time combined hard manual labor with healthy doses of theology and classical liberal arts education. The fifteen-year-old Upton, by all accounts, hated the liberal arts but thrived on the hard work, read military history whenever possible, and learned from hours in church and at revivals that the world was in darkness and that those who had seen the truth were under the solemn and pressing obligation to bear witness and evangelize God's truth abroad.

After two semesters at Oberlin, Upton won an appointment to the U.S. Military Academy. By the time Upton arrived at the academy, it was over a half-century old. For the last seventeen of those years, it had been headed by Sylvanus Thayer, who had turned its limited, undistinguished engineering program for army officers into one of the finest higher education programs in the United States, if not the world, for training potential officers. Thayer developed rigorous military training that was combined with broad scientific, mathematical, and liberal arts education.

Upton thrived on the academy's discipline. By his own admission, he loved West Point and wanted no other life. As he wrote to his sister, "I am passionately attached to West Point, and would not give up my appointment here for a million dollars."[9] Yet, he also readily admitted to her, "The army is a hard place to practice religion; though few scoff at it, yet a great majority totally disregard it. Still, through the prayers of others, I hope to lead a Christian life and do as much good in the army as in any other profession. I do not think that Christians have ever disgraced the profession of arms, on the contrary, they are those who have most ennobled it."[10]

In spite of the personal challenges of professing his faith combined with espousing his strong abolitionist and temperance convictions within the confines of West Point, which at the time housed a majority of southerners in its classes, Upton felt comfortable in that atmosphere. "It attacked," as one historian put it, "none of his basic beliefs, maintained a strict discipline that was familiar and therefore comfortable to him, and promised to give him the training he felt he would need to improve the world. . . . It encouraged his ambition."[11]

If Emory worked hard at Oberlin, he worked even harder at the academy, finding military policy, tactics, and history highly stimulating. The training also instilled pride and elitism into the youth. West Point imbued in Emory a sentiment of aloofness from and superiority toward civilians; it taught him to take great pride in the achievements of academy graduates and of the regular army. Emory extended this pride into a feeling of hostility toward nonprofessional civilian soldiers.[12] Much like a seminary prepares the would-be minister to take up the call and wear the cloth, so too this impressionable youth was "anointed with" or, to use a more modern term, "socialized into" the professional ethos of the military, an outlook from which he would never waiver.

Historic accidents are vital to shaping human destiny, and Upton's life was certainly no exception. The Civil War broke out in 1861, the same year that Upton graduated. Emory actually foresaw the coming of the war and wanted to graduate early so that he might get into action from the first shots of battle. Graduating early would also mean he would obtain a commission ahead of the many civilians who were flocking into the army ranks and thus avoid service under a civilian superior. Upton, along with twenty-nine other West Point seniors, petitioned the secretary of war for early graduation and immediate assignment in the army. On May 6, 1861, the petition was granted, and they received officer commissions. Because Emory graduated in the top 20 percent of his class, he could select the military branch in which he wanted to serve. He chose the artillery because he claimed that it promised quick promotions. Thus, at age twenty-one, Upton became a second lieutenant in the Fifth United States Artillery.

Throughout the war, Upton saw some of the toughest, most deadly battles, including those at Bull Run, Chancellorsville, Cold Harbor, and in the Wilderness campaign. He was seriously wounded on two occasions. Almost everyone found him to be the embodiment of an ideal soldier: brave in combat, quick and astute in planning tactics, fair with his subordinates, attentive to the soldiers' health and safety in every way, yet also strict as a disciplinarian and precise in giving orders with the expectation that his commands would be carried out to the letter. Likewise, his superiors thought well of him. Not only was he picked again and again for difficult and increasingly responsible command assignments, but also he was promoted swiftly throughout the ranks, becoming one of the few men during the Civil War, on either side, to lead troops into battle under three different branches—artillery, cavalry, and infantry.

His last commander during the war, Major General James H. Wilson, said that Upton's actions were "the most heroic . . . that came under my observations during the war" and that he was "incomparably the best tactician of either army."[13] Wilson cited as a case in point Upton's incredible heroism when General Lee detached General Early to threaten Washington, D.C., along the Maryland border in 1864. Upton's cavalry brigade in Wilson's Sixth Corps was sent to cut off Early and defend the capital:

> It was in this charge that the heroic General David A. Russell, commanding the division, was mortally wounded. He was promptly succeeded by Upton, who pressed the division forward with conspicuous ability and energy. In the full tide of success the gallant young commander was severely wounded on the inside of the right thigh by a fragment of a bursting shell. The muscle was frightfully lacerated and the femoral artery laid bare, but, instead of retiring, as he was fully justified in doing, and indeed he was ordered to do by General Sheridan in person, he called his staff surgeon and directed him to stanch the bleeding wound by tourniquet. As soon as this was done, he called for a stretcher, and had himself borne about the field thereon, still directing the movements of his victorious division, and did not leave it or give up the command till night had put an end to the pursuit. The fortitude displayed by him upon this occasion was heroic in the extreme and marked him as a man of extraordinary nerve. It was in notable contrast with what had come to be customary on such occasions.[14]

Although he was never rash in his displays of heroism, Upton remained in the heat of battle "a remarkably cool head."[15] As another officer observed: "[Upton is] a thorough student of military science, and is also a master of the details of military life. He is quick to see and use the material at hand."[16] Yet, he was not above using purple rhetoric to rally his troops to the cause, as when he took back the U.S. arsenal in Augusta, Georgia, in 1865. After all, according to Upton, it was the Lord's work: "Soldiers! Four years ago the governor of Georgia, at the head of an armed force, hauled down the American flag at this arsenal. The President of the United States called the nation to arms to repossess the forts and arsenals which had been seized. After four years of sanguinary war and conflict we execute the order of the great preserver of the union and liberty, and today we again hoist the stars and stripes over the United States Arsenal at Augusta. Majestically, triumphantly she rises!"[17]

Out of these varied, intense wartime leadership experiences Upton later fashioned invaluable lessons for shaping his philosophy toward military professionalism. Like many of his generation, the horrors of the Civil War were firmly etched in his memory, but unlike anyone else, Upton turned these experiences into important precepts for fundamentally reorganizing the postwar army so that it could meet its future challenges. For instance, he saw the main cause of so many Union defeats as directly due to ill-trained, incompetent leadership. As he wrote to his sister during the war, "I am disgusted with the generalship displayed. Our men in many instances have been foolishly and wantonly sacrificed."[18] Older generals, he came to believe, were incapable of making swift, decisive choices, inspiring men to take aggressive action by stirring speeches, or leading in the heat of battle from the front of the line. After Cold Harbor, Upton observed, "I have seen but little generalship during the campaign. Some of our corps commanders are not fit to be corporals."[19]

Upton also came to believe that well-trained, well-disciplined regular troops, led by professional careerists—not volunteers or politically appointed generals—were essential for victory. That basic truth was gleaned for Upton out of innumerable, often bloody, and disastrous battlefield encounters. His famous dictum summed up his own fundamental faith in the superiority of professionals over amateurs in wartime: "20,000 regular troops at Bull Run would have routed the insurgents, settled the question of military resistance and relieved us from the pain and suspense of four years of war."[20] Perhaps this statement was an exaggeration because most likely neither the South would have been deterred by twenty thousand U.S. regulars nor Congress would have been motivated enough to raise that many regulars before the first battle of the war. Yet, in a larger context, the Uptonian preference for regulars over volunteers during wartime contests of any sort was convincingly argued and succinctly phrased and ultimately became the dictum of most postwar military professionals.

By the end of the Civil War, Upton had risen to the rank of major general. At age twenty-six, he was the youngest major general in the army and recognized by his peers, even then, as destined to make his mark on the military. He married, though it was a brief, tragic union. His wife, Emily Martin, died within two years of a lung infection contracted on their honeymoon in Italy. Upton mourned her loss the rest of his life and never remarried. For all practical purposes Upton afterward "married his career."

In the post–Civil War era, with limited command opportunities available except on frontier forts defending territory against Indians,

Upton was reduced in rank to lieutenant colonel. In rapid succession he was stationed at a string of small forts: Lenoir, Tennessee; St. Louis, Missouri; and then Denver, Colorado, fulfilling traditional peacekeeping constabulary roles. Throughout these years, Upton could not let go of the awful events he had witnessed and endured during the war: volunteers refusing to fight because their contracts were completed; professional soldiers pushed aside for political favorites; state governors withholding promotions from deserving men; incompetent leaders, both professional and amateur, in command of army corps; and inexperienced militiamen running from the ranks at Bull Run. With the great moral crusade of the war now won, Upton turned his attention to another cause, reform of the military. He planned first to reform military tactics and second to reform overall military policy.

His opportunity to institute reforms arrived on June 5, 1866. He was ordered by the War Department to return to West Point, where he spent the next four years designing a new system of military tactics. There, with righteous zeal, he set to work on creating a new approach learned from his wartime experiences that he hoped would eliminate future American waste and needless bloodshed. The Civil War had been fought with essentially eighteenth-century French military methods, which emphasized rigid, linear tactics; the soldiers would advance lockstep in columns with simultaneous volleys of fire, using little personal initiative or inventiveness in combat. With his friend Henry Du Pont, Upton experimented with his ideas by using cadets at the U.S. Military Academy under various test conditions. He rewrote the basic concepts of U.S. infantry tactics and later amended the cavalry and artillery tactics in similar manner, specifically adapting the methods to American terrain and American battlefield experiences. His tactics also incorporated the use of new rapid-fire weaponry such as the breech-loading rifles that could keep up steady, intense fire on enemy troops. Attacks en masse, either heavy columns or rigid lines, were abandoned in favor of light, flexible units of four, later called squads, that could conform quickly to varied terrain and firepower. Tight oversight and control of troops by commanders were reduced in the Uptonian system by placing increased responsibility on the individual soldier to select a target, fire when necessary, and take cover on his own initiative.

Here was a truly original American form of military tactics that, as Upton claimed, was aimed "to shake the morale of the enemy by securing in every stage of the advance a preponderance of fire, at the same time advancing in such small fractions, up to the moment of the final rush or assault, as to reduce the casualties to the lowest limit."[21] This system not only adapted well to U.S. geography but also fit peculiar American values, especially the dominant individualist, Protestant values of the era. That is, it sought to place greater choice for action and personal initiative on the individual soldier in the line, not on the commander or higher authority.

On August 1, 1867, General Order Number 73 of the War Department formally adopted Upton's new tactics for the infantry, and later, in 1874 and 1875, respectively, the cavalry and artillery manuals were published.[22] By the 1870s Upton's name was synonymous with the state-of-the-art tactical reforms undertaken throughout the military. His new tactics manuals were also required for state militia, and because he retained the copyrights, Upton earned substantial royalties that significantly supplemented his army paycheck (in those days it was legal to do so).

On July 30, 1870, Upton was selected commandant of cadets, the second in command under the superintendent, and was responsible principally for military training and instruction. By his early thirties Upton had achieved considerable success and fame, including the highly regarded position as second in command at West Point. Nonetheless, with his tactical reforms complete, he was restless and sought new fields to conquer beyond the confines of the routines of the U.S. Military Academy. Upton proposed to the general-in-chief of the army, William T. Sherman, who was Upton's commander during the Civil War and who was a strong proponent of Upton's reforms, that he embark on a world tour to study Asian and European armies to find out what Americans could learn from military systems abroad. Both Sherman and Secretary of War William W. Belknap supported the idea. Upton, in the latter part of 1875 and during most of 1876, became an official observer for the U.S. Army, traveling around the world to study the major armies. What emerged from his extensive notes and interviews was his book *The Armies of Asia and Europe,* which is the most detailed portrait, even to this day, of the late-nineteenth-century armies in Europe and Asia. It described in straightforward journalistic prose their organizations, tactics, methods of instruction, sizes, planning processes, and means of policy formulation and civilian oversight.

Although dry in terms of statistical and factual details, and occasionally laced with Christian commentary on local morals, the book drew important lessons for Americans on the key attributes of professionalism Upton discovered from observing Asian and European armed services, especially Germany's military, namely that:

1. The regular army should be the core of the military, and regular officers must be well trained to be its leaders;

2. Entrance into the officer corps ought to be based only on graduation from a military school or by passing a qualifying exam and course of professional study;

3. Merit should be the sole basis for advancement within the military;

4. Advanced war academies need to be created to teach officers broader, more complex military strategy and tactics in preparation for senior command and general staff posts;

5. A general staff, free of civilian control and composed of officers with the best professional training, is essential for planning, coordination, and overall direction of the armed services;

6. Rotation on a regular basis between the line and general staff is important to prevent stagnation and promote the integration of the various services with the central planning function;

7. Rapid promotion must be fostered for the most talented to insure that the government profits from their skills to the utmost and rewards their professionalism, expertise, and dedication;

8. Officer qualifications should be regularly reviewed on an annual or biennial basis by evaluating which officers "show the zeal, aptitude, special qualification, and personal character." Those found wanting in these basic qualities need to be separated from service to "prevent the injury to the service";

9. Although regulars have to form the core of the military, according to Upton, adequately trained reserves are required to back up the regular army, organized in various strategic depots throughout the country and capable of rapid mobilization; and

10. "Every citizen, in consideration of the protection extended to his life and property, is held to owe military service to his government. To equalize the burdens of military service, and to facilitate the equipment and mobilization of troops, each country is divided into military districts, to which are permanently assigned army corps, divisions, brigades, regiments, and battalions, which draw from the districts all their recruits both in peace and war."[23]

Cost was also a central theme throughout Upton's writing. In his view, peacetime cutbacks were always false economies. Rather, a strong peacetime defense saved huge sums—and lives—when war broke out by making quick, easy victories possible. "Regular troops," he stated, "engaged for war, are the only safe reliance of a government, and are, in every point of view, the best and most economical."[24] Here again, he showed little love for ill-trained volunteers or political meddling from civilian officials; they only caused great harm and potential loss of life. Again and again, Upton would cite the examples of Prussia's six-week victory over Austria in 1866 and Germany's destruction of the French army within four months in the 1870s because of their superior military peacetime preparation.

Although he deplored German militarism, Upton nonetheless believed that the United States had much to learn from German professionalism. "We cannot Germanize: neither is it desirable," he stated, but the central German lesson was also clear: Americans, following the German example, should place "regulars" at the heart of the military with "sufficient strength, not merely to form the Army's nucleus but to serve as the backbone of the forces on a war footing."[25] Upton saw this military model as the best for the United States because it would prevent from recurring the human tragedy he had personally witnessed during the Civil War: the needless bloodshed, immense costs, and wanton pain and sacrifice. Above all, the military model appealed to his own religious values, the vigorous Methodism he had been reared in from childhood; that is, the world was a dark place that needed Christian enlightenment, a muscularized American Christianity, in particular, a tough, no-nonsense way of attaining God's way on earth, even if it was the Americanized version. Certainly the cause was just.

Army officers received Upton's *Armies of Asia and Europe* enthusiastically, and military journals carried positive reviews. Several of Upton's ideas became part of the Burnside Army Reform Bill of 1878, which included the creation of the general staff, rotation of officers between staff and line, and the development of advanced training schools. The Burnside bill lost in Congress, however, because by the time it came up for a vote, several of its principal backers had been defeated in the midterm elections.

Despite the setback, Upton doggedly went to work in the last years of his life on another book, *The Military Policy of the United States*. Its introduction sums up its basic message: "The object of this work is to treat historically and statistically our military policy up to the present time, and to show the enormous and unnecessary sacrifice of life and treasure, which attended all our armed struggles."[26] He noted also that "we have rejected the practice of European nations," and so "all of our wars have been prolonged for want of judicious and economical preparation."[27] In his careful, chronological review of U.S. policy toward warfare from the Revolution through the Civil War, Upton repeatedly underscored, by example after example, how ill prepared the United States was for engaging in each of the impending conflicts. He showed in a fact-filled, detailed fashion how the loss of life and resources was the result of the reliance primarily on raw volunteers with short-term enlistments who were poorly equipped and trained and led by too small of a regular cadre.

Problems also were only magnified by repeated interference of civilians in military affairs along with the promotion of "political" generals over careerists. Whereas Upton depicted the civilians in charge as the villains because of their shortsightedness and self-interested political meddling, he saw the regulars as the heroes of his tale: "Whenever the Regular Army has met the enemy, the conduct of the officers and men has merited and received the applause of their countrymen. It has rendered the country vastly more important service than by merely sustaining the national honor in battle. It has preserved, and still preserves, to us the military art; has formed the standard of discipline for the vast number of volunteers of our late wars, and while averting disaster and bloodshed has furnished us with military commanders to lead armies of citizen soldiers, whose exploits are now famous in the history of the world."[28]

Of course, his idealized version of events neatly omits names of prominent West Pointers in the Civil War who turned out to be disastrous leaders: George McClellan, John Pope, Ambrose Burnside, and Joseph Hooker, to name a few; nor did Upton cite citizen soldiers who came to be capable commanders, such as John A. Logan and Francis P.

Blair in the North and Nathan Bedford Forrest and John B. Gordon in the South. His contempt for civilian control was so extreme that at points in his book Upton seemed to prefer placing military policy solely in the hands of military professionals, leaving civilians to do little more than rubber-stamp preapproved military policy. In some places the text seems to imply that military policy should or can be made entirely in a political vacuum and that no alternative exists but to place seasoned, trained regulars in charge. Upton's history of American military policy was crafted as an elaborate argument—a polemic—to underscore the value of the regular army being at the center of future military policy-making; for Upton, the very survival of the country counted on it!

On the whole, Upton nonetheless prepared a well-written, solid history with a cogent theme. As military historian Russell F. Weigley concludes, "He did an impressive job. No similar study of American military history had ever been attempted, and to this day there is no history of American military organization and policy which fully equals Upton in the period he covered." As Weigley also notes, however, the book "was a work of deep pessimism" because the unbroken record of "American military history was the recurrent failure of civilian leaders to devote the country in peace to preparation for war."[29]

Was Upton so deeply pessimistic, though? Military historians such as Weigley have tended to view Upton as an American Clausewitz, Scharnhorst, or Moltke, who promoted professionalism because of dark visions of human nature à la the continental European conservatives. Upton, by contrast, was thoroughly American in his outlook and experiences; after all, he had witnessed the worst of the Civil War as a young man and in a tough, realistic, no-nonsense analysis had attempted to outline a remedy—that is, professionalism—to prevent such an awful tragedy from recurring.

In addition, although his ingrained Protestantism knew all too well the didactic consequences of Adam's fall, original sin, Upton believed deeply in the possibility of Christian salvation: specifically, with ample hard work, faith, *and* God's grace, one might find redemption. By cleaving to the professional model, would the army—and ultimately the United States itself—find redemption? Was Upton's professional calling, in fact, his own unconscious effort to transform his personal beliefs into reforming the wider society? Was it Upton's attempt to transmute his own religious faith into a modern secular creed?

Upton had been reared in the particular denomination of Methodism that was perhaps the most innovative organizationally of any Protestant faith. As religious historian Winthrop S. Hudson notes, it was not in terms of doctrinal creativity but rather in organizational innovation that Methodism flourished in the United States:

> A major reason for the astonishingly rapid spread and growth of Methodism was the adoption of the "circuit system" which Wesley had devised for his English societies. Thus the new church was equipped with a highly mobile ministry of traveling preachers who covered a vast territory instead of being tied to a single locality. The more intimate nurture of the flocks they gathered was provided by local lay preachers and class leaders. No system could have been more admirably designed for moving quickly into new territory, whether that territory was in older settled regions of the seaboard or over the mountains into new communities of the frontier. In both areas Methodists met with equal success.[30]

Upton's faith in military professionalism, like Methodism's practice of mobile, "professing" clerics, embraced structural originality for the good of the cause. The future of the U.S. Army and of the United States were worthy aims for which to advocate his own novel administrative changes. In addition, the timing was ripe for acceptance of his ideas. The postwar army, with its reliance on volunteers, politically appointed generals, and antiquated command structures, badly needed reform, and General William T. Sherman, the military's chief general between 1869 and 1883, admired and actively supported Upton's ideas. Moreover, the U.S. Army, numbering only twenty-five thousand in the late nineteenth century, working with budgets averaging $30 million annually, and living in relatively secluded garrisons distant from civilians, permitted a unique nurturing world for Upton's innovations. As Samuel P. Huntington writes: "The very isolation and rejection which reduced the size of the service and hampered technological advance made these same years the most fertile, creative, and formative in the history of the American armed forces. Sacrificing power and influence, withdrawing into its own hard shell, the officer corps was able and permitted to develop a distinctive military character. The [contemporary] American military profession, its institutions and its ideals, is fundamentally a product of these years."[31]

As Secretary of War Elihu Root would later remark of Upton's *Military Policy of the United States*: "His voice was of one crying in the wilderness. The Government did not even print his report, but with those of his associates it was filed in manuscript and forgotten."[32] Perhaps overlooked by civilians, though not within the closed ranks of the military during that time, Upton's manuscript was passed around among his friends. Uptonian thinking became widely known, admired, and accepted as "the gospel" by the officer corps.

As not infrequently happens in history, events occur to force action. In this case, fundamental military reforms were adopted quickly along the lines Upton proposed because of a single and sudden action-forcing event, the Spanish-American War. It lasted a mere 109 days in 1898, and although called "a splendid little war" by Theodore Roosevelt, it was hardly splendid and not much of a war. Indeed, that brief engagement showed all the flaws in the military that Upton had warned against so prophetically throughout his writings. The sinking of the battleship *Maine* in the harbor of Havana, Cuba, combined with the jingoistic "yellow journalism," whipped Congress and the country into a war frenzy for which the American armed forces were ill prepared to fight. There was no overall planning, leading to chaotic logistical support; volunteers were thrown into the ranks with short-term enlistees; state governors appointed officers who did not have military command experience or fitness for hazardous assignments; and congressional representatives and civilians meddled constantly in strategic policy-making decisions.

Fortunately, the United States faced an even weaker, more ill-prepared foe, Spain, so that of the 223,235 troops who were mobilized, only 289 Americans were killed by enemy bullets. Yet, 3,848 Americans, most of whom never saw action, died as a result of disease or improper medical attention. A war commission afterward concluded, "At the outbreak of the war the Medical Department was, in men and materials, altogether unprepared to meet the necessities of the army, . . . [and] the shortcomings in administration and operation may justly be attributed, in large measure, to the hurry and confusion incidental to the assembly of an army of untrained officers and men, then many times larger than before, for which no preparations in advance had been or could have been made because of existing rules and regulations."[33]

Of course, Upton had issued warnings that this catastrophe would happen, but his words had been ignored by the civilians in charge—until now. By good fortune, President William McKinley appointed a new secretary of war, Elihu Root, after the Spanish-American War to institute changes in the military. A Wall Street lawyer by profession, Root knew little about the army, but he possessed a keen, analytical mind and was deeply committed to finding some way to improve the American armed forces. He was given Upton's unpublished manuscript to read, and he was impressed.

Beginning in 1902, Root, supported by President Theodore Roosevelt, initiated reforms along the professional pattern that Upton had outlined more than two decades before; that is, creation of a general staff, rotation of staff and line officers; institution of advanced education for senior commanders; establishment of a new personnel system designed to weed out incompetents and promote the best officers; better pay; retirement provisions; strict limits on political involvement by officers; a modernized command structure with a professional system of education from preliminary to advanced levels required for filling staff-line posts; development of a reserve force to support the professional regulars; and, through the use of federal subsidies, a strengthening of professional standards and training for state militias (now the National Guard). Upton's ideas were not entirely accepted, but the majority were adopted by the 1920s, especially his overall ethos of professionalism, which decisively shaped such leaders of the old "brown shoe army" as George Marshall, Omar Bradley, George Patton, and their ilk, who later led the U.S. military in World War II and the immediate postwar era. These "sons of Upton" and the Uptonian-inspired reforms that Root sponsored enabled the United States to fight successfully on a global scale in World War I, World War II, and the cold war—and win.

In a broader sense, though indirectly, Upton's ideas also invaded the civilian world, where instruments of planning and professionalism, modeled largely on the military experience, came to be grafted onto various key civilian institutions such as the Bureau of the Budget (later the Office of Management and Budget) at the federal level as well as budgeting, planning, and policy units at the state and local levels. More fundamentally, classic organization structures with clear lines of authority, top-down command, and strong provisions for control and responsibility so characteristic of many modern public bureaucracies are largely (yet certainly not wholly) products of Uptonian (military) designs. The ripple effect of Uptonian thought has been widespread, though largely uncharted, throughout twentieth-century American government and public administration.[34]

At 8:00 AM on Tuesday, March 15, 1881, Upton's Chinese servant, Ah Sing, came to call the colonel for breakfast. He found Upton slumped over his desk, with pistol in hand and blood around his head. Word of Upton's suicide quickly spread throughout a shocked military community.[35] Had he died because he saw no future for himself in the military? Or was his death caused by the strain of the throbbing headaches from a sinus condition for which he repeatedly sought treatment? Or was he deeply depressed because his reform ideas had not yet made progress toward adoption? Was it possible that he foresaw little hope for their acceptance in the future? Or, ironically, had his own religious perfectionism, which had driven him on to such a successful military career, amazing feats of wartime heroism, and postwar intellectual brilliance, turned against him and destroyed his life in the end? Perhaps we will never know, but what we do know for sure is that Upton's ideas remain very much alive and pertinent today in shaping the professional ideals within the modern American administrative state.

5

Jane Addams
The Call from the Inner Light
for Social Reform

Jane Addams, 1860–1935
(from the Jane Addams Memorial Collections,
Special Collections, The University Library,
The University of Illinois at Chicago)

The Settlement Movement is only one manifestation of that wider humanitarian movement which throughout Christendom . . . is endeavoring to embody itself, not in a sect, but in society.
—Jane Addams
Twenty Years At Hull-House

By the end of her life in 1935, Jane Addams had become one of the most honored and revered women of her generation. At the age of twenty-nine, with her friend Ellen Gates Starr, Addams founded Hull

House, a settlement house in the middle of one of the worst Chicago slums. For the next forty-five years, Addams devoted herself to uplifting the lives of the immigrant poor—Poles, Germans, Italians, Russian Jews, and others—who flocked to the United States and settled in the neighborhood near Hull House. In the process of beginning the settlement movement in the United States, Addams pioneered innovative, comprehensive methods in social work and in the wider fields of women's rights, labor negotiations, and world peace (for which she shared the 1931 Nobel Peace Prize with Columbia University president Nicholas Murray Butler). At the time of her death, surveys ranked her ahead of Susan B. Anthony, Helen Keller, and Amelia Earhart as the greatest American woman.

With regard to the creation of the modern welfare state in the United States, Addams, more than any other individual, should be credited with conceiving and spawning, in the words of Theda Skocpol, "a maternal welfare state," that is, caring, compassionate, and comprehensive institutions for dealing with the urgent problems of women, mothers, children, and the urban poor.[1] Her Chicago Hull House model, begun in 1889, started experimenting with innovative ways to deliver human services to the needy at a time when government welfare was nonexistent. Addams's ideas quickly spread to other communities. By 1891, 6 settlement houses existed; by 1897, they totaled 74; by 1900, they numbered more than 100; and by 1910, more than 400 existed throughout the nation. Addams's ideals of essentially local volunteerism and self-help became elevated to the federal level by her disciples in the 1910s and 1920s as the social welfare model for the U.S. government, seen in the Children's Bureau, the Women's Bureau, and the Sheppard-Towner Act and still later in elements of the 1935 Social Security Act. Equally important, Addams's Hull House trained the next generation of women social service leaders by helping them hone their political skills, nurture their informal networks, and develop their policy agendas and by imbuing them with a deep idealistic commitment to social welfare reform that remains to this day a central ethos of the social work profession.

What makes her enduring achievements so remarkable is that Addams had to overcome major, if not almost overwhelming, personal obstacles from childhood onward that would have stopped most people from doing anything with their lives. Recall that in the late nineteenth century women had few career options. They were expected to either marry and raise children or become spinster schoolteachers or governesses, generally considered unwanted, underpaid vocations. We also tend to forget that medical authorities in those days claimed that women were the weaker sex and warned them against pursuing careers because such aspirations would expose them to "brain fatigue." Few colleges or graduate schools admitted women, which drastically limited their career options. The United States in the late nineteenth century was hardly hospitable for supporting women's advancement, let alone opportunities for able women such as Jane Addams. Yet, if those harsh realities did not create enough roadblocks, Addams also faced special debilitating hardships that placed considerable physical impediments on her from birth.

Jane Addams was born the youngest child of John Huy and Sarah Weber Addams, on September 6, 1860, in Cedarville, Illinois. Her mother was a widely respected member of this northern Illinois farming community, but Jane hardly knew her because Sarah died when Jane was just two years old. John Addams was, like Sarah, widely respected in Cedarville, having become relatively wealthy through real estate transactions and small-business ventures. He served for sixteen years as a Lincoln Republican in the Illinois state legislature and was noted for his integrity and intellectual abilities. As Jane's autobiography recounts, without a mother, her father became an overwhelming force in her life. He was "the cord which not only held fast my supreme affection, but also drew me into the moral concerns of life."[2] Her earliest thoughts, she explained, were directed toward him, so much so that she claims to have exhibited "a dog-like affection"[3] toward her father, even going so far as to emulate his physically deformed thumb. "I believe I have never since wanted anything more desperately than to have my right thumb flattened, as my father's had been."[4] Her frantic attempts to identify completely with her father gave her, as a result, only a heightened sense of her own inferiority in relationship to him. In her youth Jane thought of herself (incorrectly, at least as depicted by her photos) as "ugly"—"a pigeon-toed little girl whose crooked back obliged her to walk with her head held very much to one side."[5] She sensed immense shame in public next to her father: "I simply could not endure the thought that 'strange' people should know that my handsome father was around this homely little girl."[6]

In addition to this deeply felt sense of shame, Jane Addams suffered throughout her life debilitating physical illnesses. She had a curvature of the spine as a child, perhaps resulting from spinal tuberculosis, which caused her considerable pain and obesity in later life (weight of more than 175 pounds on a thin-boned, five-foot, three-inch frame). She had frequent physical breakdowns, with the first occurring in 1882 at the time of her father's death. Some speculate that the breakdowns were psychosomatic in origin, but others claim that they were genuine. In 1888, while visiting Rome, Jane contracted sciatica rheumatism, and she was incapacitated for several weeks. Then several other illnesses developed: in 1915, pleuropneumonia; in 1916, tuberculosis of the kidney with complications of diabetes; in 1923, while in Tokyo, breast cancer, resulting in a double mastectomy; heart trouble in 1926 while lecturing in England; an ovarian cyst in 1931, which was removed at Johns Hopkins University Hospital; and ovarian cancer, of which she died in 1935.

In addition to these physical limitations, Jane had to cope with complicated family relationships throughout her life. She hated Anna, the woman her father married when Jane was eight. Not only would Jane now have to share her father with another woman but also she would have to struggle with her belief that the woman seemed to be the antithesis of the ideals of her morally perfect father—in essence, a negative role model. Although cultured, well read, and musical, Anna was said to have an "uncalled for temper" or what Jane Addams's biographer has said was "a formidable, even overbearing presence."[7] Certainly, in Jane's eyes, Anna represented a useless moral life, caring only for social position, her family, and a comfortable home life. "I never saw her do anything more useful with her hands than adjust objects in a room, care for her flowers and strum the guitar."[8] Anna never made any attempt to find a career. In short, her life displayed a privileged uselessness, or the exact opposite of the Protestant moral purposefulness that Jane embraced.

Moreover, Jane's siblings were a continual burden for her. Brother Weber had a complete mental breakdown in 1882 when Jane was only twenty-two, and she had to manage both his family and business for him for the rest of his life. Her sister Mary died in 1894, and at the age of thirty-four, Jane was left to raise Mary's three children. Her sister Alice married a man who had no use for Hull House or its founder, so relationships between them were continually strained. Throughout her life, Jane faced constant family pressures not only to deal with innumerable family crises but also to forego her own professional aspirations. Given her family's size and repeated problems, it would have been natural for her to be consumed by its needs, thereby fulfilling the general societal expectations at the turn of the century of what "a maiden auntie was supposed to do." "It has always been difficult," wrote Addams, "for family to regard the daughter otherwise than a family possession."[9]

Perhaps the root of her incredible strength to overcome all these personal handicaps and contribute significantly to the advancement of public affairs can be traced to the extraordinary attachment she had to her father's moral ideals. As historian Robert Crunden has observed, "Addams united her father's ideas about life with her growing moral concerns and internalized her perceptions of his attitudes."[10] The depth of her conscious acceptance of his moral outlook is evident in the opening pages of her autobiography, in which she recounts how "from a very early period . . . I recall 'horrid nights' when I tossed about in my bed because I had told a lie. I was held in the grip of a miserable dread of death, a double fear, first that I should die in my sins and go straight to that fiery Hell . . . and second, that my father—representing the entire adult world which I basely deceived—should die before I had time to tell him. My only method of obtaining relief was to go downstairs to my father's room and make a full confession."[11]

Hell was real to this little girl, and absolution could only come on bended knee before her father. It no doubt led to her inflated sense of responsibility to humanity as a whole. For instance, Jane Addams told of her earliest dream at the age of six in which everyone was dead except herself. She alone had to invent a wagon wheel or the affairs of the world would never again resume.[12]

Her father described his religion as Hicksite Quaker. The Hicksites were the followers of Elias Hicks (1745–1830) of Long Island, New York, who had opposed the evangelistic influences on English Quakerism from Joseph John Gurney (1788–1847) as being inconsistent with the Quakers' general emphasis on merely following one's own "inner light." Many of the controversies among mid-nineteenth-century American Quakers concerned the debates between the Gurneyites and Hicksites. John was no doubt conscious of the split but exhibited little interest in such doctrinal disputes. Instead, he simply followed the more democratic, nonevangelistic path of Hicksite Quakerism. Without a Friends Meeting House near his home, John attended various nearby Protestant churches, often teaching Sunday school but never accepting a denominational membership. What he developed for himself, and Jane internalized, was a highly personal morality that sought to follow one's inner light as derived from a common set of Christian virtues, emphasizing courage, character, kindness, fairness, and love of humanity. Jane faithfully followed her father's admonition, "Mental integrity above all else," or, as she put it, "My creed is everyone be sincere and don't fuss."[13]

Although her writings say little about formal religion, her life—and work—were decisively shaped by the no-nonsense, practical Protestant values inherited from her father. She joined a Presbyterian church in college, but creeds and denominations mattered little. As biographer James Linn writes, "Her humanitarianism was too pervasive to permit entrance of any interest in dogma."[14] What mattered more in her faith was that she fuse her image of her father's morality with her own righteous ambition to make a difference in the world and to be responsible for improving the human condition in real and direct ways. Like him, she too would be earnest, ethical, independent, and undogmatic. Like him, she too would chart her own course that followed her inner light throughout her lifetime regardless of consequences—whether founding Hull House at age twenty-nine in Chicago's worst slum with little support; taking highly unpopular public stands for world peace in the midst of World War One; challenging the establishment thinking about women's rights, child labor laws, and minimum-wage legislation; or embarking on crusades for any number of innovative and often unpopular social welfare reforms. It was not by accident that Jane Addams dedicated her popular autobiography, *Twenty Years at Hull-House*, "To the Memory of My Father."

Following her father's insistence that she become well educated, Jane earned outstanding grades in high school. She wanted very much to attend the premier woman's college of that era, Smith College in Massachusetts, but she observed her father's wishes and attended the nearby Rockford Seminary, as had her two older sisters. At the time the seminary had a strong classical and religious orientation, especially promoting evangelistic conversions and missionary work abroad. Jane, in her own independent fashion, resisted studying the classics and religion, instead making a special effort to major in the natural sciences, a major that the college had just started. At Rockford she not only made top grades but also became senior class president and editor of the school magazine, the *Rockford Seminary Magazine*, and represented all the women's colleges in a national speaking competition (coming in fifth place behind a later three-time Democratic presidential candidate, William Jennings Bryan). From these experiences she learned the power of the written and spoken word, and during her lifetime she wielded the pen and oratory with facility to further the causes in which she passionately believed (today 514 citations of books, magazines, and published speeches are listed under her name). At Rockford Addams also engaged in her first effort at social reform. She pressed the seminary to offer bachelor of arts degrees instead of certificates on graduation (and she received one of the first such degrees). In 1881 Jane Addams was graduated as class valedictorian, telling her classmates in her commencement address "not to be afraid to do what you believe in doing."[15]

These brave words of advice were undoubtedly directed at herself as much as at her classmates, and the admonition indeed proved difficult for her to pursue. Her father's death coincided with her college graduation and left her grief stricken: "I will not write of myself or how purposeless and without ambition I am."[16]

Her autobiography's description of her next eight years reads like Bunyan's *Pilgrim's Progress* in recounting her own personal struggles and soul searching to find her calling. "During most of the time," wrote Jane Addams of this period, "I was absolutely at sea so far as my moral purpose was concerned, clinging only to the desire to live in a really living world and refusing to be content with a shadowy intellectual or aesthetic one."[17]

At first she tried attending the Woman's Medical College in Philadelphia, thinking that she wanted to be a physician, but her first major illness forced her to drop out after only a few months. She then took two lengthy trips to Europe with lady friends, from 1883 to 1885 and from 1887 to 1888. European travel was customary for young women in that period to learn social graces and to round out their cultural educations. Yet, she tells how these trips were neither satisfying nor fulfilling sources of what she felt most deeply about concerning the necessity for her own moral development and public service. She was pressed by Anna to marry, but she rejected all suitors. Possibly she sensed that a husband would only divert her from achieving the lofty moral aims she wanted from life, or possibly she was never emotionally or sexually attracted to men.

"The Snare of Preparation" is the title of the chapter in her autobiography covering this period of eight years of wandering and self-reflection. The term was coined by Leo Tolstoy to denote how society conspires to keep its young in a perpetual state of inactivity at the time when, in Jane Addams's words, "they are longing to construct the world anew and to conform it to their own ideals."[18] The temptation— the snare—was always to prepare and never to engage in the real work of the world. Certainly, Addams did not believe that "with all her education, she was not held responsible for anything."[19] At this time she wanted a meaningful life with moral purpose, as she wrote in a poem that was full of grim Protestant self-determination and righteous zeal:

Life's a burden. Bear it.
Life's a duty. Dare it.
Life's a thorn crown. Wear it.
And Spurn to be the Coward.[20]

Yet, this period of idleness and wanderlust allowed her to crystallize her own unique sense of her moral destiny. While in England on her second visit, she toured London's East End and "got a glimpse of how the other half lived in shocking poverty."[21] Exposed to the settlement movement in England, where Oxford students, beginning in 1884, went to these slums to live and work among the urban poor, Addams returned home at age twenty-nine committed to fostering those ideals in the United States. As she wrote in her autobiography, "I had made up my mind the next day whatever happened that I would begin to carry out the plan."[22]

And what a risky plan she chose! With little personal means other than a small inheritance from her father's estate and no contacts or support other than her good friend from college days, Ellen Gates Starr, Addams began to explore one of the poorest regions of Chicago for a place to start a settlement house. By luck, she discovered a portion of a large, run-down home built by the Hull family in 1856 in what had been at the time a prosperous suburb of Chicago. In 1889 Hull House was surrounded by one of the poorest, dirtiest, most industrial, and most crime-infested sections of the city, teeming with recent European immigrants to the United States. She convinced the heirs of the Hull estate to donate a small portion of the original Hull home (later acquiring thirteen surrounding buildings in the neighborhood).

In 1889, after soliciting money from friends and adding their own hard labor, Addams and Starr renovated the dilapidated structure and in a matter of months opened Hull House. The house fulfilled Addams's burning moral vision, which was, in her own words, "Without the advancement and improvement of the whole, no man can hope for any lasting improvement in his own moral or material individual condition."[23] The telling phrase here was "improvement in his own moral or material individual condition." Although seeking to uplift the lives of those least fortunate, Addams was also fulfilling the call of her own

inner voice, her ingrained Protestant conscience, as well as the consciences of the many whom she would eventually enlist in this cause.
This crusade would be an altruistic one that would ultimately gratify
a deep yearning within Addams and the many who rallied to the settlement movement. Addams underscored this inner motive in one of
her major addresses titled "The Subjective Necessity for Social Settlements":

> The motive which underlies a movement is based, not only upon
> conviction, but upon genuine emotion, wherever educated young
> people are seeking an outlet for that sentiment of universal brother-
> hood, which the best spirit of our times is forcing from an emotion
> into a motive. These young people accomplish little toward the solu-
> tion of this social problem, and bear the brunt of being cultivated into
> unnourished, oversensitive lives. They have been shut off from the
> common labor by which they live which is a great source of moral
> and physical health. They feel a fatal want of harmony between their
> theory and their lives, a lack of coordination between thought and
> action. . . . It is easier to state these hopes than to formulate the line
> of motives, which I believe constitute the trend of the subjective
> pressure toward the Settlement. There is something primordial about
> these motives, but I am perhaps overbold in designating them as a
> great desire to share the race of life.[24]

As she stressed in the same address, behind such idealistic motivations of youth lay a wider humanitarian movement to fulfill Christ's
message: "I believe that there is a distinct turning among many young
men and women toward this simple acceptance of Christ's message.
They resent the assumption that Christianity is a set of ideas which
belong to the religious consciousness, whatever that may be. They insist that it cannot be proclaimed and instituted apart from the social
life of the community and that it must seek a simple and natural expression in the social organism itself. The Settlement movement is only one
manifestation of that wider humanitarian movement which throughout Christendom . . . is endeavoring to embody itself, not in a sect, but
in society itself."[25]

Although Addams and the settlement movement may ultimately
have been motivated by the ideals of an applied Christianity, it should
not be forgotten that the social issues posed by the rapid urbanization
rates during this era were both real and serious. As historian Richard
Hofstadter once remarked, "The United States was born in the country

and . . . moved to the city."[26] During the 1880s and 1890s when Addams began the settlement movement, the United States was experiencing more intense rates of urbanization than it has at any other time before or since. A century before, only 3.3 percent of Americans lived in towns; during the 1880s the figure jumped to 33.3 percent, and in that decade alone, Buffalo, Detroit, and Milwaukee doubled in size; Chicago, St. Paul, and Denver tripled; and New York jumped from two to three million people.

Much of this influx was fueled by the more than five million immigrants who came to the United States during this era, but migrants from rural areas of the nation were also drawn to the cities in search of better paying industrial jobs that, in turn, were a significant source of the mushrooming urban population growth. The result: slums, crime, poverty, environmental pollution, poor public sanitation and health, transportation congestion, unemployment, and a host of other urban problems that begged for solutions. In an era dominated by beliefs in social Darwinism and laissez-faire doctrines, no federal government programs were available to alleviate such conditions. That is, unlike today, no programs existed that established public housing, minimum wage laws, child labor laws, social security, food and drug inspections, public health facilities, and the like. William Dean Howells, the turn-of-the-century realist novelist, poignantly described the ugliness of the urban scene at the turn of the century: "But to be in it, and not have the distance, is to inhale the stenches of neglected streets, and to catch the yet fouler and dreadfuller poverty-smell which breathes from the open doorways."[27]

Hull House and the settlement movement it spawned were in many ways regarded as practical responses to the harsh realities of turn-of-the-century urban life. Although the term "settlement movement" is unfamiliar to many Americans today, it was at the time a major effort to cope with what many saw as the central domestic problem facing the United States. Through privately funded, multipurpose facilities, settlement houses, with live-in volunteer and paid staff, devoted themselves to providing acculturation, education, and social services for newly arrived immigrants living in nearby neighborhoods. Hull House, which became the model for other settlements across the United States, sought to meet the basic social service needs of the urban poor without the direct proselytizing by religious missionaries, as was customary in those days (e.g., the early YMCAs and YWCAs and the

Moody-Sankey Protestant revival begun in 1874 in Brooklyn, New York).

Indeed, Jane Addams saw the settlement movement as far broader, as "an experimental effort to aid in the solution of social and industrial problems which are engendered by the modern conditions of life in a great city."[28] Like the settlements of western pioneers, these urban settlements would bring educated men and women to settle and work among the poor. Through education, work, self-help, and voluntary cooperation—the dominant Protestant values of the era—immigrants could pull themselves out of poverty and uplift their lives to achieve the rewards of the American dream. Addams's settlements would sustain the Protestant ethic without necessarily a belief in a Protestant God. Addams herself recognized the symbols associated with "settlement": "the word [settlement] still implies migrating from one condition of life to another totally unlike it."[29] Here, men and women could in the best spirit of American democracy improve themselves. So too could educated men and women, such as Addams, find their own fulfillment, improvement, and personal uplift through settlement work.

When Jane Addams and her associates first founded Hull House, the term "uplift" included a strong emphasis on exposing the poor to the beauty of good art, music, and literature. As Hull House evolved, however, it took on many of the characteristics that today we regard as the best methods used in comprehensive social service centers: job training, employment counseling, food cooperatives, day-care, kindergartens, family services, social clubs, after-school recreation, senior citizen activities, and even college courses for credit. By residing in the neighborhood where its services were rendered, Hull House could respond comprehensively to the immediate, varied needs of the poor in the locale. As Addams said of Toynbee Hall, where Oxford students worked with the London East End poor, Hull House also would be "so free from professional doing good, so uneffectedly sincere, and so productive of good results in its classes and libraries that it seems perfectly ideal."[30] Yet, unlike Toynbee Hall, it would be more democratic, open, applied, neighborhood oriented, and, especially, reflective of feminine leadership. In the United States, a settlement would come to be a sphere where educated women, such as Addams, would take the lead to create institutions and engage in the new forms of social service work that at the time the nation lacked.

Specifically, what did the settlement movement that Addams started bring to the development of the modern American administrative state? First, social settlements, as Allen Davis aptly reminds us, were "the spearhead for reform."[31] They brought significant numbers of middle-class, educated women—and men—into direct contact with the harsh realities of modern urban life and sparked their enthusiasm as well as their long-term commitment to evolving an agenda for social welfare reform. Addams's autobiography recounts essentially one highly personal experience after another of contacts with "the guests" who appeared on the doorsteps of Hull House (she always referred to them as "guests," never "clients"). From these experiences she learned important lessons about the dire conditions the urban poor faced. For example, the first guest Addams discusses was "an interesting young woman who lived in a neighborhood tenement, whose widowed mother aided her in support of her family by scrubbing a downtown theater every night."[32] Her living situation was unfortunate, but a few months' stay at Hull House provided her with the economic means and practical instruction to get on with her life, marry, and resettle in another eastern city. In this instance, like each one that followed, Addams claimed to have learned invaluable lessons or morals about how to deal with the plight of the poor. In this case, she realized she should not moralize but must realistically address her guest's situation in a direct, no-nonsense fashion. Each new case brought new learning experiences and new issues for those in the house to resolve, such as how they should become better integrated with the community, provide for the needs of the guests, deal with the official authorities, recruit good staff and volunteers, develop a political agenda, finance program goals, and take on not only popular but also unpopular causes for the betterment of individuals in the neighborhood.

Not only did settlement work in general bring many people from middle-class backgrounds into direct contact with the new social realities and therefore serve as a catalyst for social reform but also Hull House in particular became, over the years, a central meeting point, a "salon" in the European sense, for nurturing novel ideas regarding a wide range of political, economic, and social concerns. Discussions revolved around such vital topical issues as child labor reforms, minimum-wage legislation, women's suffrage, and methods of negotiating labor disputes. Frequently visitors from the nearby University of Chicago would lecture at Hull House and use it as a laboratory for experimentation. Its openness to eclectic and unconventional ideas made Hull House controversial at the turn of the century for what were considered its advanced ideas, but Addams generally was able to avoid alienating the general public. If anything, her lecture trips around the United States and abroad as well as her numerous writings did much to garner support for the settlement movement and its ideas and ideals.

Hull House also helped to foster new disciplines in economics, political science, and sociology. Indeed, the Chicago school of social science, associated with the names John Dewey, Albion Small, William Thomas, Richard Ely, and Charles Merriam, was enhanced by close, long-term involvement with Hull House. As one intellectual historian has pointed out,

> Hull House was the great catalyst to progressive social science. It, and other social settlements, reified the problems of modern American civilization for a generation of disturbed Protestant intellectuals at the same time it provided them with a definite personal alternative for action. Hull House brought the problems of the city to one place where they could be confronted, classified and organized. It provided room, board, and congenial friends. In time it generated ideas. . . . Without the inspiration of Hull House, of Jane Addams and her many friends and associates, social science as developed in America would not have taken the pattern it did.[33]

As the contemporary Hungarian novelist George Konrad has written, the best way to affect policy is to change a society's usual thinking patterns and accepted conventions. Addams's Hull House, by nurturing the new progressive social sciences and avant-garde ideas about social welfare, would fundamentally shift America's customary thinking patterns about this field as well as the tacit compacts involved with urban reform. Altering basic thinking patterns and tacit compacts thus marked another important contribution by Addams's Hull House for shaping the modern American state. It is worth remembering that beginning in the 1870s most large U.S. cities had a political "machine" or "urban boss" as the central vehicle for urban governance. Like the leaders of a corporation, the boss and his lieutenants would dispense favors, from jobs to Christmas baskets, in exchange for votes, thereby running the city as a political machine primarily for the benefit of a fairly narrow male cadre of followers.

By contrast, Addams's "lieutenants," or the graduates of the Hull House experience, were primarily middle-class, educated women. At Hull House and other settlements, these women learned how to challenge the establishment, hone their political skills, develop alternative agendas for welfare reform, forge informal networks, and ultimately take the helm of leadership for making social change a reality. In short, they developed a new form of institutional governance. As Theda Skocpol writes, Hull House and other settlements "became settings from which talented women could create and pursue an alternative kind of wide-ranging career combining social research, public education, civic activism and intermittent periods of official service."[34] Among the names of the talented women who began their careers by working for Addams at Hull House were Julia Lathrop, member of the Illinois Board of Charities and first head of the federal government's Children's Bureau; Florence Kelly, director of the National Consumer League; Alice Hamilton, first woman professor at Harvard Medical School and a pioneer in the field of female health issues; Grace Abbott, director of the Immigrant Protection League and later director of the Child Labor Division of the Children's Bureau; and Alzina Stevens, first juvenile probation officer in Chicago and national leader in reforming the juvenile justice system.

These and other Hull House graduates learned about the practical politics of challenging those in power and how to bring desired changes in the system. Addams described one such encounter regarding sweatshops:

> During the fourth year of our residence at Hull-House we found ourselves in a large mass meeting ardently advocating the passage of a federal measure called the Sulzer Bill. Even in our short struggle with the evils of the sweating system, it did seem that the center of the effort had shifted to Washington, for by that time we had realized the sanitary regulation of sweat shops by city officials, and a careful enforcement of factory legislation by satisfactory inspectors will not avail, unless each city and State shall be able to pass and enforce a code of comparatively uniform legislation. Although the Sulzer Act failed to utilize the Interstate Commerce legislation for its purpose, many national representatives realized for the first time that only by federal legislation could their constituents in remote country places be protected. . . .
>
> Through our efforts to modify the sweating systems, the Hull-House residents gradually became committed to the fortunes of the Consumer's League, an organization which for years had been approaching the question of underpaid sewing women from the point of view of the ultimate responsibility lodged in the consumer. It be-

comes more reasonable to make the presentation of the sweatshop situation through the League, as it is more effectual to work with them for the extension of legal provisions in the slow upbuilding of the code of legislation.[35]

While Addams increasingly turned her attention after 1910 to broader issues of world peace, the struggle for woman's suffrage, and other wide-ranging problems, her Hull House assistants went on to pioneer what we now take for granted as the elements of the modern national welfare system in the United States. The route was by no means direct or clear-cut. Rather, its evolution was haphazard, beginning with Progressive social measures at the federal level that created the Home Education Division in the Bureau of Education in 1911; the Children's Bureau in 1912; the Women's Bureau in 1918; and the Sheppard-Towner Act, administered by the Children's Bureau from 1921 to 1926, that gave states $1 million annually in matching grants to enhance local maternal and infant health, education, and welfare programs. Ultimately, elements of these social welfare experiments at the national level were written into the 1935 Social Security Act, which serves to this day as the fundamental framing document for the American welfare state system. As one thoughtful scholar of this topic notes, "Remarkable statebuilding successes during a period otherwise inimical to U.S. welfare state formation, the Children's Bureau and the Sheppard-Towner Act, were the joint political achievements of women reformers and widespread associations of women."[36] Or, as another student of this subject writes, "[It] is not accidental that the originators for the idea of the Children's Bureau and its first two chiefs, Julia Lathrop and Grace Abbott, had all cut their social welfare teeth in the social settlement movement. . . . People trained in the settlement's clearing house ideal had a natural affinity for experiment and they were not content with piecemeal attempts to improve the lives of children. Consequently, the Bureau was . . . something like a national settlement with a specialty in children."[37]

In the end, Addams's legacy in building the modern American state was achieved through those she had trained at Hull House. Her paid and volunteer staff learned from the local settlement experience invaluable lessons that eventually were elevated to the national level and institutionalized by various methods into a permanent agenda for social reform. Rather than design a paternal welfare state, Addams's lieutenants crafted what Skocpol refers to as unique reforms that emerged into a maternal welfare state. Its broad focus was on the well-being of families and children to provide them with educational skills for social adjustment, industrial opportunities, a living wage, and avenues for civic cooperation. In Skocpol's words:

> During the Progressive Era and early 1920s, a nascent maternal welfare state began to come together in the United States, emerging in the space left open by the absence of civil bureaucracies and a strong working class movement (the forces that were creating paternalistic welfare states in other nations). Through regulations, public benefits, and services focused particularly on mothers and their children, the nascent maternalist welfare state sought public powers to promote the well being of all American families. Women officials disproportionately staffed the government agencies charged with implementing these programs and new government functions were normally justified as a universalization of motherly love.[38]

Yet, as Skocpol also underscores, the maternal welfare state as envisioned by Addams and her followers was never quite realized. From the 1930s to the 1960s, as the United States created nationwide social insurance programs, separately administered benefits and protections for women, mothers, and children often survived, yet they were frequently subordinated and pushed to the sidelines. They were often underfunded and poorly administered, and they frequently lacked comprehensive approaches for dealing with family social issues. Male-dominated social service agencies consistently built up contributory insurance and downplayed the development of noncontributory public assistance programs, including Aid to Dependent Children and Aid to the Families of Dependent Children. Moreover, "political marginalization of female administrators, social workers, and surviving materialist programs in the era of Social Security" increased.[39]

Ironically, Jane Addams died the same year, 1935, that the United States enacted social security legislation, which today serves as a key aspect of our modern American state. If she had lived, she would have undoubtedly *not* approved of the by-product of the Social Security Act, namely, the growth of professionalization and bureaucratization of social services throughout the United States. These trends were the very antithesis of the highly personal style of social work that she had pioneered at Hull House.[40] Nor would she have liked to watch the eventual fragmentation and chronic underfunding of social service programs, especially those for families, mothers, women, and children. Above all, she would have fought bitterly the marginalization of these groups and the lack of emphasis on their needs by the social security system as a whole. The focus on meeting eligibility requirements instead of dealing humanely with the genuine problems of the poor would have angered her. Such twentieth-century trends in social policy would have violated her ingrained Christian morality, the call of her own inner light inherited from her father, involving what she saw as just, decent, and fair treatment for those less fortunate.

Nonetheless, if she were alive, Jane Addams could also take heart that portions of what she so passionately believed in were incorporated into the modern-day U.S. state. Minimum-wage legislation, child labor laws, mandatory retirement systems, public health programs, workplace safety and health requirements, workers' compensation laws, and public assistance programs are part and parcel of today's state social service system. Her Hull House nurtured the progressive social sciences, from economics to statistics, that are now central methodologies for understanding, classifying, and conceptualizing policy issues. The administrative networks of professional women who learned their skills at Hull House opened up, enriched, and democratized our governing processes. In this era of devaluation of government to local control, Addams's emphasis on volunteerism, grassroots participation, and third-party, nonprofit organizations to deliver public services look remarkably prescient. Moreover, Hull House and the settlement movement fostered an enduring ethos of social service in the United States, an outlook that was expressed succinctly by Addams: "It is the collective responsibility of society to see that the individual has the environment which will protect and nurture his best."[41]

Prophetically, Jane Addams achieved in her life what that wagon-wheel dream as a six-year-old child foretold. She invented a wheel so that the United States might move ahead—or carry on—throughout the twentieth century and beyond. The social service institutions that grew out of her moral convictions permanently transformed the way the United States cares for its poor.

6

Frederick W. Taylor
Latter-Day Puritan as Scientific Manager

Frederick W. Taylor, 1856–1915
(courtesy of the S. C. Williams Library,
Stevens Institute of Technology, Hoboken,
New Jersey)

Chairman: Mr. Taylor, do you believe that any system of scientific management induced by a desire for greater profits would revolutionize the minds of employers to such an extent that they would immediately, voluntarily and generally enforce the Golden Rule?
Mr. Taylor: If they had any sense they would.
—Hearings before the Special Investigating Committee of the House of Representatives, 1912

FREDERICK W. TAYLOR REMAINS ONE OF THE MOST paradoxical figures in administrative history. He worked entirely in the business sector and had few good things to say about government, yet his scientific management doctrines so thoroughly permeated public life that few can claim to have left a greater legacy for shaping the origins and development of the modern administrative state. Taylor was often harshly reactionary in his dealings with subordinates, but he was revolutionary in his convictions that scientific management would create a better life for everyone. He was rigorously empirical, but his doctrines were erected on massive normative beliefs. His personal habits by all accounts were obsessively compulsive, yet he had a long, happy marriage, a warm circle of friendships, and, above all, devoted disciples who served to spread his fame and ideas far and wide. An unorthodox radical who recast the very foundations of the American factory system, Taylor could equally claim the title as a man of "the establishment" because his theories literally established powerful new governing arrangements for the United States. Taylor was born into a proper mainline Philadelphia family; however, he most enjoyed working next to factory workers, grinding machine tools, and even using the salty language of a shop foreman.

Taylor's doctrines dominated business and public administration education during the first half of the twentieth century, but his ideas were renounced, even ridiculed, by academics in the second half. Nevertheless, even after his ideas went out of fashion, the institutions predicated on his doctrines remained central to governing the United States. Today it would be hard to imagine how the U.S. government—at every level—could function without the ingenious spin-offs from the Taylor system: budget systems; planning processes; work analysis; rational systems of job testing, pay, and classification; and efficiency measures. Other by-products of the Taylor system include academic disciplines such as operations research and management science and institutions that foster applied organization analysis, such as think tanks, policy shops, and in-house government research labs. Even the modern conception of managers as trainers, coaches, planners, and equipment organizers, for example, can be credited to Taylor's handiwork. His scientific management doctrines, applied to all levels of government throughout this century, decisively yet silently influenced its various activities.

Most of these applications were not made directly by Taylor; rather, they were fashioned principally in the public sector through the little-known but enormously critical work of the New York Bureau of Municipal Research. There his ideas were introduced in roundabout ways. Taylor had little contact with the bureau and did not exhibit much interest in its work. Frederick Taylor saw himself and liked others to view him as a lifelong man of business, especially at the shop level. His direct, applied innovations were confined mainly to the narrow arena of the first-line factory supervisor, but they spilled over in numerous, inexplicable ways to virtually all sectors of twentieth-century American life.

Peter Drucker, the well-known business expert, argues that Taylor, not Marx, deserves to be ranked with Freud and Darwin as the most revolutionary theorists who shaped the modern world, yet Taylor considered himself an eminently practical man.[1] He lived and worked simply throughout his life, always preferring to see the direct applications of his work in improving shop conditions. His lifestyle, manners, and dress shunned the ostentatious and favored the conventional and plain. As his biographer wrote, "He never wore anything in the way of formal morning or afternoon dress, a plain sack business suit always was good enough for him. And it was with reluctance that he ever wore formal evening dress, . . . his belief that time was too valuable to give any more of it to dress than was necessary."[2] He abstained from tea, coffee, cigarettes, liquor, and chocolate—or any excess. His lifestyle was severely puritanical.

Nonetheless, underneath his simple exterior lay a highly complex figure. A friend noted that there was always a driven quality to excel about his character; he felt that one had to get on with life and make a contribution to the world. Because he was a workaholic, friends thought of him as a "bit of a crank." His life, personal and public, centered around work. "What impressed us was his love of work. . . . Even in recreation, or anything he went into, he went into it in a most strenuous way."[3] Indeed, if there was one thing that he railed against, it was restrictions on work by subordinates, which he called by such names as "stalling," "soldiering," "goldbricking," and "quota reduction." Likewise, if superiors were not enlightened—or smart enough—to promote factory productivity by adopting *his* labor-saving techniques, Taylor would be equally furious in his denunciations, labeling them as "cesspools of commercialism" or "higglings of the marketplace."

His frequent fallings-out with his employers came more often than not over their failure to grasp his doctrine's main message, namely, that by working together and working smarter, more work could be accomplished and a better life for all would be achieved. Or, as he put it, "Scientific management is not any efficient device, not a device of any kind for securing efficiency; nor is it any single or group of efficiency devices; rather, it is 'a mental revolution,' wherein both management and labor come to see when they stop pulling against one another and instead both turn and push shoulder to shoulder in the same direction, the size of the surplus created by their joint efforts is truly astonishing."[4] Indeed, all of Taylor's inventions centered around improving work efficiency, that is, functional foremanship, time-motion studies, rational incentive systems, production planning, new high-speed machine tools, and the like.

At least in his view and in the opinion of his disciples, throughout his life Taylor was driven to perfect a system, *the* system, that would improve working arrangements, thereby improving productivity, harmony, and abundance for all. If only people were smart enough to adopt it, scientific management would be a "substitution of peace for war; the substitution of hearty brotherly cooperation for contention and strife; of replacing suspicious watchfulness with mutual confidence; of becoming friends instead of enemies."[5] Here ultimately was a plea for a new vision of universal brotherhood on earth achieved through the application of the Taylor system—a system that he and his disciples saw as capable of transforming the United States, even all of humanity.

The vision would be brought forth from the rigorous application of empirical science. As Henry Towne wrote: "Mr. Taylor was the first to perceive that in this field [of business] as in the physical sciences, the Baconian System could be applied, that a practical science could be created by following three principles: viz: the correct observation of *facts*, the intelligent and unbiased *analysis* of such facts, and the formulating of *laws* by deduction from the results reached" (Towne's italics).[6]

In essence, Frederick Taylor was a man of deep convictions that included an admittedly secular creed called "scientific management." He not only fashioned this creed but also nurtured those who were its disciples and during his lifetime strove to spread its beliefs and keep "the faith" pure.

Taylor was born on March 22, 1856, and, as he said of himself, "I was born with a whale of a New England conscience."[7] His father, Franklin, was a fourth-generation English Quaker, and his mother, Emily, was a sixth-generation English Puritan. Fred's ancestral religious roots went deep, and thus a religious outlook, though in secular form, came naturally. Both sides of his family had fled sixteenth-century England because of religious persecution for their radical beliefs and eventually settled outside Philadelphia, gaining respectability for hard work, their growing prosperity, and above all, their strict devotion to their own brand of Protestantism.

What is important to underscore about Taylor's religious heritage is that it—on both sides—can be traced to the most radical of radical Puritan-Quaker sects. His father's lineage went back to the Lollards, the fourteenth-century sect whose members were precursors of the Puritans. As historian John Fiske notes, "The name by which they were known was a nickname which might cover almost any amount of diversity in opinion, like the modern epithets 'freethinker' and 'agnostic.' The feature that characterized the Lollards in common was a bold spirit of inquiry." According to Fiske, many Lollards professed extreme beliefs for their day, that is, "that the law of the Gospel is a kind of Communism, in which Christians dwell together in freedom and equality with no distinctions of rank or privilege such as are imposed by human law or institutions."[8]

The radical pedigree was equally strong for Taylor on his mother's side. One of her forebears, Kenelm Winslow, arrived in Massachusetts aboard the Mayflower in 1629. These Puritans had been so zealous in their religious beliefs that they were not content even with the extreme (at that time) Presbyterianism but went on to become Independents, or what in the United States are now called Congregationalists. Obviously today the Congregational Church is considered a mainline Protestant church, hardly radical, but in the 1600s many of its faithful had been forced to flee from England to Holland because of their extreme Protestant beliefs. They eventually left Holland for America because of what they saw as the potentially corrupting influences of the Dutch Protestants on the youth. It was in the New World that they sought to found a "city on a hill" for the greater glory of God: separate, isolated, and free to practice their own brand of radical Protestantism.

Franklin Taylor, however, was not a religious zealot. By all accounts he was a highly intellectual, gentle man, devoted mainly to doing good civic works in the community in Germantown, Pennsylvania, where he lived, married, and raised three children. He had inherited considerable real estate and farming interests and so led a comfortable life in a fashionable section of Germantown in a large home staffed with a maid, butler, cook, and coachman.

On the other hand, Emily Winslow Taylor had a dominating influence over her son's life. Her Puritan idealism burned strongly, as reflected in her views of child rearing, which she expressed as "work, drill, and discipline." Her household was, in her view, "a thing ruled regular," and her maxim was that "her boys grow up pure in mind and body."[9] Like the early Puritans, she never set much store in using tact with people. Simple straightforwardness was her style, as it was to become Fred's. "Tact she was inclined to associate with hypocrisy. She knew her mind and spoke it plainly and to the point."[10] In the 1820s Emily would gravitate to Unitarianism, and likewise Fred would follow her religious inclinations, himself eventually marrying in and joining a Unitarian Church (though attending only irregularly because he could not talk back or argue with the minister during the sermons).

Home life for Fred and his brother and sister was therefore a potent mixture of serious religiosity and intellectualism. Fred's father would read history to the children or converse in German and French. Emily, in addition to being an expert linguist, was an abolitionist and feminist whose home was always open to the avant-garde intellectuals of that era. She personally knew Ralph Waldo Emerson, Bronson Alcott, David Thoreau, Wendell Phillips, William Lloyd Garrison, Julia Ward Howe, and Lydia M. Child. In 1842, when she was only twenty, Emily accompanied Lucretia Mott to London as a delegate to the International Anti-Slavery Convention and toiled ceaselessly for the causes of women's suffrage and the abolition of slavery. It was said that she ran her household open "to a bold sense of inquiry, dissatisfaction, resolute in a new vision, discipline and passion for making the new vision prevail." Likewise, Fred inherited her reformist zeal: "In the Taylor lexicon, ought was invariably followed by a can and will. . . . He could not be content just with discovering facts. Do not these facts clearly point to this thing? Then we will bring this thing to pass."[11] For Emily, and so too for Fred, there could be no hesitating, halfway measure; if the truth was self-evident, action must follow to turn it into reality.

The family's comparative affluence allowed Fred to acquire a superior childhood education. In 1869 at age thirteen he was sent to study in Paris, and then in 1870 he went to Germany, learning the language and then traveling extensively throughout Europe. Not only did he travel widely, but also he attended the prestigious Germantown Academy, a local private school, and then Phillips Exeter Academy, a top-notch New England prep school, where he excelled in sports, especially crew, skating, gymnastics, and baseball. He captained the baseball team and was a diligent student, earning good marks in most classes.

Taylor was also considered a rebellious student, however. He was disciplined for reading a book during chapel and was caught cheating on an exam for which he was disciplined but not dismissed from school. As he remarked later, "What I look back upon perhaps was the very best experience of my early life, namely the severe Exeter discipline, in which no excuse was taken for anything and in which everybody had to toe the line in all respects."[12] Poor health resulting from eye strain forced him to leave school during the fall of his senior year. His parents traced Fred's problem to studying too hard by the light of a kerosene lamp. Others, however, attribute his eye strain to psychosomatic disorders. Whatever the cause, Taylor had to change his plans to go on to Harvard and study law. He passed the Harvard entrance requirements with honors but had to stay home to recuperate.

Fred picked a curious way to recover from his illness—another mysterious paradox in his life that charted its future direction. Instead of choosing bed rest, touring Europe, or socializing with his circle of mainline Philadelphia friends, as was often customary in those days, Taylor became an apprentice machinist at the Enterprise Hydraulic Works, a small Philadelphia business near his home. During the next four years he worked up through the ranks beginning by, as he put it, "doing odd jobs on the floor of the machine shop. . . . I started to serve my apprenticeship as a pattern maker in 1874 and during the years between 1874 and 1878 completed my apprenticeship both as pattern maker and machinist. In 1878 I entered the employ of the Midvale Steel works as a laborer and during the period between 1874 and 1884, I occupied the positions of laborer, machinist, gang boss, assistant foreman and foreman in the machine shop in the steel works."[13] To Taylor, these experiences were hardly terrible; rather, he would later look back on these years as some of the best of his life. Indeed, he recommended that all youth, especially those who were college-bound, spend a few years "in actual hard work . . . under careful and constant supervision in a factory."[14]

Yet, it should be quickly added that Taylor was never a typical apprentice, forced to work long hours for little pay and live in humble dwellings. To the contrary, Fred daily commuted back to his parents' comfortable home, with his meager apprentice wages supplemented by an ample family allowance. During those years he carried on extensive sporting and social activities. Taylor was a member of the Young America Cricket Club and was on the winning team in the U.S. lawn tennis doubles championship of 1881. He even regularly sang in the choral society and participated in amateur stage productions. Furthermore, Taylor's rapid rise from shop boy to shop foreman at Midvale Steel Works was assisted by a family friend, William Sellers. Also, while Taylor was at Midvale, family influence allowed him to study for his engineering degree at the nearby Stevens Institute. He received his mechanical engineering baccalaureate in 1883 without taking any classes. Instead, he earned the degree by simply passing an examination.

Taylor's rudimentary ideas about scientific management first took shape at Midvale. The gross mismanagement by the owners, the poorly trained workers, the continual hostility between owners and workers, and the laborers' avoidance of work and their frequent lack of adequate equipment and faulty machinery appalled him. "It was a horrid life," he claimed later.[15] In fact, he was so repulsed by what he saw that he "either wanted to get out of the business entirely and go into some other line of work or find some remedy for this unbearable condition."[16]

He could not walk away from this challenge, however. He was too deeply imbued with the reformist zeal of his family, and so he chose the latter alternative as his life's calling, namely, searching for a new order that would bring harmony and accord to the workplace as well as improve its productivity. During the 1880s at Midvale, he experimented in an incremental manner with various methods to reform the factory workplace that evolved into the basic components of scientific management. Such elements included time-motion studies; use of the stop watch; a rational incentive plan for pay; and functional foremanship that divided shop management into eight positions rather than one, including a time clerk, inspector, gang boss, shop disciplinarian, and instruction card clerk. He began also his quarter century of experiments with high-speed cutting tools to improve the technical performance and efficiency of the machine tools then used by workers.

During this period, Taylor earned for himself the reputation as being authoritarian in his relationships with subordinates, especially those who opposed his ideas, those who were too slow to learn them, and those who placed informal restrictions on work or Taylor's experiments being performed. Nothing would or could obstruct his zeal to reform what he called the "horrid" conditions he found. He became a man obsessed with a mission, and no one, workers or management, was allowed to stand in the way of his reformist passions. And like any reformer possessed by his own ideas, Taylor became dogmatic about his beliefs, which hardened into "the one best way solutions," or, as he later wrote: "The key to harmony was to discover 'the one best way' to perform a task, determine the optimum daily pace of tasks, train workers to do the task in the prescribed way and at the prescribed pace and review successful completion of the items."[17]

Taylor's emphasis on the word "prescribed" is a clear indication of the author's intentions, that is, the idea should rule—his "prescribed" idea—and none other in order to achieve workplace harmony, peace, and productivity. In this period he drove himself and his subordinates relentlessly, conducting such microexperiments as finding the right size of a shovel and analyzing the minute motions of shoveling efficiently. Taylor sought to replace rules of thumb (i.e., general, common sense notions, in this case regarding work and its measurement) with general laws of scientific management based on empirical reductionist experimentation; detailed, unbiased observations; systematic knowledge; and evaluation of the facts (which he later termed "the science of shovelling"). No one—not workers, not management, and certainly *not* those who spoke out against the Taylor system—was allowed to stand in the way of finding "the one best way" to do work efficiently and of evolving a science of management.

Taylor's work was immeasurably aided by the time in which he lived. First, as Taylor biographer Daniel Nelson points out, Taylor arrived on the scene at the advent of the new factory system "that enlarged the realm of the manager and enhanced the possibilities for managerially defined social relationships."[18] In particular, the rapidly increasing use of a new power source, electricity, at the turn of the century allowed manufacturers to widen their control over the factory environment. Previously, plants had to be operated during the daylight hours and be located next to power sources such as a stream. These requirements restricted the ability of plant managers to arrange men and materials for producing the most efficient forms of outputs. Because of the electric light bulb, however, plants could now operate twenty-four hours a day. Manufacturers could now build plants anywhere and in any way, arranging workers in new locations and configurations that could greatly improve the handling of materials, reduce costs, and increase the speed of production. Thus, the dawn of the age of electricity introduced increased flexibility over working conditions that suddenly required choices, that is, new choices on the part of management to decide on the most efficient ways to produce goods.

Second, this era of change from old to new factory systems created chaos that Taylor could see firsthand on the shop floor, chaos created by the inability of managers to deal with the rapid technological changes in the workplace, resulting in the workers' "horrid" lives. The main mode of management prior to Taylor's reforms was for managers simply to show displeasure and to tell a foreman or his workers to improve performance or face dismissal. No exceptions were allowed; one had to shape up or be out of a job. No effort was made to analyze the task and suggest alternative approaches, nor did anyone keep detailed records that would track the quality and quantity of work performance and reward success. Training for jobs, providing feedback on what was accomplished, or planning for what should be accomplished were nonexistent. Performance was largely based on rule-of-thumb thinking, and the response by foremen to unsatisfactory work was to utter a few curses and fire the offending worker. As Harlow Person writes of this period, "A management's concept of a proper day's work was what a foreman could drive workers to do. Indeed in the steel industry foremen were called 'pushers' because they physically drove gangs to work."[19] No wonder that to many, especially his disciples, Taylor's scientific management doctrines seemed a far more humane *and* enlightened alternative to the mindless, intimidating style of rule-of-thumb management that was then so prevalent throughout industry.

Third, this era fostered the development of administrative thought and its dissemination by way of books, journals, and professional meetings as no other period before in the United States. The social sciences emerged in this period; in 1876 Johns Hopkins University offered the first doctoral degrees in the field, and Columbia followed in 1880. In 1887, the second issue of a new journal, *Political Science Quarterly,* published Woodrow Wilson's "The Study of Administration"—the first full-length essay on the subject of administration ever published in the United States. The American Economic Association was formed in 1885, and the Academy of Political and Social Sciences was created in 1889. Taylor's ideas became quickly recognized in particular through their introduction and circulation at the professional meetings of the American Society of Mechanical Engineers (ASME), an organization that had been formed just in 1880.

Taylor began attending ASME meetings in 1886 and met several of the major business theorists of that era, such as Captain Henry Metcalfe, Frank Halsey, and Henry Towne. He shared with them his new ideas, such as those in his 1895 paper titled "A Piece-Rate System."[20] Taylor published most of his papers and books through ASME and became the president of the society in 1906. Clearly, without these professional ties nurtured through ASME, Taylor could not have developed his thinking as fully or as clearly as he did, nor could his doctrines have achieved the widespread national fame and popular appeal they eventually did. As one administrative historian, Paul Van Riper, notes, the 1880s was "the decade in which the budding, if not full flowering of administrative thought took place in terms recognizable today."[21] Certainly, Taylor benefitted from the contact with other administrative theorists in the field at ASME meetings, and he remained loyal to that organization as his professional home throughout his career.

Fourth, not only did Taylor enter an era where a new factory system was emerging, where the conditions of factory life cried out for reform, and where professional associations such as ASME grew up to nurture and spread his scientific management doctrines, but also the Populist and Progressive political movements at the turn of the century provided a welcoming national environment for his new ideas. Historian Richard Hofstadter aptly labelled this period as, above all else, "the age of reform," especially moral reform. Political reformers of this era tended to talk in "moral rather than economic terms"; they set "impossible standards"; and they were "victimized, in brief, by a form of moral absolutism."[22] Presidents Theodore Roosevelt and Woodrow Wilson were in many ways symbolic of this period because both saw themselves as moralists and viewed morality as the central issue facing American politics. They often spoke in absolutes about the necessity for waging the fundamental fight for morality. Taylor's thinking in many ways fit perfectly with this age of reform in which public discussions focused on morality, impossible standards, and moral absolutism.

Ultimately, Taylor's own dogged determination (some say obsessive compulsion[23]) to develop and advance scientific management against often difficult, even impossible, opposition must be credited with a major share in its achievement of popularity. For example, in 1890 Taylor left his successful work at Midvale, and during the decade of the 1890s he encountered considerable difficulties in advancing his cause. Taylor made some contacts with the U.S. Navy, which led to his association with the Manufacturing Investment Company, a firm that made wood pulp from lumber by-products. Here he found that the firm's leadership was more interested in improving its financial position than its productivity and that his hard work in instituting his system was not only unappreciated but deeply distrusted. He left Manufacturing Investment in 1893 with a dim view of big business and embarked on a career as a consulting engineer, introducing various aspects of scientific management to several companies. He had only limited success at consulting, however. Businesses tended to want only bits and pieces of the Taylor system and often for short-run financial advantages only, not the long-term goals Taylor had in mind. Perhaps his most productive consultancy was at the Bethlehem Steel Company in 1898, where he installed a system of functional supervision and production management that incorporated most of the ideas of scientific management. Even there, however, Taylor had frequent clashes and an eventual falling-out with management.

By good luck, new-found affluence gave Taylor greater independence from consulting work. At Bethlehem Steel, he developed a new high-speed machine tool that turned out to be perhaps his most important and lucrative invention. It earned him a substantial personal fortune, thus allowing him to retire in 1901 and to devote the rest of his life to publicizing and advancing the cause of scientific management. Retirement gave him the luxury of time to nurture his cause—the Taylor system—by lecturing, writing, and sponsoring a close-knit group of devoted disciples.

By the turn of the century, Taylor had, through his various experiments at numerous firms, a bundle of techniques—loosely woven into a philosophy—aimed at making industry more efficient. The basic conceptual components of the Taylor system included the following:

rationality, or the application of reason, based on research into "the facts" of a work situation, applied to an organization, management, and activities of people;

planning, or the establishment of goals and objectives to determine future work programs;

specialization, or the division of labor among workers and the development of specific tools, materials, and machines for labor to fulfill their tasks;

quantitative measurement, or the accumulation of data and its application based on unbiased analysis applied to elements of managerial operations, particularly the qualifications of individuals to do specific tasks;

"one best way," or the belief that one single method of doing a job and one best tool, material, and worker could be developed for performing work most efficiently;

standards and standardization, or the belief that after the one best way is discovered through systematic research, then standards can be designed and rigorously followed; and *managers,* or well-selected, trained, and competent people to apply uniformly the principles of scientific management.

All these elements added up to improving work efficiency or, in other words, the maximization of output for a given input or the minimization of costs for any given output. And improved efficiency was certainly what many Americans were looking for in reforming public services in cities at the turn of the century. Cities, with their "bosses" and "machines," became the target of many government reformers during the Progressive era.[24] Also, most of what Americans spent on government went to the local level. In 1902, nearly three-fifths of all direct public expenditures were consumed by cities and counties. If national expenditures for defense were excluded, that figure jumped up to three-fourths. Moreover, most of the activities carried out by city government in that era were relatively routine physical ones, such as fighting fires, maintaining streets, and collecting trash, which made efficiency principles via Taylorism seem, for many, a worthwhile and eminently practical doctrine to apply to public activities. After all, had not the Taylor system already proved its success in business? Was that not evidence enough that it could—should?—work well for government?

Scientific management ideas therefore came to be in high demand and naturally seemed to find their way into the public sector, given both what many saw as an urgent need for greater efficiency in the public sector and the central preoccupation with efficient work methods advanced by the Taylor system. Ideas have their own peculiar route they choose to travel or are compelled to travel, however, and so too with the Taylor system's introduction and growth within government. It entered and then dominated public administration during the first half of the twentieth century by unexpected paths, though hardly on account of any direct efforts from Taylor himself. Taylor did achieve considerable national press attention from the testimony he gave before a special investigating committee of the House of Representatives in 1912 on behalf of scientific management, yet these remarks brought him comparatively fleeting notoriety. His two books, *Shop Management* (1903) and *The Principles of Scientific Management* (1911), were certainly important for spreading his Tayloristic principles, but in reality they represented only a small fraction of the growing flood of 240 business management texts published in the first decade of the twentieth century. His chief assistant, Carl Barth, initiated the application of scientific management techniques for the U.S. Army at the Watertown Arsenal in Massachusetts in 1909, with the enthusiastic support of General William Crozier, then head of the army's ordnance department. These basic reforms in armament production, however, became embroiled in controversies with the unions over the use of the stop watch and other Taylorite efficiency techniques applied on the job. Thus, their direct application for the U.S. military was short-lived, and in fact the use of scientific management methods was prohibited by congressional legislation in 1915 primarily because of the negative publicity from the Watertown experience.[25]

Taylor's most trusted lieutenant, Morris Cooke, who assisted Taylor's widow in preparing a two-volume biography of Taylor, had his own distinguished public service career as director of Philadelphia's Department of Public Works (1911–1915), director of the Water Resources Section of the National Resources Board (1934), and administrator of the Rural Electrification Administration (1935–1936). Morris Cooke wrote prolifically about scientific management theories in the *Annals*, the *American Political Science Review*, and the *American Society of Mechanical Engineers Transactions*. In addition, he edited a volume on public utility regulation and such popular books as *Our Cities Awake* and *How About It?* Cooke's writings, however, had little influence on the public administration literature of that day and thus did not bring Taylorism to the forefront of public administration, nor did Cooke himself develop basic administrative institutions predicated on Taylorism.[26] Rather, the job fell to a small but highly talented circle at the New York Bureau of Municipal Research to advance the Taylor doctrines within public administration and develop them in creative ways for government. How did this occur? The scene must now shift from Taylor's life to New York City.

The New York Bureau of Municipal Research was incorporated in May 1907 as a privately funded government research organization. Supported by such prominent businessmen as financiers R. Fulton Cutting, Andrew Carnegie, and John D. Rockefeller, the bureau was created out of the climate of urban reform that engulfed the major American cities at the turn of the century. The New York bureau in particular grew out of what its organizers saw as a logical extension of electoral political reform. In 1904, New York's first reform mayor, Seth Low, had been defeated, and those seeking change were left groping for new urban reform strategies. Soon after Low's defeat, in 1905, his supporters at a New York reform club, the Citizen's Union, set up the Bureau of Civic Betterment as a committee of the union.

During the next two years, the bureau developed under the leadership of William H. Allen, Henry Bruere, and Frederick Cleveland (nicknamed the ABCs), all of whom brought elements of Taylorism to the organization. Two of them, Allen and Bruere, had begun their careers in what was then called scientific charity work. Allen was hired by the Association for Improving the Condition of the Poor (AICP) immediately after receiving his doctorate at the University of Pennsylvania. Bruere received his law degree from Harvard and was employed directly out of law school to devise relief programs for the poor for the McCormick family charity in Chicago. He joined the staff of the AICP in 1903. The "scientific charity" movement that both Allen and Bruere participated in used quantitative techniques such as surveys to evaluate relief work and to document the effective use of charitable funds. Allen, as secretary of the AICP, began adapting the ideas of Taylor's *Shop Management* to the efficient and economical management of welfare agencies and their funding.

Cleveland was equally important for bringing Taylor's ideas to the bureau. Cleveland had received his doctorate in economics from the University of Pennsylvania the same year as Allen and worked as an accountant with the firm of Haskins and Sells. He was soon recognized as a specialist in municipal financial accounting. During the course of his work as a consultant, he prepared accounts and reports for the AICP and became closely associated with its activities. He held strong beliefs about efficiency and economy as a necessary part of government activities and even brought Frederick Taylor to lecture at the bureau a few times.

The early application of Taylor's thinking to welfare reform became an instrumental precursor for attracting the initial support for the bureau's development. As Jane Dahlberg writes, "When Mr. Cutting, along with other political 'do-gooders' lost faith in the reform movement, Dr. Allen convinced them that improved methods were needed in government as well. He reasoned that the city was the largest philanthropist of all, and that all of the combined philanthropic contributions could not equal the amount of money *wasted* each year by the city" (Dahlberg's italics).[27] Rather than concentrating on getting good people into leadership posts at city hall, the reformers soon shifted the focus of their reform priorities to systematic quantitative research as a central means for improving urban life.

After two years of existence, the committee gained independence from the Citizen's Union and became the New York Bureau of Municipal Research. Largely on the promise of bringing more efficiency and economy into city government, Allen convinced Cutting to begin modestly supporting the bureau by a contribution of $1,000 per month (later significantly expanded with Rockefeller and Carnegie funds). The first two purposes of the bureau, as noted in its articles of incorporation written in May 1907, stressed the need "to promote efficient and economical governments and to promote the adoption of scientific methods of accounting and of reporting the details of municipal business."[28] It was pure Taylorism.

The bureau's work was begun, like Taylor's, literally from the ground up—with potholes. As Jane Dahlberg writes,

> Bruere, with an assistant, set about trying to match repair contracts with the work done. For example, they charted all holes in the pavement on Eighth Avenue from Forty-second to Fifty-ninth Streets before and after repairing was done. Often the streets would be recorded as repaired, but with no effect on the holes. . . . The Bureau obtained sufficient evidence from observations of the work of the Borough President's office to show incompetence. No office in the city government, however, seemed interested in hearing about the Bureau's findings. It proceeded therefore to publish its data in a pamphlet entitled, *How Manhattan is Governed,* thus exploding a bomb in city hall, and ultimately leading to the removal of the Borough President then in office.[29]

Here was the beginning of the applications of Taylorism to municipal administration, that is, close, detailed rational analysis of work practices; the application of quantitative methods; record keeping; unbiased evaluation; and publicity about the empirical results for improving services and lowering costs. What evolved from the hundreds of studies by bureau personnel were not only the first comprehensive, detailed examinations of administrative practices from inside government but also new techniques that fundamentally changed the way Americans managed, organized, and controlled government. For example, through their consulting work with the city's Health Department, the bureau invented a new approach to planning, controlling, and directing public resources, that is, the basic techniques of public budgeting that became the model for other cities, states, and even the federal government's budget system. For the first time, budgets, thanks to the bureau, became meaningful plans for future government actions presented to the public for their direct oversight and control. Also, within the Health Department, the bureau pioneered new ways of collecting statistics and planning for program goals and objectives. They experimented with and evolved, again based on applications of Taylor's methodology, new designs for personnel classification, wage standards, efficiency systems of personnel ratings, accounting practices, and government purchasing processes. Within a relatively short period of a few years, the bureau put into place these important administrative inventions, largely inspired by Taylorism, and fostered the spread of these ideas throughout the United States.

What were the primary spin-offs from the work of the bureau for the development of the American administrative state? First, as one scholar of Taylor, Hindy Lauer Schachter, underscores: "Taylor's primary lesson for Allen and his associates was his implicit assumption that questions of organizational planning and implementation are researchable, that information collection and use is both possible and salutary for future performance. The underlying rationale for Taylor's work is that research-based intervention has positive performance consequence, that knowledge gained through specific experiments can be used to alter day-to-day production realities. Bureau research accepts this assumption as its most basic premise."[30]

Politics might be irrational and emotional, but administration need not be. Administration was potentially a *science*, rooted in the value of efficiency that was based on systematic research and the application of unbiased principles. Taylorism fired the imagination of the bureau to move local governments out of the depths of corruption and wasteful practices and into a new era of moral reform and civic advancement. The New York bureau became the model for similar agencies in Chicago, Cincinnati, Milwaukee, and many other communities, later advancing into the university-based bureaus at the University of Wisconsin at Madison (1909), the University of Illinois (1911), the University of Washington (1912), the University of California (1913), the University of Oklahoma (1913), and the University of Minnesota (1913). By 1914 these proliferating government research agencies established a national federation, the Government Research Conference. In 1917 the conference developed a permanent secretariat that became a central office and clearinghouse for the conference with a monthly bulletin that circulated essentially Taylorite ideas throughout the nation. By the 1920s there were nearly forty bureaus nationwide. Generally their work was funded not by public agencies but by private sponsors, primarily financed through philanthropic agencies and individual philanthropists, just as Rockefeller, Carnegie, and Cutting had supported the New York bureau. Taylorism in practice literally "bubbled up" from the grass roots, mainly spreading throughout U.S. city halls by means of voluntary and private or nonprofit, university-connected bureaus. Even today most remain university-connected or private foundation-based research enterprises (though the word "bureau" has gone out of fashion as their label).

Second, Taylor's ideas via the bureau's work had, in turn, an enormous impact on the American civil service system at every level of government. In the words of Frederick C. Mosher:

> In its application to governmental personnel, scientific management greatly added to the substance of civil service administrations. Jobs could now be studied in terms of the duties involved and the qualifications necessary to execute them: they could be systematically differentiated one from the other and standardized into classes having similar requirements. This became the basis for *position classification examinations* that could be framed to measure these qualifications objectively and competitively. Merit acquired a substance beyond honesty, basic education, general intelligence and political neutrality. Thanks in part to the aptitude testing of the U.S. Army in World War I, personnel testing by civil service organizations became perhaps the most nearly 'scientific' of all activities in the personnel realm. *Training* became an approved personnel function as long as it was restricted to the provision of knowledge and skills necessary to specific classes of positions, a restriction which is still applied in many American jurisdictions. A new near-science of *efficiency ratings* was developed to provide a more objective basis for supervision and (often in conjunction with competitive examinations) as a determining force in promotions. By 1930, these activities had become the core of public personnel administration in the civil service (Mosher's italics).[31]

Still today these elements—classification, examinations, training, and ratings—form the hub of civil service processes, much of it derived from the work of Frederick Taylor, as translated into the public sector by the New York bureau. Such elements not only gave content to the meaning of merit but also, as Mosher suggests, effectively and permanently depersonalized American personnel administration.

Third, the governing structure of the United States on the national level was also decisively changed by the bureau's application of scientific management ideas when Frederick Cleveland was appointed by President William Howard Taft in 1910 to head the President's Commission on Economy and Efficiency (known as the Taft Commission). Although previous committees had investigated national administration, the Taft Commission was set up "to inquire into the methods of the public business of government . . . so as to attain greater economy and efficiency."[32] The Taft report would be the first comprehensive national study of the executive branch. Drawing on the work of the bureau in devising budgeting processes for New York City, the commission, as Jane Dahlberg writes, "considered a national budget as fundamental to reorganization and lasting benefit. . . . In conference with department representatives, it worked out classification expenditures, appropriations, and estimates, and developed an executive budget for the President."[33]

The Taft Commission followed the New York bureau's methodology to the letter by detailed fact gathering, rational examination of work performed, quantitative measurement, unbiased analysis of findings, and belief in one-best-way solutions. The commission issued a total of 110 reports between 1910 and 1912 on virtually all major aspects of the federal government, making numerous recommendations for detailed labor-saving and cost-cutting efficiencies. Yet, it was the proposal for a national budget that perhaps was the most lasting and significant product of the Taft Commission. For the first time the executive budget idea was advocated for the federal government.

In February 1913, President Taft sent to Congress a report prepared by the commission that included a national budget proposal. The report, "A Budget for the Fiscal Year 1914," saw the budget as a key tool for promoting efficiency and included four parts: (1) the financial condition and operating results as a basis for considering present and prospective financial conditions; (2) summaries of estimates for considering revenues and expenditures in relation to government policy; (3) a summary of proposed changes of law for greater economy and efficiency; and (4) schedules supporting the budget statements, the need for a bureau of the budget, and other recommendations. The Taft proposal was pigeonholed by Congress primarily because of a party change to the Democratic presidency of Woodrow Wilson in 1913. Almost a decade passed before the proposal was enacted into law as the Budget and Accounting Act of 1921, which was, as Herbert Emmerich remarked, "probably the greatest landmark of our administrative history except for the Constitution itself."[34] The "budget movement" spread nationally, largely through work of local bureaus. States and cities would soon require executive budgets modeled on the 1921 act. The achievement of the 1921 act, however, in the words of Henry Bruere, "can be related back to the work that Mr. Cleveland did, and that in turn found its source in the work of the Bureau of Municipal Research."[35]

As important as research, civil service reforms, and national executive budgets were for American administrative development, a fourth product of the bureau, also based on scientific management ideas, was equally critical for establishing the modern administrative state, namely, developing trained public managers. With the financial support of Mrs. E. H. Harriman and the leadership of such prominent scholars as Charles Beard, the bureau created the Training School for Public Service, the first such educational program in this country. Mrs. Harriman had been to England and had been impressed by the public service education offered by the major universities in that country. When she attempted to donate funds to Harvard, Yale, and Columbia to promote public service education, the Ivy League schools scorned her proposed financial contribution, equating government service with "dirty politics" at its worst and "nonacademic" at its best.[36]

The New York Bureau of Municipal Research thought differently. Its training school would educate a new breed of men and women in efficiency techniques applied to the public sector that could advance not only the established goals of particular government agencies but also the broader needs and goals of communities. Following the model of the Taylor system, the bureau trained young men and women to make honest decisions based on fact, not personal whim, and to devise one-best-way principles of administration from their research. Many of the training school's early graduates became the future leaders in public administration, including Robert Moses, Luther Gulick, A. E. Buck, and C. E. Rightor, to name only a few.

In 1924 the training school moved to Syracuse University and established the first public administration university degree-granting program in the United States, the Maxwell School of Citizenship and Public Affairs. Under the deanship of William E. Mosher, Maxwell became, ultimately, a model for public administration education throughout the United States, remaining a leader in this field even today. Heavily salted with Taylorism, the basic classes in budgeting, planning, personnel, administrative analysis, organization, and management and the internship experiences (often studying city halls and county seats from the inside) were derived from the initial educational program designed by bureau personnel to provide government with trained and efficient public managers.[37]

Finally, the governing system of the United States in the twentieth century would be indelibly recast by the transformation of an offshoot of the bureau into the Brookings Institution, which in turn became the prototype of the modern-day Washington think tank, a source of what some call "the new policy elite."[38] Now more than one hundred think tanks thrive in metropolitan Washington, D.C. Through the development and promotion of their policy agendas and administrative ideas, these organizations play powerful roles in shaping the priorities of the nation. As James A. Smith sums up the multiple roles that think tanks play today in Washington:

> As scholar-statesmen, they can speak with an authority that former elected officials rarely command (some ex-presidents excepted). As specialists in various fields, they formulate the broad concepts through which social problems are defined and investigated and train other specialists who may have an even more direct impact. As consultants, they monitor the programs and policies already in place and increasingly find opportunities to advise the private sector. As government experts, they collect the raw data that allows a modern bureaucracy to function and provide day-to-day analysis needed by governmental officially. As interpreters, they speak to both policy-makers and the public and set the contours for policy debate, sometimes momentarily widening its parameters, and sometimes narrowing it to practical choices. And as entrepreneurs, they direct financial resources and intellectual personnel into specific policy areas, work to broaden the policy agenda, and create new mechanisms for bringing the expert into play.[39]

In a nutshell, concludes Smith, "Over the long term, experts in their various roles have first defined and then reshaped the institutional structures by which knowledge is brought to bear on policy."[40] Again, the lineage of this new structure for American governance can be directly traced back to the New York bureau's experience. After 1913 several bureau personnel tried to keep their ideas alive in Washington when they finished working on the Taft Commission report by establishing a Washington-based connection for the bureau. In 1916 they created a privately funded Institute for Government Research, re-named and expanded in 1927 to the Brookings Institution. Originally funded by the Rockefeller Foundation, Brookings sought to maintain a neutral policy stance by broad representation from liberal to conservative, businesspeople to academics, and even a balance of east-west geographic interests. Its first director, William Willoughby (who drafted the 1921 budget act), promoted studies of efficiency within federal agencies. Robert S. Brookings's work, however, raised the substantial endowment and widened the policy agenda into such fields as foreign affairs, labor-management, and international economics. A wealthy St. Louis businessman, Brookings came to Washington during World War I as a "dollar-a-year-man" (a term given to individuals who were recruited into government service during World War I and paid one dollar annually because they donated their services) and devoted the rest of his life to building the institution that bears his name. Brookings himself was an enthusiast of Taylorism, believing in—and promoting—his institution's agenda that the only way to lower taxes and reduce the national debt was by making government more efficient. The efficiency theme helped immensely to garner numerous contributions Brookings solicited on behalf of his institution, and his national fundraising campaign to influence public policy agendas has become the model for many think tanks in Washington and around the country. Placing a special premium on the expert and expertise, Taylorism via the work of the bureau thrives now in many forms and guises. Again, as James A. Smith explains in metaphoric terms:

> The enterprise of experts has grown like a coral reef built by countless busy organisms. Not only does it create its own ecologies environment, harboring various delicate flora and fauna, it often changes the passages between sea and shore. Like a fantastic underwater growth, these institutions have created bridges between the public and private sectors and have filled in almost every known space in our fragmented governmental system. This growth has fed upon itself: private research groups have prodded the government into adding specialists to executive departments, the expertise of the executive branch has compelled Congress to set up its own research units, government agencies have used contractual research arrangements to foster nongovernmental research centers, and universities have set up new research and training to respond to the shifting need for public specialists. New venues and arrangements for the expert are continuously opening.[41]

The configurations and permutations of the efficiency movement that Frederick Taylor began and that the bureau fostered were numerous, varied, and long-lasting throughout public life in the United States during the twentieth century. Indeed, the effects remain so vast and often hidden from view that they are impossible to chart fully or even partially, as the foregoing quotation from James A. Smith suggests. Taylorism, as Judith A. Merkle writes, even stimulated worldwide "the spread of a new world vision of the proper goals for industrial and industrializing societies." It fostered "the reorganization of the world industry of an integrated, planned, mass basis for the promotion of broad-scale social efficiency."[42]

Ironically, all these massive changes in the way Americans—and the world—govern themselves in the late twentieth century derived from a man who had little liking for or appreciation of government. His faith and that of his disciples was rooted firmly in finding the one best way for business managers, particularly first-line shop managers, to run their affairs most efficiently and economically.

Like the early radical Puritan saints of his forebears, Frederick Taylor believed in a highly rational, volunteeristic "city on a hill," a Saint Simeon vision for improved social advancement based on an empirical science, one that would remake the world by fostering peace, prosperity, and cooperation among all people—if only they would believe in his system and adopt its principles.[43] After all, what better way was there to bring about God's kingdom on earth? Like the early Puritans, Taylor insisted there could be only *one* rational creed (scientific management), *one* ritual (empirical science), *one* set of commandments (the principles), and *one* test of discipleship (do you believe in *my* method?). All other gods, such as rules of thumb, were deemed false and were forbidden to be practiced. All resisters were vilified as "soldiering," "goldbricking," or "cesspools of the marketplace."

The absolute *oneness* that Taylor demanded of his faith and faithful gave inordinate power and intensity to his beliefs that cast a long shadow of influence throughout the twentieth century and beyond. Nevertheless, like Puritanism, whose faithful quickly split into various fractious, dissenting denominations, Taylorism also came to be interpreted and applied in different ways. At the bureau, its doctrines took on new, unpredictable, and innovative applications to public sector practices that probably Frederick W. Taylor would find astonishing today.

7

Richard S. Childs
Minister for the Council-Manager Plan

Richard S. Childs, 1882–1978
(from Yale University Archives, Manuscripts and Archives, Yale University Library)

A Reformer is one who sets forth cheerfully toward sure defeat. . . . His persistence against stone walls invites derision from those who have never been touched by his religion.
—Richard S. Childs
  National Municipal Review, July 1927

RICHARD CHILDS LIKED TO REFER TO HIMSELF as the "minister who performed the marriage ceremony between the city manager plan as first thought of in Staunton, Virginia and the commission plan in Des Moines, Iowa."[1] Certainly no person in the twentieth century more tirelessly spoke for the gospel of urban reform. Throughout his adult life, from age twenty-one until his death at age ninety-five, Childs crusaded ceaselessly for a wide range of state and local reforms that included the short ballot, nonpartisan elections, improved judicial selection processes, reform of the coroner's office, municipal charters, and revision of archaic county governmental structures.

What most fundamentally transformed the landscape of municipal government in lasting ways, however, was his "invention" of the council-manager plan and his remarkable mission to press its adoption throughout the United States. Today roughly half the American cities with populations of more than ten thousand operate under the plan, a form of local government that puts a professional manager at the helm of day-to-day administrative operations. The plan not only introduced a new profession of city management into public life but also brought together a package of important administration reforms and served as a key vehicle for putting the changes into practice at the grassroots level. The reforms included civil service systems, planning processes, public budgets, and nonpartisan elections.

Childs's handiwork can also be found even in "unreformed communities," or those without the council-manager plan. Bits and pieces of the plan came to be grafted onto these municipalities through such novel institutional adaptations as chief administrative officer, a position designed to bring professionalism to those localities that never adopted, for various reasons, the entire package of the plan. Childs maintained a remarkably consistent, fervent belief throughout his lifetime that a well-conceived structure of government was the key to, in his words, "a democracy in truly workable form."[2] To that end, he focused his considerable energies, first as a part-time avocation and then perhaps as the longest-running vocation in the twentieth century, as the foremost American urban reformer.

Ironically, few specialists in government know his name today, let alone the millions of Americans who live and work in council-manager communities. Even city managers rarely hear of the man who fathered their careers. It is puzzling why this single individual who so profoundly—and successfully—transformed the basic pattern of local institutions in the United States under which millions of Americans are governed should be a largely forgotten historic figure. Perhaps even more puzzling are the following: What drove Childs for more than seven decades to pursue so tenaciously his urban reform agenda even when it became highly unfashionable in the post–World War II era?

In the end, how did he so thoroughly succeed at his mission of chang-ing local government in the United States when his ideas were largely discredited by many academics, even other civic reformers? What did all his grassroots reforms mean for the broad development of the American administrative state?

Richard Childs was born on May 24, 1882, in Manchester, Connecti-cut, to William Hamlin Childs and Nellie Spencer Childs. His father was a self-made millionaire, one of the cofounders of the Bon Ami Com-pany (their cleansing powder is still sold today and is known for its label of the little chicken and the motto, "It hasn't scratched yet!"). The Childs family heritage can be traced back to Benjamin Childs, who came to Roxbury, Massachusetts, from seventeenth-century England during the Puritan Revolution. Some of Richard Childs's earliest memories of his social life revolved around the North Congregational Church, where his parents "were genuinely devout, faithful attendees which was a matter of course for them and for all the people they knew."[3] Small-town life for the Childs family, as for many in the nine-teenth century, involved active church membership; "faith in the Holy Bible was implicit, literal, and unquestioning."[4] William Childs taught in and served as Sunday school superintendent. Richard idolized him: "His piety was simple and genuine and to the end of his life he would tuck down briefly to his knee—one knee—in prayer before he left his bedroom in the morning."[5]

The religious devotion of the father left no small imprint on his son. In a loving portrait written of his father after his death, Richard re-vealed a deep-seated affection for this homespun religious man, whom he described as devoted to "good works," an "eager beaver" in any church or community activity who was driven to involve himself in all kinds of local service such as organizing the Young People's Society for Christian Endeavor and pulling together the citizens of Manchester to build the first town water system.[6] William poured the same energies into other ventures, such as founding the highly successful Bon Ami Company and his not-so-successful backing of civic reform politicians such as Seth Low for mayor of New York City. William not only fur-nished Richard with inherited wealth that made his lifelong reform avocation possible but also, and more important, imparted a strong sense of Christian idealism, namely, beliefs in mission, service, faith, optimism, and progress, which shaped Richard's own calling through-out his life.

When Richard was ten, the family moved to Brooklyn, New York. He attended private schools, Adelphi Academy and later Polytechnic Preparatory School, which was then one of the best academic high schools in the city, where he excelled in courses on literature and current affairs. After he was graduated in 1900, he went on to Yale, concentrating on literature and the social sciences, and received his bachelor of arts degree in 1904. A family friend landed Richard a starting job with Erickson Advertising Company, where he learned the ad trade from one of the masters of the business at that time, Alfred Erickson (who also happened to hold the Bon Ami advertising account). Because of family connections, combined with hard work and a flair for writing appealing ad copy, Childs rose to junior partner in the firm within a few years. By 1911, his career had brought him back into the family business, where he quickly became Bon Ami's general manager. He served briefly in World War I as a "dollar-a-year-man" (the term coined for someone who donated his services and was paid one dollar a year) in the War Department and then returned to Bon Ami. In 1928 he left Bon Ami to become assistant to the president of A. E. Chew, an export firm, and in 1929 he was named to the board of directors of the American Cyanamid Company. He later rose to become the executive vice president of one of the company's major subsidiaries, Lederle Laboratories (a company that primarily manufactured drugs and medical supplies) from which Childs retired in 1944.

That business career was his official vocation, and if that was all Childs accomplished, he would certainly not have merited mention as a significant public figure today. Rather than business affairs, however, Richard's real love, genuine enthusiasm, and boundless energies during his adult life were devoted to the cause of local civic reform. Again, his father served as a role model by working as a leader in the New York State Progressive party and chief backer of Theodore Roosevelt's presidential campaign on the Bull Moose party ticket in 1912. At roughly the same time, Richard, while starting his first job at Erickson, paralleled his father's ardent boosterism by opening a one-man office next door to Erickson to promote the short ballot, an office that eventually broadened into becoming the chief organizational sponsor of the council-manager plan. In addition, for more than fifty years, both before and while working at Bon Ami and Lederle, he served as a volunteer for the national council of the National Municipal League (now the National Civic League), including acting as the league's president from 1927 to 1931 "at a salary of nothing and well worth it," as he described later.[7]

Like his father, who was deeply involved in volunteering for various civic causes throughout his life, so too Richard followed a similar path, although not via church or party affiliations but by means of nonpartisan associations, reform clubs, civic leagues, and the power of the pen. Even at age ninety-five, he was still vigorously working for civic reform, commuting regularly from his Brooklyn Heights apartment twice a week to work at the league's downtown Manhattan office as an unpaid consultant.[8]

How Childs led a silent reform in the American urban landscape can only be understood against the backdrop of what urban government was like prior to 1900. The last two decades of the nineteenth century witnessed faster rates of urbanization than at any time—past or present—during American history: hamlets became towns, towns grew into cities, and cities turned into metropolitan communities. As late as 1850, little more than 15 percent of Americans lived in villages of more than twenty-five hundred. In 1800, only 3.3 percent of Americans lived in towns of any size. By the 1880s the number of Americans who lived in cities rose one-third; by 1900, the number was nearly 40 percent, and by 1920, more than half of all Americans lived in cities. The massive shift from a predominantly rural to urban population was unprecedented—for which the United States was wholly unprepared.

Much of the increase was fueled by the influx of more than five million immigrants. At home perhaps an even larger, though unknown, number moved from farms to towns, a movement that resulted from two factors: the push of the closing of the frontier and the pull of rapid technological change. The closing of the frontier pushed many into cities while increased agricultural productivity and the advent of industrial mass production translated into massive employment opportunities and thus pulled others off farms. Cities had to respond to these heretofore unprecedented urban-industrial population shifts in numerous ways. For example, as Lent D. Upson has pointed out, between 1860 and 1920 Detroit added 228 new activities to its municipal government, including the "development of zoning plans, inspection of food handlers, public health nursing, community centers, electrified street lighting, motorized fire and police services, public airport facilities, dental care for school children, mandatory grade school—and later high school education."[9]

Although these new local public services were swiftly grafted onto municipalities at the turn of the century, they were often added piecemeal and haphazardly, and the actual management of these services left much to be desired. As administrative historian Leonard White wrote of this era:

> Low standards of municipal accomplishment, waste and misapplication of public funds, lack of vision with regard to the City's future and lack of energy in pursuing even the most limited objectives, government by political machines, for the purpose of maintaining controlling power of the machine rather than by independent officials for the good of the community, jealousy, and ill-will between communities even where cooperation was essential, concealment of the real condition of public business rather than frank recognition of the right of the public to know the facts of public affairs—all cooperated in varying degrees to produce discontent, distrust, and suspicion of the mayor and or commission.[10]

The muckraker journalist Lincoln Steffens put it more graphically in his classic exposé, *The Shame of the Cities:* "Franchises worth millions were granted without one cent to the city. . . . Companies which refused to pay black mail had to leave, citizens were robbed more and more boldly, pay-rolls were padded with the names of non-existent persons; work on public improvements was neglected, while money for them went to the boodlers. . . . Behind the corruptionists were men of wealth and social standing, who, because of special privileges granted them, felt bound to support and defend the looters. Independent victims of the far-reaching conspiracy submitted in silence."[11]

The actual day-to-day worries of those who lived in the rapidly growing cities of the United States in that era, however, were far more immediate than academic. Problems resulting from slums, crime, poverty, environmental pollution, poor public sanitation and health, substandard education, inadequate public transportation, and unemployment cried out for solutions.

By 1900 civic reform associations flourished in most big cities, propounding various solutions to the then-apparent urban ills. More than eighty such associations existed by 1894, sixty of which had been founded since 1890. More than a dozen were located in New York City alone, most of which had been established to combat corrupt city bosses and machines such as Tammany Hall. As Bernard Hirschhorn, Childs's biographer, has noted, "The reformers' objectives included the promotion of honest, efficient and economical government, the suppression of vice, charter reform to include home rule and strong mayor government, civil service, the prevention of election frauds, the separation of municipal from state and national politics, nonpartisan and businesslike government, the elimination of politics as the basis for the selection of candidates for municipal offices, and simplified, centralized city government through short ballots and at-large elections."[12]

For a young man of means coming of age, imbued with religious ideals and fascinated by Progressive reform issues, it was a grand time to be alive. Childs recalls the excitement: "Political reform was boiling! Novel devices were fondly advanced for ending political machines and their alliances with privileged and vested interests. The Progressive Party was in the making and assailing the so-called invisible governments with varied programs of reform. Oregon reformers were making a bold pioneering trial of the initiative, referendum and recall. Direct primaries were displacing party conventions in a dozen states with more to come."[13]

Although he recounts it in secular terms, Childs describes his first voting experience (when he "saw the light") as almost a religious conversion. Like Saul on the road to Damascus, Childs claimed that he was "mortified" that he had to vote for nineteen different candidates and that he recognized only four of the names. In fact, his father knew less than he did, and it pained Richard that his father recommended that he simply vote the straight party ticket.[14] "I decided then that the trouble with our municipal government was not voter apathy. . . . The trouble was that the ballot was too long."[15]

Richard Childs called that voting process "a travesty on democracy."[16] In his mind the process came to be associated with an inherent evil that had to be rooted out so that the people as a whole might rule and democracy prevail. Just as Childs's Puritan forebears must have perceived the Reformation in stark terms as a battle between themselves and what they considered the corruption of the true faith by the pope and his followers, so too Childs's Manichaeistic Progressive faith saw the world in black and white with little gray in between. There could be no hairsplitting or fine-tuning a political philosophy: democracy was in jeopardy, and that meant war! Just as his forebears must have railed against "popish plots" and "the evils of Rome," Childs called for war on "political rings," "unelected bosses," and "corrupt machines."

Warfare, for Childs and many of his fellow Progressives, just as for the Protestants of the sixteenth-century Reformation, took the shape of moral reform, that is, "purifying" what they viewed as corrupt public organizations via civic activism and reform associations; effective propaganda campaigns to expose wrongdoers; and rational organizational structures to promote "clean" democracy. After renting an office next to the Erickson Ad Agency where he worked, Childs hired a research staff of one person; secured well-known sponsors such as Woodrow Wilson, then president of Princeton University; and used his creative pen that he was honing on writing advertising copy to send out a steady stream of eye-catching publicity.

His materials advocated a reformed election process that would *not* essentially disenfranchise voters by requiring them to vote for a host of unknown candidates in a multitude of petty offices. Childs formally established the Short Ballot Organization, which sought to reduce the length of the ballot so as to permit voters to make better and presumably more rational choices from among fewer candidates. His propaganda skills as an ad man and pamphleteer that he learned next door helped him orchestrate a masterful advertising strategy. In little time, Childs mounted a successful national campaign for short ballots with few resources at hand. He accomplished his goal through the illusion of high-level support while having little more than a mail drop for an office. His well-crafted, pithy slogans were effectively targeted at small-town audiences throughout the United States. Childs also showed unusual zeal for a cause that at the time captured immense public interest. He expressed himself in clear, quotable prose, usually combined with incredible horror stories about bosses and machines to make his case convincing.

Later, he produced a book, *Short Ballot Principles,* that became widely circulated and was used even in college classes.[17] Its publication brought him national recognition among academics and reformers, as well as an increased network of reform support and funding for his work. He joined some of the influential and prestigious reform clubs of that day: the City Club of New York, the City Union, and the National Municipal League. By the time he was twenty-six, his life had taken on what others later called "a split personality—a drive to prove himself in business coupled with what he'd rather do than eat: civic reform!"[18] Again, Childs, like the early Puritans, seemed to have no problems reconciling his capitalistic spirit with his reformist faith. He was a young man on a quest, one of the youthful "eager beavers" (just as he had described his father) in both business and civic reform. Surprisingly, while carrying on all these activities, he still found time to marry, have three daughters, and pursue an active social life.

Nevertheless, Childs and other Progressives came to realize that shorter ballots were not enough to insure that qualified individuals got elected. They saw that even more was needed to promote good government. Quite by accident, a new alternative form of local government emerged that caught the eye of many reformers: the commission plan. First created in 1903 in Galveston, Texas, after the disastrous hurricane of 1900 that destroyed much of the downtown area, the commission plan was hailed by many of its proponents as the chief vehicle for Galveston's speedy recovery from the devastation. Whether its achievements in Galveston were overblown is hard to say, but for Childs it was attractive by virtue of its simplicity. It could be "sold" to voters easily, he later claimed. By its very definition, commission government required the election of a small board of five, seven, or nine full-time commissioners to represent the entire city collectively while being individually responsible for administering municipal functions. Here was, in Childs's view, "conspicuous responsibility—and hence accountability—of all elected officials to the people."[19] The number of officials would be so few that the voters could select them easily and rationally and then could directly hold these same officials responsible for how well—or poorly—they ran city affairs as a whole. In many ways the commission plan was a logical extension—and improvement—on the short ballot concept because it kept the electoral offices limited and placed voter attention squarely on deciding the broader policy questions for the entire community. It also introduced the idea of full-time commissioners managing the community effectively.

Although Childs began urging cities to adopt the commission plan as part of his campaign for the short ballot, even referring to municipalities with the plan as "short ballot cities," its defects were becoming readily apparent to reformers. In practice, accountability was diffused among the commissioners. For example, it was often difficult to tell who was in charge and who was to blame when things went wrong: all commissioners? a few? or just one? In addition, good people were not always elected commissioners. To the astonishment of many reformers, the old party bosses also ran for office—and won!

Despite the increasingly obvious defects, commission plan adoptions gained steam. Especially after large cities such as Houston, Texas, and Des Moines, Iowa, passed city charters patterned on the idea and bolstered by Childs's victorious campaign from his storefront Short Ballot Organization, by 1915 more than five hundred communities had adopted the commission plan. The plan was short-lived thereafter, however, because a new competitor gained prominence, again thanks to the work of Richard Childs. Historical accident also played a part. What happened next to Childs's ideas occurred by chance in a small, out-of-the-way town, Staunton, Virginia.

In 1906 Staunton, Virginia, a town of 11,336 people at the head of the Shenandoah Valley (and the birthplace of Woodrow Wilson), became a first-class city under Virginia Commonwealth law. Having passed the ten thousand mark according to a recent census, the community was forced to reorganize its government from a unicameral to a bicameral legislative body. The new bicameral body grew from twelve to twenty-two members, and the municipal government suddenly came under the direction of more than thirty legislative committees. At the same time, Staunton had no full-time city employees, and so the enlargement of its chief policymaking organ into a bicameral body brought what work was being performed almost to a standstill. As one commentator observed, no one could agree on what should be done or how the work should be administered, which left "the various city departments drifting without leadership."[20]

Moreover, an enormous backlog of public works projects awaited action. Eyewitness Henry Oyen described the situation of Staunton's city streets in graphic terms: "Each of these streets had a single track laid on ties, at one side. The rest were plain mud. In wet weather wagons went hub deep in the mire, and it was a feat to make the crossing on foot. . . . As for the side streets, picture a red clay country road with a gully washed out in the middle."[21]

With the streets a mess and the city government crippled by indecision, on August 7, 1906, a legislative committee of the city council recommended a solution for Staunton's problems, namely, the creation of a position of municipal director and the placement of all administrative work "in the hands of some competent salaried official."[22] This report was sidetracked, however, while another legislative committee examined the then-popular commission plan as an alternative. After a year of study and deliberation, the committee concluded that adopting the commission plan was not feasible. They pointed out first that the plan would add five new commissioners to the existing unwieldy bicameral legislature, thus compounding the present administrative chaos. Of more significance, they noted, because the commission plan had recently been found unconstitutional under Virginia law, Staunton was left with no other alternative than to appoint a general manager as an expedient means of coping with the pressing community dilemmas.[23]

Thus on January 16, 1908, the two bodies of the city council passed an ordinance establishing an office of general manager who would have "entire charge and control of all executive work of the city in its various departments."[24]

From the tenor of their arguments, clearly many supporters of the general manager idea wanted the city to run more like a business. Its major sponsor, Councilman Hugh S. Braxton, argued, "Regarding Staunton simply as a business corporation . . . it is evident that the same principles should be applied as would be applied in the case of any ordinary business concern."[25] Editorial comment in the *Staunton Daily Leader* also backed the same "self-evident" business principles: "a municipal director is a man who has charge of and runs the city on business-like principles. Some cities have three directors and some have five. Staunton has twenty-two, and they all try to run it in a different way."[26]

What did the Staunton experiment represent? Many saw it as the first city manager community in the country. With the appointment of a civil engineer, Charles E. Ashburner in 1908, Staunton, for all practical purposes, had effectively appointed the first city manager. The manager concept had been discussed previously, however. In 1899, in an editorial in *California Municipalities*, Haven A. Mason, one of the founders and first director of the League of California Cities, proposed the establishment of the post of business manager within California municipalities. Professor Charles E. Merriam, chair of the political science department at the University of Chicago, while serving as a member of the Chicago Charter Convention (1905–1906) unsuccessfully advocated the idea of an appointed chief executive for Chicago. Ukiah, California, had already created the post of chief executive officer, with the person to be selected by the city council on the basis of merit criteria (although no one was appointed, nor was the post explicitly called a manager).[27]

Thus council-manager government did not begin in Staunton because already it was being discussed in reform circles and even had been adopted in a modified version in Ukiah. Staunton's experiment, however, not Ukiah's, caught the eye of one eager, young Progressive reformer, Richard S. Childs. He documented and publicized the idea widely as the *best* plan for cities in the United States. In a fascinating letter to Lawrence M. Conant, associate editor of *World's Work,* dated May 1, 1931, we glimpse Childs's own account of how he brought to prominence and nationally publicized the Staunton idea:

Shortly after I saw your article [in *World's Work*] on Staunton, I conceived the idea that the city manager feature united to the commission plan would provide a new plan analogous to the business corporation and to the German burgomaster [sic] setup, which would be very much superior to the commission plan, which, at the time was coming rapidly into vogue and bringing with it some advantages as well as some serious defects of organization.

I was then a volunteer secretary of the National Short Ballot Organization, which I had organized . . . with Woodrow Wilson as President. I was also secretary of the New York Short Ballot Organization whose mission was to push for the application of our short ballot ideas in the State of New York. In the latter capacity, I laid out a program for an optional municipal government law, which would make the commission plan available to all the smaller cities of the state, in a form ready for adoption by referendum. I twisted the standard commission form to provide for a city manager and an elaborate bill was drafted by my assistant, H. S. Gilbertson.

I did this without consulting the governing board of the New York Short Ballot Organization and brought the bill to them as a finished piece of work for their endorsement. They declined to endorse it for publication, as part of the association's program, preferring to keep the simpler strategy of trying to get the minor state officers made appointive—one task at a time, so the bill was left on our hands. Looking around then for someone to father it, we got it sponsored by the Lockport Board of Trade, which introduced it in the legislature. The National Short Ballot Organization, forthwith gave it generous publicity in its press releases; secured for it the attention of charter commissions all over the country; Woodrow Wilson mentioned it in one of his speeches on a western tour, it was put into a technical loose-leaf "Digest of Short Ballot Charters"; papers on the "Lockport Plan" were gotten into various civic conventions and magazines; and thus the idea was put on the map in a campaign which went on for ten years under my personal and enthusiastic direction.[28]

The letter tells us much about Childs's tactics and strategy simply by the action verbs and phrases he used to describe his own work: "gave it generous publicity," "push for," "twisted," "father it," "keep the simpler strategy," and "put on the map." Here was someone not beneath using enough guile and slight of hand to get his way if he believed the cause was just. Moreover, his letter omits certain facts or at least does not give the whole story. He paints himself as merely "a volunteer secretary of the National Short Ballot Organization" with "Woodrow Wilson as President." In fact, Childs was pretty much *the* organization, whereas Wilson was more or less a figurehead. It was Childs who got Wilson to mention the idea in his Seattle, Washington, address; it was Childs who put it into the loose-leaf "Digest of Short Ballot Charters," terming it "the Lockport Plan"; and it was Childs who worked tirelessly to publicize it nationally and fashioned it into an easy-to-adopt format for cities. Furthermore, and perhaps most critical, it was Childs who understood better than anyone else at the time—and this was where his advertising background proved invaluable—that to sell the council-manager plan effectively he had to make it conform to the popular, indeed dominant, metaphors of the day, namely, business symbols.

Childs recognized that the commission plan could never be sold as being "just like a corporation with a board of directors" unless it "would appoint a manager." So he added a "manager" to the "commission" idea and put the word "council" in front so that no one would confuse the new plan with the old one. As Childs aptly said, "This catch phrase has converted whole cities."[29] In addition, although he likened himself often to "the minister" who joined the commission plan with the manager plan and "converted whole cities," he in fact did far more. As Don Price noted, Childs was an astute "manipulator of symbols" who figured out just the right words to convert the public to his cause and accomplished this feat so surreptitiously that even today few city managers or administrative scholars have ever heard his name.[30]

Richard Childs worked especially hard between 1910 and 1920 promoting manager government. Although the New York legislature failed to pass the bill that would have allowed Lockport to adopt the plan, Childs generated enormous press coverage in the process. Indeed, he created so much interest that numerous towns across the country adopted the idea of the plan, referring to it as the most modern form of municipal government, even though only a few localities at that time actually implemented it. First to adopt council-manager government was Sumter, South Carolina, in 1912; then Dayton, Ohio, followed in 1913; and by 1918, nearly one hundred communities could boast being council-manager communities.

Childs generated all of his materials from his New York City Short Ballot office and often did not know where or how his press releases and publicity were being used. As John Porter East, one of Childs's biographers, has noted: "Childs . . . played no specific role in the Sumter victory until after the South Carolina legislature had approved the plan and the people of Sumter had accepted it by referendum. In brief, his materials were used extensively in that crusade, but he was unaware that they were being used and he played no personal part. After acceptance of the plan, Childs did assist the new council in the preparation of an advertisement for a manager."[31]

After crystallizing the manager concept into popular form and giving it national publicity, Childs capped off his efforts by institutionalizing the plan in a way that remains to this day the preeminent form of local government advocated by the leading civic reform organization in the United States. The specific nationwide sponsoring association was the National Municipal League (now called the National Civic League), whose Standing Committee on Commission Government included such prominent scholars of that era as William Bennett Munro of Harvard University; Charles A. Beard of Columbia University; Ernest S. Bradford, author of a history on commission government; and Clinton Rogers Woodruff, the league's secretary.

In 1898 the league had supported the strong-mayor form of government in its pamphlet titled "The Model City Charter." In 1911, its Committee on Commission Government reported that the commission plan "had brought about democratic control of municipal government through unification of powers."[32] A year later, however, Childs became a member of that committee, and, as W. F. Willoughby wrote: "By 1913, influenced by the Lockport Plan . . . and by Childs, the committee at the League's Toronto conference switched its approval to the commission-manager idea. Accordingly, a reactivated committee on Municipal Program was instructed to draft a new Model City Charter that prescribed the commission-manager form of government. At the 1915 conference, held in Dayton, the first large city to adopt the manager plan, this innovation was approved."[33]

Willoughby gave the credit for adoption of the new "Model City Charter" to the young men in their twenties and thirties, such as Lent D. Upson of Detroit and Frederick P. Gruenburg of Philadelphia, and others led by Richard Childs, who persuaded the older men in the league, such as Charles E. Merriam, A. Lawrence Lowell, Frank J. Goodnow, and A. R. Hutton, to endorse the council-manager idea. In addition, Childs convinced the league to undertake a major national education campaign on behalf of council-manager government. In modern parlance, Childs proved himself an adept behind-the-scenes organizational networker.

By the 1920s the plan had generated so much momentum on its own in finding community support for adoption that it was well beyond Childs's capability to influence its direction. Later, when post–World War II suburbs flourished throughout the United States and required effective managers, the plan provided the entire package of ready-made reform elements, that is, modern civil service, public budgets, planning instruments, professional management, and the like, so the suburban entities could function and grow in the complex and urbanized postwar United States.

A City Managers' Association (later called the International City Managers' Association and now the International City/County Management Association [ICMA]) began in 1914 and developed into a powerful lobby that even to this day works on behalf of promoting the plan. The ICMA developed research, training, and professional development programs for city managers. Furthermore, the National Municipal League (now the National Civic League) continued to press through its various editions of the "The Model City Charter" (now in its seventh edition) for the plan as the ideal local government structure.[34] Intellectuals lent their scholarly support early on as well, from Harry Toulmin's *The City Manager* (1915) to Leonard White's *The City Manager* (1927) to Harold Stone, Don Price, and Kathryn Stone's *City Manager Government in the United States* (1940).[35]

Today, all states except Indiana and Hawaii offer the plan as an option for communities to select as municipal charters for local government. The reasons for the continued enthusiasm for manager government vary from region to region and community to community, but clearly the plan serves a variety of local interests across the United States in finding a practical means for governing more effectively in a changing and increasingly globalized world. It is sustained no doubt today for the same reasons that Staunton, Virginia, found it invaluable in 1908, namely, because cities now, as then, find institutionalized professional managerial skills essential to operating in a complex, modern world.

Yet, if Childs's only contribution to creating the modern administrative state was to bequeath to Americans simply another governing form, admittedly the most popular form of local government today, that alone would probably not qualify him to be labeled one of the significant modern American state founders. What he achieved—perhaps quite unwittingly—was a far broader, more pervasive revolution in U.S. governance as a whole, one that probably even he did not envision—or want! Certainly, he fought any variation in the plan, *his plan,* when cities failed to conform to its—*his*—specifics. For example, he would never concede that Staunton was the first manager community. Rather it was Sumter, not Staunton, according to Childs, that should be anointed with that honor. Staunton failed to qualify, in Childs's eyes, because it retained the strong mayor and bicameral legislative format and thus was not true to the plan, *his plan.*

Childs, the perpetual, dedicated reformer, however, could not hold back the grassroots managerial revolution he started. When San Francisco proponents of the plan failed to get their charter ratified by voters in 1932, a compromise was worked out that led to the creation of the CAO, the Chief Administrative Officer, within municipal government. The CAO grafted elements of professionalism onto the top levels of city hall without all of the features of the council-manager plan. Soon large and small communities alike began tinkering with the plan, adapting variations of it to suit the particular needs of their communities. In the process, both the plan and its myriad of amended imitations brought increased professionalization in numerous ways to U.S. localities. Experts multiplied, bringing with them new techniques and technologies to solving local problems. Here, in reality, was the profound, far-wider transformation that Childs's handiwork wrought within the U.S. political landscape. Until the twentieth century, American municipal affairs were conducted largely within the purview of elected amateurs. Childs can be credited with triggering a massive professional transformation of twentieth-century American urban life via his plan's invention and his own forceful advocacy of it throughout his lifetime. As Frederick C. Mosher noted sometime ago, "For better or worse—or better *and* worse—much of our government is now in the hands of professionals."[36] And much of this professional public management revolution can be traced to when twenty-one-year-old Richard Childs was confronted by a long, confusing ballot that neither he nor his father could figure out.

In truth, however, that revolution began earlier, before the voting booth encounter and before Childs went to Yale or moved to Brooklyn. Rather, the formative influence that so fundamentally transformed the wider world began in his childhood, within a Congregationalist Sunday school where he was imbued with his father's Christian ideals of service, moral uplift, and civic reform. Here his mind was ignited by the word of God's basic creed and doctrines along the Congregationalist lines that would shape the direction of his future reforms.

Congregationalism is a church that traces its roots and beliefs back to the Puritans and the Protestant Reformation. Within this reform tradition Childs was raised, and he clung tenaciously to those values as an adult, values that he often proclaimed in secular form, as noted at the beginning of this chapter: "A Reformer is one who sets forth cheerfully toward sure defeat." However, Congregationalism, via his father's larger-than-life parental ideal, came to be fashioned into a far more complicated, secular version by Childs's creative talent for combining public relations with moral zeal. The church historian J. Paul Williams has written of Congregationalism: "They believed in the gathered church, practiced the covenanted relationship, insisted on the right of the local congregation to choose its own pastor, opposed the use of the [Anglican] prayerbook. . . . [It was] a church of Christians where the congregation governed."[37]

Here was a model of church government that Childs transformed into a plan, the council-manager plan, where "the gathered church" became the "compact community"[38]; where the covenanted relationship became the reformed charter; where the chosen pastor became the city manager; where the elect became the elected at-large, nonpartisan council; where opposition to the Anglican prayerbook became opposition to the corrupt, unreformed machine-style politics; and where the self-governing Christian community would become the democratic self-government in local communities that Childs fervently hoped would prevail if the plan was adopted. Indeed, as noted earlier, Childs even likened himself to a minister who performed the marriage to make this event happen. He did not make the claim in the narrow sense, that he was merely marrying the Staunton experiment with the Galveston commission government; rather, he saw his role in a much larger context—that his lifelong mission was to convert whole cities by his catch phrases to the faithful, just as the Puritan divines had strived so ardently to do more than two centuries before.

8

Louis Brownlow
Apostle of Administrative Management

Louis Brownlow, 1879–1963
(courtesy of the International City/County
Management Association, Washington, D.C.)

I look upon my profession as city manager in exactly the same way that a
minister of the gospel looks upon his mission, and I believe that as a city
manager endeavoring to make the city for whose administrative affairs I
am responsible better in every way for every boy and girl in it, I am doing
the work of the Master.
—Louis Brownlow
  A Passion For Anonymity

LOUIS BROWNLOW ROAMED OVER MANY FIELDS during his lifetime: local politician, printer, journalist, editor, author, advisor to presidents,
world traveler, commissioner for the District of Columbia, city manager, planner, and association director. Above all, however, he was an

administrative innovator who created some of the most important public institutions for governing the United States during the twentieth century. As president of the International City Managers' Association (ICMA), he turned this weak, fledgling association of city managers into a strong, effective public management association that became a model for other public professional groups and that acquired broad influence within the U.S. governing processes. Later, he set up and directed the Public Administration Clearing House (PACH), which advanced the cause of professionalism and public administration nationally in numerous yet subtle ways. Then, as chair of the President's Committee on Administrative Management (nicknamed the Brownlow Committee) for President Franklin Roosevelt from 1936 to 1937, Brownlow and his committee, most scholars agree, refashioned the American presidency more profoundly than at any time since George Washington's first administration. The Brownlow Committee was a prime mover in creating the administrative apparatus of the Executive Office of the President (EOP), which fundamentally transformed the presidency from a weak office with a few staff assistants to what we know it as today, that is, one of the most powerful chief executive positions in the world. Some even argue that without the committee's reforms, the United States could not have successfully fought World War II or the cold war or achieved the level of postwar prosperity and free world leadership witnessed today. Throughout the postwar era, most national task forces set up to study federal reorganizations, as well as many state and local ones, largely followed Brownlowian prescriptions, at least until the 1980s.

Yet, ironically, perhaps no one except for a few dedicated students of public administration or the American presidency or twentieth-century historians recognize his name. History books routinely omit references to Brownlow's achievements. He chose to work in the background throughout much of his life, giving others the credit for his achievements. As the second volume of his autobiography is titled, his work is characterized by *A Passion for Anonymity*.

During his lifetime, he was a remarkable administrative innovator, institution builder, and even one of the primary architects of the modern managerial presidency who brought about major reforms as a quiet insider. By all accounts, "Brownie," as he was known to friends, was a superb storyteller, raconteur, writer, tireless worker, and organizer, and he was artful at convincing people to accomplish new tasks that he wanted done—often without their realizing it. Many would find

Brownlow's smiling face hidden behind successful reforms that were put into place, but Brownie's imprint was recognized only well after the changes were made. He was a master at what Fred Greenstein would later label "hidden-hand leadership."[1] Brownlow, if he were alive, would no doubt scoff at such a pretentious label applied to himself, however. After all, he had "a passion for anonymity" (a term Brownlow actually borrowed from Tom Jones, who at the time was the British cabinet secretary).

Certainly, he was a product of humble, anonymous origins. Born on August 29, 1879, Louis Brownlow even liked to joke that he was literally born into government at a post office. His father, Robert, was a postmaster third-class in Buffalo, Missouri, and the family lived above the modest setting of the small-town, midwestern U.S. post office. Buffalo, the county seat of Dallas County in the Ozark Mountains, was in the geographic center of Missouri, with eight hundred inhabitants. If Brownlow grew up in a family of modest means, his formal education was even more simple. Brownie never graduated from elementary school, not even first grade. Childhood rheumatic fever, contracted in the spring of 1885, kept him home. He was forbidden to participate in strenuous activities, play, or do chores. It was believed—wrongly—at the time that his health would be severely impaired if he tried to perform activities and that he could not lead a normal life.

Although he lacked formal education, Louis more than made up for it in other ways. An intelligent, gregarious youth with a photographic memory, he read widely and was free to wander around town, talking to anyone, helping out people here and there. Louis liked to learn from everyone, young, old, and middle-aged, and all the townsfolk became his contemporaries—and mentors. "I was a social being," he wrote of himself, "gregarious by nature and never content to be alone with myself."[2] Indeed, the first volume of his autobiography, *A Passion for Politics,* recounts colorful stories, one after another, from his youth up to age thirty-five when he entered public administration. The tales usually start with a sentence such as "I remember that I was sitting in Mr. William L. Morrow's lap, listening to a tale of pioneer days."[3]

Brownlow's childhood, at least the way he describes it in his autobiography, shares considerable parallels with Mark Twain's famous fictional character, Huck Finn, also a product of late-nineteenth-century, small-town Missouri life. Both boys missed formal schooling and were free to wander around their hometowns and learn from the stories and events they encountered that seemed larger than life. Both could spin fantastic yarns about the colorful characters they met and often got these people to do things for them that they normally did not want to do on their own accord. Although he did not run away from home or have a drunken, abusive father like Huck did, Brownie immersed himself in small-town Missouri life, learned from it, loved it, and for the rest of his life carried within him its values, characteristics, and habits of associating with others.

For instance, he always relished learning about the various details of individual personalities, both nefarious and angelic. He knew from an early age where the best sources of gossip were in town and liked to frequent those spots. As Brownlow wrote, "The barber shop was the center of where juicy bits of scandalous gossip about the more respectable people of the community were carefully nurtured and disseminated."[4] He would develop a keen sense for news and a realistic understanding of human nature that would serve him well in his later careers of journalism and public administration. Louis also cultivated others, his contemporaries and superiors, with a mature openness and ease beyond his years that helped him move among many types of individuals and learn from all of them. "There were social values to learn," as he wrote, "manners, morals, customs which were an important part of my young life." He quickly picked up town gossip about who was acquiring several interesting new books or "the sordid details of the pregnancy of an unmarried girl . . . [where] the putative fatherhood of the occasional illegitimate child was determined."[5]

Small-town Missouri life was an ongoing morality play where the eager, astute Brownie came to be instructed on the basic lessons of life. Yet, here too was an absence of violence, war, or deep personal tragedy to scar permanently a childhood sense of security and optimism about the future and its possibilities.

Brownlow, from an early age, also exhibited an enormous appetite for the printed word. He enjoyed any kind of reading, almost without direction. "To read was my passion—overwhelming, compelling, ruling," he said.[6] The town did not have a library, so he supplemented the standard childhood fare by borrowing from various family attics, parlors, and even the saddlebags of circuit-riding preachers. Everything in Buffalo was fair game to read. There seemed no limits on what interested him; he would read current magazines, dime store novels, basic science texts, and great classics. For instance, one summer in his early teenage years Brownie listed his reading as follows: *Robinson Crusoe, Pilgrim's Progress*, a modern chemistry textbook, a romance novel, a summary of the U.S. census of 1880, and portions of the ninth edition of the *Encyclopedia Britannica*. Like town gossip, his voracious, eclectic reading habits would delight in individual tidbits of human interest stories as well as moral lessons derived from these stories that were generalizable and applicable to his own life.[7]

Increasingly small-town politics became a focal point of Brownlow's youthful enthusiasm. Without the modern-day distractions of television, radio, movies, phones, or video games, Brownie's childhood was rooted in the give-and-take of local politics. "I know there never was a meal at which politics and public affairs was not discussed," he later wrote.[8] Political talk flowed freely around the family dining table each night. The discussions of this close-knit family of three children and two parents were intense; the group knew firsthand how politics had in fact altered their lives. Brownlow's mother, Ruth Adelia, and his father, Robert, had both been born in Tennessee. Although they had come from well-educated, prosperous homes of that day, Brownlow's family were southern supporters whose lives had been dramatically uprooted by the Civil War and Reconstruction. Forced like many southerners to flee in the postwar era to the midwest, both spun endless tales of the hardships they endured as a result. Ruth was a Democrat who had opposed slavery and had endured ostracism for her point of view. Robert had fought in the Civil War and was almost fatally wounded in a shooting while jailed in a northern prison. He married and resettled in Buffalo to find a new life after being left impoverished by Reconstruction. Buffalo was a place they believed they could begin life over again.

Robert rejected both his geographic and his political roots; he no longer was a Democrat but also could never be a Republican. Rather, he always searched for something better, showing a special affinity for every passing third party that came along, from Greenback to Anti-Monopoly to Union Labor to the Farmers' Alliance to Populist. As Louis watched his father's twists and turns along the political spectrum and his ebb and flow of passions over newly created third parties, he always saw moral lessons to draw. Nevertheless, his mother's more conservative and certainly consistent Democratic affiliation won his affection as well as his lifetime commitment. By the age of five, Louis knew he was a Democrat and remained so for the rest of his life.

For the thirteen-year-old Brownie, 1892 was a watershed year. The presidential election between Grover Cleveland and Benjamin Harrison became his all-consuming interest: "I spent my days around the courthouse and the stores on the square listening to and breaking in on the political debates."[9] He was apprenticed by a family friend, Frank Furth, the Democratic county chair, to clip articles from the local newspapers, report on political affairs, and run errands for the Democratic candidates. The Democrats lost Dallas County, but Cleveland won the presidency, which meant that Louis, a loyal, hard-working Democrat, was awarded a minor political patronage job. The county Democrats could appoint a new postmaster, and Louis, needing a job, was appointed his assistant. For many in Buffalo, this appointment of a young teenager to a job that paid adult wages was outrageous (a $25 monthly salary was considered hefty wages in small-town America during the depression era of the early 1890s).

The ethical lesson from this political controversy was not lost on the youthful Brownlow, namely, that public office is central to community affairs and that the choice of people for these offices is very much tied to the values and outlooks of the community they serve. Public administration stands at the heart of community life and is inextricably intertwined with fundamental community norms and standards of conduct.

In small midwestern towns of the late nineteenth century, these fundamental norms and standards of conduct that Brownlow absorbed so thoroughly into his own moral outlook sprang from the religious life of the community, which was then overwhelmingly Protestant. Typical of this era, Buffalo was dominated by five Protestant churches—Presbyterian, Baptist, Christian, and two Methodist. Just outside the town limits resided other denominations—"hard-shell" Baptists, Missionary Baptists, and one northern and one southern splinter denomination. No Jews or Catholics lived there—all had been driven away by the hateful vengeance of the Know-Nothings a decade or two before. Protestantism was the all-encompassing faith—and force—influencing communal life; there was no rival. As Brownlow wrote, "I would find myself in Sunday School, in church, and breathing an air that admitted no other thought than that [the Protestant] church was the center of the true and everlasting life."[10]

Disputes over Protestant doctrines raged in this period. Although they now seem so foreign to late-twentieth-century minds, these issues were taken with utter seriousness by the youthful Brownlow and most residents of Buffalo: Should baptism be done by sprinkling or full immersion? Can infants or only adults be baptized? Should pipe organ music be played in church? Is predestination or Arminianism the correct doctrine? In many ways this era in the United States was closer to the sixteenth-century European Reformation considering the intensity with which those arcane religious disputes were debated.

Religious arguments, as with politics, spilled over into family dinner table discussions and made Brownie not only highly conscious of denominational differences but also tolerant toward all. "The fact that Mother was a Methodist and Father, a member of the Disciples of Christ," Louis wrote, "called in everyday speech the Christian Church, kept me from being a sectarian, as otherwise I might well have become." He added, "It operated to keep open the door to theological and religious matters when my curiosity was engaged, in a manner that might have seemed impious, or even sinful, had I been drilled in any one faith, as the true faith."[11]

The endless wrestling over the merits of various denominational faiths led Brownlow to develop his own discriminating moral conscience and keen ethical sensitivity. "I was not sure which of the churches were right, if any," he wrote, "and I early found the supreme solace of conscious superiority when I distanced myself to join any of the doctrinal disputes."[12] His independent mind would nurture a sort of superior self-criticism about these matters that would allow him to see all sides of the debates and reach his own conclusions. Nonetheless, he would always retain a rock-hard protestantism, with a small "p," as his own essential outlook and conviction, especially in his view that morality is important, that responsible behavior is expected, that progress can be anticipated, that life on earth is temporary and full of challenges, that one is ultimately judged on good work and hard work, and that neither money nor fame but only service for the betterment of humanity is what counts in the end.

Just as he developed his eclectic reading habits, Brownlow would sharpen his own moral conscience by sampling widely from the various local Protestant denominations. He usually attended the Presbyterian Sunday school in the afternoon after having been to a Christian Sunday school in the morning and to a Methodist Church for noon services. Later in the evening he would attend a Christian Endeavor Society Meeting for its young people's activities. Not only did he try to learn from all of the services, but also he came to understand how to negotiate and navigate successfully among the competing faiths, creeds, and doctrines. This attribute would later serve him well as he sought to negotiate and navigate among the diverse faiths, creeds, and doctrines within public administration. He would understand them all so well that he would become an acknowledged expert, yet recognized as fair-minded and neutral, even in the eyes of the "true believers."

The teenage Brownlow became so respected for his understanding of the Bible and denominational topics that he taught adult Sunday school in several churches, just as later as an adult during his public administration career, he would be held in such high regard that people looked to him for his expertise and for an honest hearing. As he said of religion, "All these [religious] matters were of great concern to me. They affected me profoundly and radically because since I was not a partisan of any of these schools [of religion] and therefore tended to listen with tolerance to all of them . . . I was molded in my thinking toward the conclusion that none of these narrow questions of doctrine and of practice made any real difference. All this helped to turn me into a liberal."[13] He added, however, "It may be in this matter all of us find ourselves more determined than determining."[14] He would never fully escape from the reformed faith of his youth. Nonetheless, he found a way to transcend its narrow creeds and doctrines, becoming ultimately an apostle of a new faith, administrative management, that would serve humanity broadly by reforming American government. Brownlow remained therefore a believer throughout his life, but his set of beliefs was an unusual amalgam of protestantism—always with a small "p"—that he uniquely transformed into "the faith I sought, this the faith I found, and this the faith I hold."[15]

Brownlow's ingrained protestantism would also inspire an unquenchable drive and ambition to succeed. Just as the beliefs of the sixteenth-century Protestant saints became the driving source for organizing modern capitalism, so too Brownlow's religious values instilled in him an immense self-confidence, appetite for hard work, and desire for success. Part of this ambition was exemplified at an early age by his zeal for work. He learned to set type while working for the town's newspaper, the *Buffalo Reflex*. In 1892 the People's party, to which his father belonged at the time, believed it was necessary to start an opposition paper to the Republican's *Reflex* and founded the *People's Paper*, on which Louis was hired to work. Then, when the Missouri Populists could no longer support the costs of publication because of the panic of 1893, the editor and publisher gave the paper up, and Robert Brownlow, now without a job (the post office job had since gone to the Republicans), made a deal with the party to buy the press and type. He changed the name to the *Dallas Record* to attract a broader readership, and the newspaper soon appeared with the names Robert Brownlow and Louis Brownlow listed as coeditors and copublishers. Together they ran the paper for the next four years. During this time, Louis became a passable printer, experienced reporter, and astute writer and editor.

Now an apprenticed newsman, Brownie left Buffalo at age eighteen to find newspaper work—and his future—in the "big city" of Nashville. He chose Nashville as his destination because of family connections. Some of his mother's family had remained there, and he could find temporary residence with them. Also, as an ambitious youth, he believed that he had exhausted his opportunities for advancement in Buffalo and saw Nashville as an expansive new horizon. Life was not easy, however. After three attempts at trying to find work, interspersed with retreats home to Buffalo, Louis landed a job on a leading Nashville paper, the *Nashville Banner*. He started as an unpaid cub reporter, but within a matter of months he was posted on a regular, prestigious, and paid beat at the state court house.

Next came a series of moves—all upward. After two years on the *Banner*, Brownie went to Louisville for a year as a senior reporter for the *Courier-Journal*. From there, at age twenty, he went back to Nashville as city editor of the *News*, and then he returned to Louisville to become city editor for the *Times*. After just six months on the *Times*, the owners of the *Nashville Evening Post* merged with their rival, the *Banner*, and lured Brownlow back with yet another prestigious assignment, that of being their Washington, D.C., correspondent. He went off to report from the nation's capital, but shortly thereafter he was lured back as an editor-in-chief of a small town paper in Paducah, Kentucky. Thus in February 1905, at the age of twenty-five, Brownlow took charge of an entire newspaper. Without a staff, however, he had to carry the entire administrative, editorial, and writing burden. He tired quickly of this job and was next enticed back to Washington by the Frederic Haskins Syndicate to write about Washington and international events. Here was his dream assignment. As he said, "Even the most fantastic of my childhood dreams in Buffalo, Missouri, could not have anticipated the world which my work with Haskins . . . opened me up to."[16]

Originally, Brownlow submitted articles on a piecework basis to Haskins, fitting them in around other part-time correspondent jobs, but within two years he became a full-time Haskins correspondent, traveling tirelessly around the country—and the world—in pursuit of any sort of human interest story that attracted his fancy. He relished this peripatetic life and learned the utility of writing under a pseudonym (all his stories were written under the Haskins byline). Anonymity gave him more freedom to write what he pleased and in the manner he wanted. As historian Barry Karl has observed, "His articles for the Haskins Letter, syndicated throughout the country, were often models of clarity, artfully woven into miniature designs; but the subject matters naturally depended upon where he happened to be at the time and could range from the daily habits of a Manchu princess to the early experiments with refrigeration in Florida."[17] Indeed, Brownlow liked to compare himself to a badly trained bird dog who ran after everything but usually ended up with the quarry.

His reporting increasingly drew him toward administrative topics. As he said, "Interested as I had been in politics, national and international . . . , my early city hall, court house, and state capitol experience had inclined me toward an insatiable curiosity about administration."[18] Brownlow never really outgrew his small-town Buffalo curiosity about everything, especially his attraction to colorful human interest stories about the inner workings of community life, and for him, increasingly, administration represented the insider's inside story.

His gravitation toward administrative topics was evident in 1911 when he published his first book, titled *The American Government*, under the pseudonym Frederic Haskin.[19] This basic introduction to U.S. government became an extraordinary bestseller in part because it explained the operations of the federal government clearly and concisely. It was also popular because, unlike other basic textbooks, this text emphasized more than just the three branches of government. Instead, of the thirty chapters in Brownlow's book, only one discussed the presidency, three examined Congress, and two addressed the Court; the rest dealt with the structure and operations of various federal departments. Without any particular method or design, Brownlow concentrated on describing the unique features, work, and people in the major agencies and offices.

Hidden beneath its chatty, journalistic prose was Brownlow's own view that government was *not* embodied in presidential platforms, congressional debates, or court decisions. Rather, public administration, especially the various people working in numerous offices for the common good of all citizens, was what mattered most in making government work. As he had first observed in Buffalo, Brownlow could see through the formalities of public life and describe the realities of what made a community or, in this case, a nation function, namely, its public administration and those working for the common good of all citizens.

By 1910, Louis Brownlow had emerged as one of Washington's star journalists, and as a result, like modern-day television star news anchors, he became well connected with the Washington establishment, regularly dining with the elite of the Hill and the White House at such posh spots as the Cosmos Club. He developed an extensive, loyal network of friendships; one friend in particular just happened to be the president of the United States, Woodrow Wilson. In 1910 Brownlow had been impressed by Wilson's remarkable campaign that he waged for governor of New Jersey and thought that Wilson would make a strong president. With a friend, Tom Pence, Brownlow set up the preconvention "Wilson for President" publicity campaign. Brownlow thus became part of a small, powerful inner circle of backers who were intimates of Wilson.

After Wilson's election in 1912, Brownlow "managed to keep in touch with Mr. Wilson himself."[20] One day, as Brownlow explained, he read in the newspaper that Wilson intended to appoint him to be one of the three District of Columbia commissioners, who at the time collectively comprised the governing body of Washington, D.C. He was surprised, he claimed, because he did not know he was even being considered. On January 20, 1915, Louis took the oath of office as a D.C. commissioner. As Brownlow wrote of that event, "I was thrilled with the prospect of attempting to put into effect some of the notions about municipal administration that I had elaborated during my many years of increasing interest in local government."[21]

So at age thirty-five, Brownie left journalism to enter public administration and to quit being "a taker of notes" and to become "a responsible actor." The first day on the job "reminded me that no longer was I to look in city hall, ready to write with cheerful nonchalance all news I could find. . . . It brought in upon me with great force my new awareness of the great gulf between the irresponsibility of even the most conscientious and careful reporter and the grave responsibility of a government official charged with a high obligation."[22]

His phrase "the grave responsibility of a government official" sounded almost like a religious conversion, that is, the words of a sinner who suddenly found the faith. Previously Louis perceived himself as irresponsible. Now he described himself as possessing a "grave responsibility" and being "charged with a high obligation." Previously his life was seen as looking in from the outside; perhaps one could even say it was without meaning, a bit provisional and aimless, or, in his words, one "with cheerful nonchalance." Now as a government insider, he acquired a clear purpose, with real work to accomplish for the public welfare. Government itself took on for him a special aura, a higher calling of the public trust, where a special few (administrators) are chosen to serve (the elect?) to benefit many (the public). The Protestant values instilled during his youth had found a home where they could be applied, though transformed and played out on a far broader stage as a public administrator, perhaps even within what might be referred to as his new "church" called public administration.

During his five years as a commissioner, Brownlow learned about his new calling as a public administrator. His work also reflected his activist, creative style of reform leadership. During his tenure, Brownlow initiated administrative innovations on many fronts. Some of his reforms were procedural, such as setting up biweekly (as opposed to monthly) meetings of the commission to reach more quickly the decisions that required their concurrence. That simple change reduced the flow of paper folders that passed among them and increased the speed of their decision making. Other changes were substantive, such as creating a women's bureau within the police department to deal with the rising female crime rates in the district. Some reforms were long-range and fundamental, such as designing, with the help of citizens' groups, a comprehensive zoning ordinance.

The intensity of World War One's industrial and military mobilization during Brownlow's tenure brought enormous social and political problems to the city government's doorstep: How should they handle the rapid influx of workers? How should they provide for public services in a period of tight economic rationing? How should they deal with draft resisters, militant women suffragettes, police strikes, and rapid postwar demobilization? Brownlow relished tackling even the most mundane or difficult municipal issues. His exercise of administrative authority benefitted from congenial working relationships with the other D.C. commissioners, the city department heads, and the president of the United States.

In the last case, the special working relationship with Wilson decidedly shaped Brownlow's view of what ideal political-administrative relationships ought to be: "The President . . . when necessary, either bore or ducked responsibility for specific actions, but in any case supported Brownlow against public criticism as occasionally arose."[23] Unqualified presidential backing gave Brownlow uniquely wide latitude to act responsibly as an appointed public official and fixed in his mind the virtues of professional administrative management clearly differentiated from, yet supported by, the democratically elected leadership. Here was a model, *the* model, for sound municipal government. As he wrote of his years of service as D.C. commissioner, "I came into that position still convinced that what we most needed to meet my views of greater service to the people was the election of the right people to proper legislative bodies and the enactment of laws which would require a more liberal approach. Six years later I was inclined to believe that an enlightened, informed public administration was the basic requirement of better living for all citizens, great and small."[24]

Brownlow's definition of public administration in essence became what he had uncovered from his work in municipal administration—those structures and working relationships that he had learned from and was successful at in Washington, D.C. Its unique patterns of governance had, in Brownlow's mind, furthered the values of progress, democracy, prosperity, and general welfare for all citizens, great and small. In his view, no dark sides were evident: no worries about the possibility of excessive expansion of municipal bureaucracy; no concerns about centralization or hierarchy that resulted from such growth; no issues voiced concerning the increased control by experts; and no possibility of reduced citizen participation and involvement in government when the experts took charge. Brownlow embraced what he had experienced without reservation. He soon became its arch-advocate.

If Washington, D.C., was a unique training ground for learning the lessons of public administration, so too was Petersburg, Virginia, Brownlow's second administrative assignment, where he became the city's first city manager in 1920. He embarked on this job not only with the same enthusiasm but also with considerable citywide support, high esteem, and a clear mandate to improve city services across the board. With great dispatch and typical zeal, Brownlow went about accomplishing this broad mandate, fulfilling most popular expectations by instituting a new budgetary and accounting system; providing better garbage collection and street repairs; instituting the first use of patrol cars; and even hiring the city's first black police officer to improve policing in the black section of the community. Many of these civil reforms were highly visible to the public, and he was dubbed "a miracle-worker."[25] When he left for another position, Brownlow was perhaps Petersburg's most revered citizen and best compensated (in addition to earning a comparatively high salary, he had been given a home by the city to live in free of charge). So confident had he become of his new occupation that by now he even compared his line of work with that of a Christian minister: "I am doing the work of the Master," he wrote of his career during this time.[26]

Yet, the opposite experience awaited him in 1923 at his next city manager's position in Knoxville, Tennessee. Since Civil War days, Knoxville had been rife with partisan politics and corruption. The council-manager plan had been adopted only a few months before Brownlow arrived. It had been approved largely as a reaction to the corrupt practices of commission government—and then only by a narrow margin of the electorate. Nonetheless, Brownlow confidently set about initiating a wide range of municipal reforms, big and small, in the same manner as he had in the previous two communities, that is, a modern budget and accounting system, new police and fire services, garbage collection, street repair processes, and the like. Many of these municipal reforms were even more successful here than in Washington and Petersburg in cutting costs, increasing operating efficiency, and finding badly needed solutions to pressing municipal issues. Despite all of the new energetic reforms, the city politics were radically different here, however, and the opposition mounted quickly to defeat Brownlow's initiatives. This place was no Washington, D.C., or Petersburg, Virginia, where clear, solid mandates for change existed. Powerful private interests in Knoxville undercut his formula of establishing effective municipal reforms. Banks and businesses that had developed profitable, long-time relationships with the city were threatened by Brownlow's cost-cutting efficiency measures. He was dubbed "King Louie" by the press and his opponents. By 1925 many were calling for his resignation.

A photo of him at a long conference table in Knoxville shows Brownlow very much in charge, surrounded by the bright, eager young staffers he had hired.[27] They were mostly outsiders, with such neatly labeled titles as director of law, director of welfare, director of public works, and so on. Brownlow had brought to Knoxville the best, most efficient city management practices of that era. Nonetheless, in June 1926, under incessant public attack, Brownlow resigned. It was a bitter experience, but he had been taught an invaluable lesson: community politics, not just the contents of "correct" administrative reforms, can make all the difference between success and failure.

From this apparent failure, however, Brownlow emerged as the preeminent national leader among public administration practitioners.

He earned respect for upholding the ideals of professional city management while being criticized and achieved much recognition for what he had accomplished. Brownlow's stature within the field propelled him into increasingly responsible positions during the next decade. In this period he left three important permanent legacies for the creation of the modern American administrative state, critical contributions that serve to label him as one of its key founding figures.

First, Brownlow's leadership reshaped the fundamental components of public professional associations into what we now know as their vital policymaking roles within the overall schema of American government. Associations of public professionals started in 1872 when Stephen Smith, a medical doctor who served on the staff at Bellevue Hospital in New York City, founded the American Public Health Association to share professional knowledge and advance the practices of public health medicine. Other associations of public professionals around the turn of the century were organized: the Association of the Chiefs of Police (1893), the International Association of Fire Chiefs (1893), the American Society of Municipal Engineers (1894), the Municipal Finance Officers Association (1906), the National Recreation Association (1906), the National Association of Public School Business Officials (1910), and the National Organization for Public Health Nursing (1912).

In an increasingly segmented and specialized society, these groups connected dispersed, yet growing, clusters of professionals across the nation to share ideas and pursue their collective education and research agendas. Until the 1920s, these groups were largely weak associations that did little to advance their professional callings other than issue newsletters or organize annual conferences. They were loosely linked, exercising little or no impact on national public policy formulation.[28]

In the 1920s Brownlow, through his role as president of the International City Managers' Association (which had been founded in 1914) brought new, wider, and more purposeful roles to public professional associations. Like other such groups, the ICMA for more than a decade had remained a weak, informal network of city managers. Brownlow envisioned—and recast—the ICMA into a far stronger professional group concerned with better management, not lobbying for the city management form of government. To that end, Brownlow set up the first full-time executive staff for the association; established a high-quality research journal for public management, a well-crafted code of ethics with enforcement provisions, and links to major scholars and university programs; and enhanced professional conferences by drawing on academics, experts, and others outside the ranks of city managers. He left to others, such as the National Municipal League, the municipal reform agenda of promoting the passage of the council-manager plan. The ICMA would be an influential national professional body, pressing for the advancement of general administration management ideas, not civic reform techniques.

As Brownlow wrote, "My plan was to bring about a greater exchange of information among all such organizations everywhere. . . . It was to keep in touch, not only with organizations of governmental practitioners but also with universities, research institutions and other groups to which [information] could be distributed for the general benefit."[29] By instituting this enhanced exchange of information, Brownlow sought to create generalizable ideas for the field that would establish a common respected language for public administration and that, in turn, would allow the field to become a force at the grassroots level in the area of administrative innovations as well as within the arena of national policy making. Furthermore, the ICMA's professionalism eventually would become a model for other groups to emulate for advancing the cause of the public sector.

Brownlow's second important contribution was to escalate this general professional model of administrative management, that is, the top executive management model that he had essentially learned and crafted from his city management experiences, created at the ICMA, and then later re-created in another national institution, the Public Administration Clearing House in Chicago in 1930. After leaving Knoxville and recovering from poor health, he worked briefly again in journalism, writing a national column on municipal reform and planning issues, and later assisted in founding "the new town" experiment at Radford, New Jersey (one of the earliest planned communities). Brownie also continued to expand his network of friendships, establishing contacts with Charles Merriam, chair of the political science department at the University of Chicago, and Beardsley Ruml, administrator of the Laura Spelman Fund, a forerunner of the Rockefeller Foundation. Brownlow succeeded in persuading the University of Chicago and the Spelman Fund to cosponsor the PACH.

From his initiation of the PACH in 1930 until his retirement as its director in 1945, Brownlow worked diligently to bring together, on a voluntary basis, the major public associations of that era. He also worked to strengthen their neutral professional competence and promote links between them and linkages with universities, especially the University of Chicago, to foster a common research agenda as well as a common language and national presence for public administration. Brownlow, using military metaphors, saw the mission of the PACH as follows: "The Technicians are rapidly organizing for the Big Push. Soon they will be ready, and when that zero hour does come, the war will be won and the day of the amateur at city hall will be over. . . . It will come when Technicians become professionals. And that is what they are rapidly becoming."[30]

PACH would lead the "big push," and Brownlow would be "the minister" to end "the day of the amateur at city hall" and to transform technicians into professionals via the new faith he preached, "administrative management."[31] He would build PACH from behind the scenes, however. For instance, Brownlow insisted on keeping the identities of the dozen professional groups he attracted to PACH separate and never referred to PACH except by its street address near the University of Chicago campus, 1313. In this way, none of the organizations would feel their existence threatened. PACH, through Spelman monies, would provide offices and staff assistance for the associations, create an excellent library, map gaps in the knowledge base among these professional groups, create a vigorous common research agenda, create new associations in those fields identified as needing them, and link together local practitioners with university scholars and government officials at all levels. Brownlow proved masterful at making such complicated, nationwide interconnections possible. He saw that "with this support of their own self esteem, their prestige will begin to increase. And with prestige will come recognition and with recognition, power."[32]

This power would be realized ultimately by Brownlow's third administrative achievement: chairing the President's Committee on Administrative Management. Here he brought administrative management ideas to the pinnacle of national prominence by fundamentally refashioning the highest office in the land, the U.S. presidency. The opportunity came with the election of Franklin Roosevelt in 1932. FDR's New Deal political agenda brought a plethora of new federal programs to cope with the immense economic crisis of the Great Depression. The president had no staff or support at that time, however, to study how to create organizations that the new administration needed. PACH, thanks to Brownlow's connections, found the funding and individuals to do many of the necessary organizational studies. Brownlow's ample network of friendships inside this new Democratic administration allowed him to carry out projects far beyond simply contracting administrative studies. For example, he was called on by the secretary of commerce, Daniel Roper, and the secretary of interior, Harold Ickes, to play a lead role in formulating and setting up the National Recovery Administration and the Public Works Administration, two key New Deal relief agencies. Brownlow, through personal friendships with engineers, planners, and public works managers throughout federal, state, and local levels, helped significantly to plan, staff, and implement the programs for these agencies.

Brownlow became increasingly enmeshed with advising on the New Deal's various economic recovery programs. The programs' dramatic expansion in size and scope during Roosevelt's first term made their administrative direction more and more unwieldy. Even the president, who was never especially interested in organizational issues, came to appreciate these managerial problems. Roosevelt, the consummate politician, sensed that his political opponents might seize on the apparent administrative weakness of his presidency to embarrass him during the upcoming 1936 election. Possibly FDR had this concern uppermost in his mind when he appointed the trusted Democrat Brownlow as chair of the President's Committee on Administrative Management.

By 1936, government reorganization was not a new idea; it had been a theme of federal government studies since the late nineteenth century.[33] Generally, though, previous commission studies on this topic focused on cost savings through reorganization or fairly low-level workplace improvements in job efficiency through personnel reductions or simply applications of new technologies. To Brownlow and his two committee associates, Charles Merriam and Luther Gulick, the emphasis of any reorganization study should be placed on improving overall administrative effectiveness, not administrative cost cutting. They believed, in short, that the focus ought to be on administrative management, that is, management at the top, to improve the overall effectiveness of the federal government. The challenge, as Brownlow expressed it, was to "provide the president with simple but effective machinery which will enable him to exercise the burden of responsibility imposed on him by the Constitution."[34]

Surprisingly, the office of the presidency of 1936 had changed little since 1789 when George Washington was first inaugurated. Not only was the office without much staff support, but also presidents up to that time viewed themselves—and were viewed by the general public—*not* as managers but rather as politicians, chief diplomats, commanders in chief, or party leaders. When Roosevelt established the committee on March 20, 1936, perhaps even he, the canniest of politicians, did not realize what far-reaching implications Brownlow's prescriptions would have for fundamentally altering the presidency by adding another role, the administrative management function. Brownlow's study would eventually create one of the most powerful chief executives in the world.

After the appointment of the committee, Dr. Joseph Harris, from the political science department at the University of California at Berkeley, was selected to serve as the committee's chief of staff to direct twenty-six people, mostly young academics under forty years of age, all of whom held Ph.D.s in the social sciences. The young academicians were urged by Brownlow to conduct studies on various aspects of presidential management, not carry out extensive, in-depth examinations of particular federal agencies. They were to take the best of existing knowledge about high-level management practices to prepare general think papers. Staffers were cautioned that their studies were for the president's eyes only and not for general circulation (only one person violated this confidentiality). In actuality, the staff had little contact with Brownlow, Merriam, or Gulick, the three members of the committee, until late in the summer when they presented their findings (which some participants claimed were conducted much like intensive Ph.D. dissertation defenses). After several months of working and reworking the drafts, the committee presented the final report to the president right before the Seventy-fifth Congress convened and he started his second term. Roosevelt read it, simply said, "That's great," and then signed it.[35]

The president was so elated by the committee report, he said later, because it allayed his fear that the opposition might attack his greatest political vulnerability, namely, the administration of New Deal programs. Roosevelt had anticipated an attack by the Republicans, but it had never come. Now with a sweeping electoral victory, winning forty-six of the forty-eight states, as well as two-thirds of both houses of Congress, Roosevelt had both a political mandate and a clear agenda to remedy the New Deal's weakness. He also knew well ahead of time what the report contained, so there were no surprises. On November 5, Brownlow wrote a memo to the president that contained the recommendations covered by the report and provided an outline for the committee's discussions with Roosevelt. Following informal discussion, the committee went to work on the final revisions to assure that the president's concerns were addressed in the final report. That report was signed by the president on January 3 and went to Congress on January 12, 1937.

In brief, the report recommended the following: (1) expand the White House staff to six administrative assistants responsible to the president; (2) strengthen and develop an Executive Office of the President with agencies such as budget and personnel offices to serve as staff arms to the president; (3) expand the merit system to cover all nonpolicy personnel throughout the federal government; (4) consolidate all independent and regulatory agencies into a dozen cabinet departments; and (5) revise the fiscal system to improve accountability by Congress and the president.[36] Here was the grand synthesis of administrative management principles Brownlow had learned—and passionately believed in—from his previous two decades of government experience now institutionalized at the top of the federal structure, the U.S. presidency.

At Roosevelt's request, Brownlow drafted legislation containing the report's recommendations for presentation to Congress. The legislation called for the president to be given nearly complete authority over the organization of the executive branch by issuing executive orders that would become effective unless they were disapproved by both houses of Congress within sixty days. The timing of the introduction of this bill, however, could not have been worse. The legislation became associated with the president's proposal to increase the number of Supreme Court justices from nine to fifteen. Critics of the "court packing" scheme soon linked the reorganization proposal to an overall presidential strategy to increase his authority. Brownlow's measure came to be dubbed a "dictator bill" by opponents.[37] Although the reorganization plan passed the House in 1937, the furor held up its passage in the Senate. By 1938, the controversy had turned into a political firestorm too great to gain approval by the Senate. The next year, after the election of a new Congress, a much amended Reorganization Act became law.

By preparing the report, Brownlow had finished his work and thus had little to do with the ensuing controversy and the eventual passage of the substantially revised Reorganization Act. In May 1939 he suffered a heart attack, which kept him on the sidelines of any active leadership. By 1940 major elements of the Brownlow report found their way into institutional practice in piecemeal fashion: presidential authority for initiating executive reorganizations, though exempting a number of agencies from his authority; extension of the merit system, though without the vast changes proposed by the report; and creation of the

Executive Office of the President, which included increased presidential staff and the addition to the White House of the Bureau of the Budget (which had been created in 1922 as part of the Treasury Department). It did not include, however, shifting the extensive personnel authority to EOP or reorganizing all the federal agencies into only twelve cabinet departments as suggested by the report.[38]

In the end, Brownlow may have gotten only a portion of the reforms for which his committee had called. In retrospect, however, Brownlow and his committee did far more in the long run than they or anyone possibly could have hoped for at the time. They permanently transformed the general American conception of the presidency. A central proposition contained within the report, as James Fesler, a veteran committee staffer underscored, "was that the President, constitutionally the head of the executive branch, is the Chief Administrator."[39] In other words, as the last sentence of the report reads, "Thus the President will have effective managerial authority over the Executive Branch commensurate with his responsibilities under the Constitution."[40]

In the committee's view, centrifugal forces were tearing apart the executive branch to the point of its emasculation. The proliferation of new depression-fighting programs meant the presidency had to be modernized. Presidential oversight and authority were in urgent need of being reasserted. Thus, the Brownlow Committee envisioned a new role for the twentieth-century American president, that is, as a chief administrator, a position few had considered before. After World War II some presidents would turn out to be more effective than others at assuming this task, but, to be sure, administrative management remains a significant part of the job description. That managerial task has even expanded into other key fields, such as "manager of the economy." Not only did the committee succeed in fundamentally redefining—or rather enlarging—the presidential role, but the subsequent strengthening of White House executive authority made the presidency an important, perhaps the most important, actor in U.S. governing processes during the last half of this century. How the nation could have survived—or prospered—without the institutional capacity to permit the chief executive to function effectively as chief executive would be hard to comprehend today.

Ironically, these institutional reforms to strengthen the presidency would later be seen, in the 1960s and 1970s, as the source of the "imperial presidency."[41] Certainly, "dictatorship" and "imperialism" were not what Brownlow had in mind because such terms negated the very ideals Brownlow most passionately believed. Just as he served as administrator in three cities, president of the International City Managers' Association, and founding director of the Public Administration Clearing House to improve people's lives, so too he sought to strengthen the presidency to allow that institution and its occupants to serve the American people better. In all these capacities, he saw himself "doing the work of the Master." By being an apostle for administrative management, Brownlow could minister to what he saw as the nation's most pressing needs in the darkest hours of the depression and later World War II. Certainly Brownlow's deeply ingrained Protestant ethic would have found subsequent misuse of presidential authority—violating laws, engaging in unsavory foreign policy adventures, and pushing the limits of what most consider legal and ethical behavior—repulsive, indeed a refutation of what his whole life represented.

The root of the word "administer" is, after all, "to minister" or "to serve." Brownlow, like every devout Protestant, would profess his faith by ceaselessly striving to minister or serve others, to dedicate his own life to the calling of public service much like a minister is called to the faith. Administrative management would be his substitute for the Apostles' Creed, and the ritual for its fulfillment would be achieved not through weekly organized worship but rather by good works regularly performed with a passion for anonymity as a public administrator. Sound administrative work could only be the sure testament of his own faith. *Results* were what counted most. All other doctrinaire disputes would seem meaningless, just as they had been in his youth in Buffalo.

From the days when the early Pilgrims landed at Plymouth Rock to the time in the late nineteenth century when people of faith lived in the small midwestern towns like the one where Brownlow grew up, Christian belief in salvation was not something that one could earn by doing good deeds now and then. For the faithful, redemption was achieved by continuous striving to serve others selflessly in the footsteps of Christ. The work of salvation, as the great Puritan divine Jonathan Edwards wrote in 1740, must be for each person "not only the business of Sabbath days, or the business of a month, or a year, or of seven years . . . but the business of his life . . . which he perseveres in through all changes, and under all trials, as long as he lives."[42] In other words, the convert's obligation to God was not satisfied by a coin in the Sunday church offering, but by hard work, twenty-four hours a day, throughout a lifetime in order to justify his faithfulness to his maker. Administrative management came to be associated, in Brownlow's mind, as his way, possibly his only way, to fulfill Christ's message of service.

Brownlow died as he had lived. He suffered a fatal stroke on September 27, 1963, while addressing a meeting of local public officials at the Army-Navy Country Club just outside Washington, D.C., in Arlington, Virginia. It was a typical Brownlow speech, full of wit and wisdom, highlighting the worth of public service.

9

Conclusion
American State Creation
as Moral Transformation

In America everything had a Protestant beginning.
—Philip Schaff
   America: A Sketch of Its Political, Social and Religious Character
of the United States of North America, 1855

EXECUTIVE ORDER NUMBER 8248 (1939) is titled "Establishing the Division of the Executive Office of the President and Defining their Functions and Duties." Like most mundane federal executive orders, its detailed, technical language hardly provides interesting reading; it outlines the specifics of setting up the White House staff for the American presidency; the functions and duties of the major units; and when, why, how, and for what purposes this reorganization will take place. Yet, buried within its legalistic prose were the essentials of the Brownlow Committee's recommendations. Ironically, only two years earlier these proposals had been decisively rejected by Congress. Through the back door of an executive order, so to speak, on September 11, 1939, the Brownlowian managerial reconceptualization of the American presidency quietly slipped into U.S. government and took effect.

Here the elements of the modern administrative state were established at the pinnacle of the national government without much fanfare or public notice. Nonetheless, in many ways that often-overlooked executive order ranks alongside the Constitutional Convention of 1787 as a landmark political event. By serving as the capstone of an administrative revolution, it brought into full fruition the modern American administrative state. At least until the 1980s, subsequent postwar reports on the organization and management of the United States government largely echoed Brownlow's prescriptions, extending and refining these ideas, or, in the words of Herman Finer, were "Mr. Brownlow's children."[1]

To be sure, most of the ideas behind the recommendations contained in the report of the President's Committee on Administrative Management were not original to that report but, as the last chapter suggests, were more or less a synthesis of administrative innovations that stretched back more than a half century, back to George William Curtis and the first Civil Service Commission, back to Charles Francis Adams, Jr., and the sunshine commission, back to the work of Emory Upton, Jane Addams, Frederick Taylor, Richard Childs, and certainly Brownlow himself. The American administrative state literally bubbled up from the grassroots experimentation of several, often anonymous, administrative inventors. Bits and pieces were added here and there to cope with particular problems. Then they spread elsewhere in frequently unsystematic ways, at times by accident. Also at times they were refined and synthesized and next moved to other places and levels of government in a slow, fragmentary, and almost imperceptible manner, at least one that was invisible to most citizens. This piecemeal process of state building from the grass roots upward culminated in the virtually forgotten Executive Order Number 8248 that presidential scholar Clinton Rossiter once properly called "an accomplishment in public administration superior to that of any other President."[2] Ironically, as Rossiter also observed, this accomplishment came from a president hardly respected for his administrative prowess. FDR was more often chastised by foes—*and* friends—for his neglect of organizational matters.

Roosevelt had no choice, however. Administrative state building in the United States had to be conducted, from the start, sub rosa. No votes were to be gained from doing it. As Richard Hofstadter presciently observed, Americans from the early pilgrims to the radical right today have always been hostile to statism. Only reluctantly, and only when believed absolutely necessary, did they buy into state building. In Hofstadter's words (written in 1955 but ones that ring even more true in the 1990s): "The growth of the national state and its regulative power has never been accepted with complacency by any large part of the middle-class public, which has not relaxed its suspicion of authority, and which even now gives repeated evidence of intense dislike of statism. In our time this growth has been possible only under the stress of great national emergencies, domestic and military, and even then only in the face of continuous resistance from a substantial part of the public."[3]

The main motivation for this institutional development that sneaked into the United States surreptitiously over many decades prior to 1939 is now clear or certainly clearer today than in 1939. Whereas some contemporary scholars point to war, politics, economics, or other numerous factors as the primary sources for the origins of the modern American administrative state, at the root, as the preceding chapters have attempted to show, were critical, yet neglected, moral factors. Much of the innovation and drive for the ideas behind the fragmentary, evolutionary development of the American state came from the work of a handful of morally motivated, principled men and women imbued with the small-town Protestantism of the nineteenth century, who creatively transformed their own deep-felt religious morality into modern secular administrative ideas and institutions that serve to govern the United States today.

The importance of religion in American life is hardly a profound or new observation. Astute foreign observers of the American character have long stressed the primacy of religion in shaping the United States. As Alexis de Tocqueville observed in 1830: "There is no country in the world where the Christian religion retains a greater influence over the souls of men than in America."[4] As a mid-nineteenth-century British traveler pointed out, in the United States "religious assemblages were being held at practically one place or another all the time. . . . Donations were constantly being made for religious purposes. America was basically a very religious country. . . . Church services were always crowded on Sundays."[5] In 1844 another observer, Robert Baird, said, "In no other part of the world do the inhabitants attend church in a larger proportion than in the United States; certainly no part of Continental Europe can compare with them in that respect."[6] Several observers from abroad specifically pointed out the importance of Protestantism that predominated the religious life in nineteenth-century America. The German theologian Philip Schaff, for example, wrote in 1855, "In America everything had a Protestant beginning."[7] Another foreign observer, André Siegfried, said of the United States, "Protestantism is the only national religion . . . [and] to ignore that fact is to view the country from a false angle."[8]

The census data of that era bears out such claims. The 1890 U.S. Census, for example, reports that of the total 62,622,250 inhabitants, only approximately 5 million were *not* communicants or adherents to some religious domination. The vast bulk, or 49,630,000, were identified as Protestants.[9] Such dominant religiosity in American life led one foreign commentator, G. K. Chesterton, to quip that the United States "is a nation with a soul of a church"[10] and inspired another, later European to joke, "You don't have a country over there, you have a huge church."[11]

Recent American historians of the nineteenth century have tended to reconfirm what earlier observers suggested, namely, that compared with other influences, the religious factor most decisively shaped national events throughout that era. Some Progressive-era U.S. historians, such as Charles Beard, had argued that "economics explains the mostest," whereas others, such as Frederick Jackson Turner, believed that "the closing of the frontier" was the defining factor in shaping the United States.[12] Today religion, as an explanatory variable for understanding nineteenth-century U.S. history, is at the forefront of historical analysis. In the words of one historian of this period writing in the 1990s, "The exciting development in American political history in twenty years is the recognition that religion was the key variable in voting in virtually every election until at least the Great Depression."[13] Or, as Richard Jensen's careful, probing history, *The Winning of the Midwest: Social and Political Conflict, 1888–1896,* concludes: "Religion shaped the issues and the rhetoric of politics, and it played the critical role in determining the party alignment of the voters."[14] Also historian Paul Kleppner in his award-winning *The Cross of Culture* argues, "Political choices were derived from beliefs about God. . . . Citizens were not robots, but reflective beings whose value systems had been 'sanctified' by family, friends, and congregations."[15]

What was true for American political life in general was also the case for state formation in that century, namely, that American state development cannot be understood properly, or at all, without an appreciation of the religious dimension. At least, one may possibly view this problem of state formation "from a false angle," as noted by Siegfried earlier, without adequately accounting for the influence of the dominant faith of nineteenth-century Americans, Protestantism. In essence, Protestantism stressed the primacy of the Bible ("sola scriptura") in defining the faith; individual interpretation of "the Holy Word" without intervention by a priest or pope; the close connection between the spirit of individual conscience and personal religious liberty; the link between the role of the self-governing congregation and political democracy; and an intense opposition to an established state religion. The root of the word "Protestant" is of course "protest." Hence, a Protestant is one who protests or, during the European Reformation, one who protests against the established Catholic or Anglican faith.

Not only was the United States first settled by Puritans who were religious refugees from the Reformation, but as Samuel P. Huntington points out, America "is the only country in the world in which a majority of the population belonged to dissenting Protestant sects. Protestant values reinforced republican and democratic tendencies in the eighteenth century and provided the underlying ethical and moral basis for American ideas on politics and society."[16] Protestantism also shaped fundamentally the sources and substance of American state development.

On the basis of the foregoing biographical sketches of several key founders of the modern administrative state, what generalizations then can be made about the religious factor in influencing the formation of the American state? In what ways specifically did the Protestant ethic foster the creation of the modern administrative state?

First, all these founders were reared in the galaxy of Protestant morality. The images, values, and vocabulary of the United States in the nineteenth century centered on Protestant ideals and ideas. Words such as "atonement," "baptism," "faith," "gospel," "heaven," "hell," "judgment day," "miracle," "predestination," "trinity," and "the Word" had real conscious *and* unconscious significance that moved the hearts and minds of believers. As Max Weber, Robert Tawney, and other scholars have demonstrated, the roots of modern capitalism sprang from sixteenth-century Puritan religious zeal and hard work[17]; so too the American state makers lived within a God-centered society and were motivated deeply by Protestant values. The reformist faith in "the priesthood of all believers" imbued notions of active, democratic participation. It drove men and women adhering to these religious ideals to be involved with their communities and to make a difference in the world through moral uplift.

Each state founder, however, came to his or her faith by a different route. Childs derived his faith from his father who, as noted earlier, "tucked down" before his bed every day; Taylor idealized his strong-willed religious mother; Jane Addams revered her Hicksite father; and Charles Francis Adams, Jr., was burdened by several generations of Adamses who foisted their heavy Puritan consciences onto him. Nor was Protestantism monolithic. Rather, in the United States in the nineteenth century, faith came in many denominational forms: Upton was raised in rock-hard Methodist fundamentalism; a no-nonsense, applied Christianity informed Jane Addams's morality; and an Emersonian transcendentalism shaped the outlook of Curtis. Some, such as Curtis, did not encounter their religion until the teen years, whereas others, such as Upton, inherited at birth their Protestantism. Some, such as Taylor, rarely darkened the Unitarian church door (as noted earlier, he was upset that he could never talk back to the minister during services), whereas Curtis preached occasionally to his local Unitarian congregation, and Brownlow, as a teenager, on his own absorbed the Protestantism of small-town Buffalo so well that he became acknowledged as a Biblical expert and taught adult Sunday school in various local churches. All were moral to a fault, and all were driven in both their personal and their professional lives by the sting of a profound yet refined Protestant conscience. The Protestant mind-set for these state makers thus was derived from diverse denominational sources and manifested itself through a variety of secular ideals: a merit system for Curtis, a sunshine commission in the case of Adams, and a council-manager plan with Childs. Each founder therefore drew on his or her ingrained Protestant values in unique ways to address the specific problems of the time.

Second, just as the Puritans during the century of reformation challenged the established church because of its corruption, greed, and power, so too American state inventors confronted the societal changes in their era—that is, urbanism, industrialism, political change, technological and economic developments—with similar moralistic fervor. They often characterized their opponents, the established order, as immoral, even demonic forces, with such terms as "corrupt bosses," "evil rings," "higgling of capitalism," "gold-brickers," and "dirty politicians." They spoke not so much in an economic or political language but in an apocalyptical religious vernacular, with "moral crusades" "to root out evil" or "to reform the wicked." Each state maker, to a greater or lesser degree, painted the opposition symbolically as sinful demons, whose wrongdoing should be publicized, reformed, and rooted out, just as the Puritan forebears had said three centuries earlier when they fought the established church. And just as Protestantism is a religion that centers on preaching "the Word," especially with passion behind preaching "the Word," so too the nineteenth- and early-twentieth-century administrative state founders in the United States passionately used a Protestant vocabulary to demonize their enemies in no uncertain terms, to expose their "evils," and to motivate their allies to rally to "the cause." All these men and women were articulate in their prophetic utterances of both the written and the spoken word and wielded strategically a Protestant morality—often with passion—against opponents to advance their political agendas.

Third, if the American state builders pictured their opposition in powerful negative symbols, they also held out positive hope for change that likewise was conceived in Protestant theological terms, that is, "to bring a new heaven and a new earth." The idealized administrative state that the reformers argued so passionately for erecting by various routes was infused with such Protestant values as "merit," "calling," "service," "public interest," "mission," "sunshine commission," and "nonpartisanship." Sometimes the Protestant normative beliefs were transformed into institutional arrangements such as the council-manager plan, where the linkages between Protestant doctrine and the plan lay not too far underneath the surface symbols. Church and state may well be formally and institutionally differentiated in the United States, but the denominational sources that forged various normative elements of the modern administrative state and undergird its day-to-day operations are closely interrelated in practice. The reformers' creative genius, as each of the foregoing chapters describes, was in fashioning the denominational Protestant beliefs in which they were reared and raised into powerful secular administrative instruments for modern state governance. The Reformed faith was infused into the forms, symbols, and even the methods of the various reformist movements in the late-nineteenth-and early-twentieth-century American state making. Indeed, the very banner under which reformers crusaded so zealously, that is, "public administration," had "to serve" or "to minister," as the root word for "administration" indicates.

Fourth, unlike European states that were founded on unitary, rational designs, usually at one time and from the top down, the American state was put together over several decades in bits and pieces, from the bottom up, and often in ways that were ill fitting, illogical, and contradictory. Much like contending Protestant sects, with their doctrines and creeds that are at times more competitive than complementary, so too the American state is an amalgam of diverse, poorly fitting, even competing organizational forms that are constantly open to further change and reform. The American state builders mostly rejected unified, rigid continental European state forms in creating the American state as being "undemocratic" or "unconstitutional." After all, denominations such as the Presbyterians, Congregationalists, Quakers, Unitarians, and Methodists were essentially in their own origins *organizational reforms* to return to a "true faith," especially the "true faith" of early Christian fellowship in which the faithful met in close-knit groups to worship their maker directly. So too, state making in the United States was in essence a continuation of the Protestant zeal to "protest and purify." Certainly American state makers rejected such words as "bureaucracy" and "state" to describe what they were doing or wanted to do because such terms smacked of the very European authoritarianism from which they had escaped. The reformers instead devised their administrative changes to solve particularistic problems they encountered and did not seem to worry too much about whether their individual state-building innovations added up to a neat, rational whole. Just as Puritan congregations were governed locally and democratically by their members, American administrative state developments were rooted as well, at least at first, in voluntaristic, local, and democratic experiments. These various independent, democratic designs, forged mainly at the grass roots like the Puritan "City upon the Hill," later bubbled up to redesign the entire national government. Recall that Executive Order Number 8248 (1939), discussed at the outset of this chapter, came as a capstone to American state creation, rather than being its starting point, as was the case in most continental Europe state development.

Fifth, at the root of Protestantism was—and remains—the ardent belief that everyone should be able to read and interpret the Holy Word according to his or her own individual conscience without the intervention by a higher authority. In short, one's faith should be grounded on "sola scriptura." Likewise, creation of the American state rested on simple, clearly written fundamentals, at times called a plan or set of principles, that could be easily understood by all citizens. This written Word would be open for all to read, interpret, and understand for themselves so that they could be directly *and* democratically self-governed. "Machines," "pols," or anything that stood in the way of direct, individual participation in democratic life were vehemently targeted for reform, just as the Puritans had attacked the priests and popes during the Reformation. Thus, there paradoxically contained an inherent potent antistatism within the peculiar American moral values that framed its new state. The "Word" would make the state, yet state could be "unmade" by the "Word." It was—and is—always a two-edged sword. Belief in the Word may serve as the cornerstone on which to found the modern American administrative state, but each individual was allowed freedom of conscience to decide what that Word meant. Like Protestants who still today hotly dispute among themselves various doctrines, creeds, and rituals, so too state reformers argued at times heatedly among themselves regarding just what was the correct interpretation of "plan" or "principle" and who were and were not the faithful. All agreed that there should be a written plan or principles on which to create the administrative state and direct its administrators.

The need for a fundamental written word was accepted as a given by the reformers, but in each case they conceptualized a way of thinking about the problem at hand, a theory if you will, that persuaded others to follow their leadership. They fashioned their ideas, both by pen and by oratory, in such ways that made sense and attracted support from their followers: Adams and his regulatory approach, Taylor and his scientific management, and Curtis and his merit ideals. American state makers were, first and foremost, idea creators whose ideas proved ultimately powerful sources of American state building.

Sixth, and equally critical, the Protestant ethic on which the modern American state was predicated never challenged the fundamental capitalistic economic order so dear to the hearts of many in the United States. Without an ordered, centralized bureaucracy, capitalism could thrive and even reign supreme. Indeed, the American state would aid and abet its hyper-development and dominance in innumerable ways. A Protestant ethic that advanced state building from the bottom up, not the top down, as well as persistently stimulating an enduring antistatist hostility toward such "an evil," fit perfectly with fostering small-town individualistic entrepreneurialism. Protestantism advanced state building, but it advanced the cause of capitalism even more by its own built-in antipower bias. The American state would never be allowed to stand in the way of the pursuit of individual economic gain, just as it could never impede the way of any individual's religious worship. Furthermore, the American state building values rooted in such concepts as "merit," "the work ethic," "neutrality," and the like were hardly serious ideological impediments to capitalism. If anything, the notions served to support and enhance its private-regarding ends by obscuring problems of distribution of power. More often, the ruthless self-interested aims of capitalism ironically served to undercut the very public-regarding Protestant norms on which the American state was erected, or at least the moral ideals of its founders.

Finally, just as Calvinism was "a politics of party organization and methodical activity, opposition and reform," so too was the process of formulating and founding the American state in the late nineteenth and early twentieth centuries.[18] The American state builders were few in number and often faced large, powerfully entrenched interests. Their success came largely from outorganizing and outreforming their opponents. In part they won from the certainty of morally "knowing the truth," but, to prevail, their truth required incredible leadership skills, talent, drive, and strategizing to turn their small cadres of followers into winning coalitions. American state founders individually and collectively were masterfully skilled at organizing associations, networks, leagues, and groups of loyalists. Their "crusades" were not achieved at one time or in one place but in most cases normally occurred over an entire lifetime of "principled" dedication to furthering "the cause." As H. Richard Niebuhr has written of American Protestantism, its success came through "waves of successive organized reformation, regeneration and renewal," so also much the same pattern followed for American state creation.[19] The American state was—and still is—a product of "waves of successive organized reformation, regeneration and renewal." There is no such thing as a once-and-for-all-time "big reform" to solve with finality the issues confronting administrative state formation, such as occurred in continental Europe, say, with the French Revolution or Fifth Republic of France. Rather, American state making was—and remains—a continuous, ongoing, open-ended process or set of piecemeal transformations, that is, "crusades." These crusades came to be labelled by various names, such as "civil service reform," "the council-manager plan," "the personnel movement," "the reorganization movement," "the regulatory movement," and so on—again, in Niebuhr's words, "waves of successive organized reformation, regeneration and renewal."

The downsides of an American state predicated on the normative values of the Reformed faith are readily apparent today: weak, fragmented, competing organizations, often too small and poorly funded to fulfill their assigned mandates, frequently lacking clear-cut direction from the top down, without adequate power to sustain long-term public policy agendas free of private interest group "meddling," and easily open to more change and more reforms. The intrinsic temporary and reformist character of the American state today is a product of its Protestant past.

Americans, let alone foreigners, do not understand this jerry-built, ad hoc administrative state. Often the very complexity and messiness of its design serves to confuse public responsibility. "Who's the boss?" is often hard to tell. Sustained action is even harder to secure, and the results of its activities are even more difficult still to evaluate properly. Its fragmented structures only compound the difficulties of coordination, direction, follow-through, and follow-up. Problems are raised and discussed, frequently with little relationship to how administrative systems then should be designed and put into place to solve the problems under review. Or, if new administrative systems are constructed, they run a great risk of being reconstructed, or reforms are stopped altogether before they are tried or before they are given much time to begin to operate. Americans, again thanks to their distant reformist heritage, are constantly tinkering with and tearing up their administrative enterprise to the point that few things are given a long-term chance of working—or working for very long.

This unique administrative state design also frustrates the effective generation of adequate political power necessary for decisive executive action. Here again is the price Americans pay for creating a state built on a powerful antipower or antistatist ethic of the Reformed faith. That faith sought to stamp out the corrupt establishment, not vest more power in existing governmental institutions. The Puritan "City upon the Hill" remains a compelling institutional ideal of an independent, voluntaristic, free association of individuals who escaped European authority to worship so zealously their own God in their particular individualistic ways. Americans, from the Puritans to the radical right today, continually seek to escape from the state, not strengthen it.

Ultimately, the American state in its present form increasingly frustrates Americans themselves. Americans constantly "damn the bureaucracy" with intensity, although paradoxically they simultaneously have become ever more dependent on its services. President Reagan nicely captured this ingrained historic American frustration in his first inaugural address when he said simply, "Government is the problem." Ironically, the very openness and malleability of the American state that allows it to add on new layers of reforms so easily, once again thanks to its reformist past, makes it an ongoing popular target for criticism, even scapegoating. In the words of Charles Goodsell, it serves as a "splendid hate object" in our minds, possibly because we never seem to be able to get a handle on it or make it work the way we want.[20] It seems increasingly large, remote, forbidding, and unable to respond to our wishes. The founding norms of a reformist faith put the American administrative state in a double bind: it is a product of so many complex layers of reforms that it now seems "over-towering," even "demonlike," yet in turn it also beckons for more reforms that only serve to heighten public anxiety toward it.[21] The term "catch-22," coined by the novelist Joseph Heller for a person caught in a bureaucratic double bind, might well be applied to the American state itself.

In addition, if all that is not bad enough, the moral reformers invented the administrative state more than a century after the U.S. Constitution was ratified by adding bits and pieces of institutions to fill in the gaps and its insufficiencies and, in the end, permit our constitutional order to work for the next century. They added a new personnel system based on merit here, a regulatory approach there, and a budgeting process elsewhere. In the words of Woodrow Wilson, their handiwork served "to run a constitution."[22] Thus, the founding of the American administrative state never seemed to be quite a legitimate enterprise. Its inherent positive-government prescriptions would always be at odds with the norms and needs of our Enlightenment-inspired U.S. Constitution that sought to curb political power via checks and balances, periodic elections, federalism, and so forth. As Dwight Waldo put it so well, "We did not *want* a European-style state, we did not *need* a European-style state, and we did not *develop* a European-style state" (Waldo's italics).[23]

Public debates even erupt today over whether this or that administrative activity is "constitutional."[24] Of course, an activity may not be regarded as constitutional to someone who believes the United States is governed *only* by the great charter of 1787, whereas it certainly is if one accepts the legitimacy of the governing institutions founded by the modern administrative state. Legitimacy of the American administration state itself remains perpetually open to debate precisely because of the way the reformers had to sneak it in through the back way a century *after* the founding of the American constitutional system. This debate, again, derives from the antistatist core of Protestantism on which the American nation was erected. Our American state, thanks to its Protestant framing of values, remains so elusive and ephemeral that it is difficult to define where it is, what it is, or even whether a "there" exists. Indeed, after almost a century of social science debate, no scholar has succeeded in defining the American state in any meaningful or authoritative manner.

Nevertheless, we can find some pluses from this American state founded on a reformist faith. It is a highly innovative, open system that can easily change and adapt to new circumstances as they arise. As Wallace Sayre noted, "The Europeans have produced a more orderly and symmetrical, a more prudent, a more articulate, a more cohesive and more powerful state bureaucracy . . . [whereas the United States has] a more internally competitive, more experimental, a noisier and less coherent, less powerful . . . governmental system, but a more dynamic one."[25] As a result, Americans created, perhaps unwittingly, a state that Woodrow Wilson argued prophetically for a century ago in his famous centennial essay "The Study of Administration," that is, for an administrative framework that fits well within our existing constitutional design, essential (even now) "to run a Constitution."[26]

Perhaps, however, even that statement reflects a somewhat modest viewpoint about the American administrative state's achievements. This administrative state has not merely run a Constitution; among other achievements, it has also in this century fought two world wars and numerous smaller conflicts successfully; helped cure the Great Depression; secured prosperity for millions; nurtured abundant technological and material progress; and now governs as the last global superpower. Indeed, civilized life within our constitutional democracy would be difficult to comprehend without the immense services performed by an administrative state in some highly innovative, complicated ways—from space exploration to hometown public library video rental services. It is also difficult to imagine how freedom—*real freedom*—could continue in the United States without such administrative safeguards as meat inspections, child labor laws, welfare payments, fire safety codes, public education, and police protection. Even more basic is that the American state, rooted in antistatist Protestantism, would not become a tempting target for revolutionaries as was the case in Europe. Marxism could never gain much of a foothold in the United States perhaps because its state would always be so elusive, always in the process of reform, always evolving. Marxism needed a stable objective for inciting hatred that the American state would simply not supply. The result, ironically, was that the American state would create a more stable state in the long run, or at least would outlast most of the Marxist states. The record of the American administrative state is therefore not all that bad, but whether it will be all that good in the future is another matter.

And what will the future hold for the American state founded on small-town Protestantism of the last century? As Americans rapidly become more heterogeneous—ethnically, culturally, and morally—and far removed from their relatively cohesive, nineteenth-century religious roots, what will happen to the U.S. state? Can the American state founded on such historically remote, indeed geographically isolated moral values survive? Or will it continue to transform itself in new, unforeseen ways to participate in, even remain a key leader in, tomorrow's world order?

Answers to such questions will largely turn on yet another question, namely, what will the international state system become in the next century? Today, unlike a century ago, the American nation is intrinsically intertwined, economically, technologically, politically, and militarily with the rest of the world. Its modern administrative state today no longer operates apart from others. Indeed, it is now a truism that in the post–cold war world the United States functions as the last global superpower. Thus the shape of tomorrow's world order may be the prime factor in deciding where the American state is headed.

Many alternative scenarios have been and are being proposed: Will we possibly have extreme anarchism, where the state system as we know it collapses entirely? Or will we see "the end of history" or "clash of civilizations" where the state is subsumed into a far larger entity or where warfare exists among cultures, not states?[27] Or will the present liberal capitalistic order continue, in which little changes and the United States hegemony remains largely unchallenged? Will we perhaps have a new form of globalism, where state political competition ends and a new "state-free" world order emerges? Or perhaps will we experience even a new "virtual state" or trading state system in which territorial expansion, production capacities, and even political power become irrelevant, and the chief state aims turn into stimulating, encouraging, and coordinating foreign investments overseas?[28]

All of these scenarios are being debated and are certainly possible. No one can predict the future, and thus we would be foolish to try to guess what alternative or combination of alternatives will prevail. We can safely assume, however, that barring the collapse or end of the state system as we know it today, America's Protestant past erected a highly flexible and adaptive state model for the United States today— and tomorrow. Throughout the twentieth century, the American state has demonstrated remarkable resiliency and strength in meeting the diverse, demanding challenges confronting it and the world.[29] This adaptability to change, in fact to reform itself enormously over the last century, may well be the greatest legacy derived from our Protestant past. Unlike Karl Marx's communist state, in which the state withers away and the proletariat reigns supreme, or a Hobbesian state in which the Leviathan never withers, Protestantism endowed the United States with a sort of protean administrative state with inherent self-reforming qualities that could not only unobtrusively transform itself into new, unimagined shapes but also continue to renew its strength and purposes to meet vastly changing global and internal needs.[30] Paradoxically, Americans, by seeking throughout their history to escape the state, may well have erected the most enduring and powerful variety of administrative state.

Ultimately, however, the American state, founded on small-town Protestant values that evolved over the last century into unique secular administrative arrangements, is probably the only kind Americans could have opted for, or accepted, given their especially intense devotion to liberty and individual freedom. Its mobile, prosperous, dynamic society, with people so fiercely devoted to protecting personal liberties, would never permit an ordered, coherent, unified, and uniform administrative state to work on these shores. It would never fit the American character or the American way of doing things. Again, the legacy from Protestant past would certainly "protest" that kind of established authority. Such is an enduring reformist mind-set that gave birth to a unique modern American state, with its unobtrusive adaptability to respond to immediate public demands of the moment while engendering rage for reform from the very same public it serves.

Notes

1. Introduction: From Whence the American State?

1. Material for this sketch of the ValuJet story was taken from several recent news accounts, especially "FAA Struggles as Airlines Turn to Subcontracts," *New York Times*, June 2, 1996, 1+; "The ValuJet Crash," *U.S. News and World Report*, May 27, 1996, 35–39; William A. Carley, "Fire Storm," *Wall Street Journal*, Nov. 14, 1996, p. 1+; and Mary Schiavo, "Flying Blind," *Time*, March 31, 1997, 54–58.

2. Dwight Waldo, "A Conversation with Dwight Waldo," *Public Administration Review* 35 (July/August 1985): 465. For the complex difficulties of defining precisely what is "the administrative state," however, see John A. Rohr, *To Run a Constitution: The Legitimacy of the Administrative State* (Lawrence: University Press of Kansas, 1986), 217 n. 11.

3. No agreed-on scholarly definition of "administrative state" yet exists; for the difficulties involved in defining this term, see Rohr, 217.

4. Beverly A. Cigler and Heidi L. Neiswender, "Bureaucracy in the Introductory American Government Textbook," *Public Administration Review* 51 (September/October 1991): 444.

5. For an important collection of essays that were critical to starting this intellectual movement in the social sciences, read Peter B. Evans, Dietrich Rueschemeyer, and Theda Skocpol, eds., *Bringing the State Back In* (Cambridge: Cambridge University Press, 1985). See especially the citations for an excellent review of the "state" literature, and for a more up-to-date overview of the extensive writings in this field, read several of the essays as well as the extensive bibliography in James Farr, John S. Dryzek, and Stephen T. Leonard, eds., *Political Science in History* (Cambridge: Cambridge University Press, 1995) or the introduction (chap. 1) in Bartholomew H. Sparrow, *From the Outside In: World War II and the American State* (Princeton: Princeton University Press, 1996). The Sparrow book is one of the recent important contributions to this impressive body of literature, but its contents only highlight the vast differences among return-to-state writers regarding such questions as: What is "the state"? When did "it" begin? How did it evolve?

6. Andrew McFarland, "Interest Groups and Political Time: Cycles in America," *British Journal of Political Science* 23 (1991): 262.

7. Richard F. Bensel, *Yankee Leviathan: The Origins of Central State Authority in America, 1859–1877* (Cambridge: Cambridge University Press, 1990).

8. Stephen Skowronek, *Building a New American State: The Expansion of National Administrative Capacities, 1877–1920* (Cambridge: Cambridge University Press, 1982).

9. Ibid., 9.

10. Ibid., 290.

11. Theda Skocpol, *Protecting Soldiers and Mothers: The Political Origins of Social Policy in the United States* (Cambridge: Harvard University Press, 1992).

12. Ibid., 525.

13. Ibid., 526.

14. Ibid.

15. Ibid.

16. Thorbjorn L. Knutsen, *A History of International Relations Theory* (New York: Manchester University Press, 1992), 2.

17. Bruce D. Porter, *War and the Rise of the State: The Military Foundations of Modern Politics* (New York: Free Press, 1994).

18. Ibid., 1.

19. Ibid., 291.

20. Ibid., 294.

21. Kenneth Waltz, *Theory of International Politics* (New York: Random House, 1979).

22. Rohr, 39.

23. Ibid., 41.

24. Ibid., 53.

25. Ibid.

26. Ibid., 56.

27. Ibid.

28. Ibid., 112.

29. Ibid., 172.

30. Letter of James Madison to Thomas Jefferson, October 24, 1787, in *The Papers of James Madison* (Charlottesville: University of Virginia Press), 10: 208.

31. Harvey C. Mansfield, Jr., *Taming the Prince: The Ambivalence of Modern Executive Power* (New York: Free Press, 1989).

32. Jack N. Rakove, *Original Meanings: Politics and Ideas in the Making of the Constitution* (New York: Alfred A. Knopf, 1996), 244.

33. James A. Stever, *The End of Public Administration: Problems of the Profession in the Post-Progressive Era* (Dobbs Ferry, N.Y.: Transnational Publishers, 1988), 2.

34. Ibid., 6.

35. Ibid., 20.

36. Ibid., 25.

37. Ibid., 19.

38. Camilla Stivers, *Gender Images in Public Administration: Legitimacy and the Administrative State* (Newbury Park, Calif.: Sage Publications, 1993), 4.

39. Ibid., 10.

40. Readers may reasonably ask why these aforementioned founders were included but not others, such as Woodrow Wilson, Frank Goodnow, or Luther Gulick, who are among those popularly viewed as "fathering" public administration. The focus of this book is on the creators of the administrative state (i.e.,

the key institutions' practices and structures that make modern government operate, rather than the administrative theories that forged the study of public administration). In essence, this book explores the origins of American administrative "institutions" as opposed to its "study."

41. Page Smith, *The Historian and History* (New York: Vintage, 1964), 30.

42. Ibid.

43. Ibid.

44. As quoted by George F. Will, "Perfume and Vinegar," *Newsweek*, December 9, 1996, 92, from an address by Theda Skocpol, "The Tocqueville Problem: Civic Engagement in American Democracy" (paper presented at the annual meeting of the Social Science History Association, New Orleans, October 12, 1996), 10–12.

45. Alexis de Tocqueville, *Democracy in America* (New York: Alfred A. Knopf, 1945), 1: 95.

2. George William Curtis: Leading Missionary for Merit

1. Paul P. Van Riper, *History of the United States Civil Service* (Evanston, Ill.: Row, Peterson and Co., 1958), 79.

2. As cited in William Dudley Foulke, *Fighting the Spoilsmen: Reminiscences of the Civil Service Reform Movement* (New York: G. P. Putnam's Sons, 1919), 29. It is noteworthy that Foulke, who was an important civil service reformer, warmly dedicates his book to Curtis. Foulke perhaps expressed best in his dedication poem to Curtis why his fellow reformers looked to Curtis for leadership:

A kindly spirit and a vision clear,
A prophet's prescience and a stateman's mind,
A face to win us and a smile to cheer,
A heart that glowed with love of humankind!
His voice was music and his words were song,
His ways were gentle but his reason just,
Quick to discern the right and encourage the wrong,
And him we followed with unfaltering trust

3. Carl Schurz, "George William Curtis," in *Speeches, Correspondence and Political Papers* (New York: Harper and Brothers, 1898), 4: 410. One can sense the importance of Curtis during his era by reading the lengthy accounts of his life contained in the two major encyclopedias of biography in the late nineteenth century: *Appleton's Cyclopaedia of American Biography* (New York: D. Appleton and Co., 1888), 2: 35–36 and *The National Cyclopaedia of American Biography* (New York: James T. Whilte & Co., 1893), 3: 96–97.

4. George William Curtis, *Orations and Addresses* (New York: Harper and Brothers, 1894), 2: 502.

5. Ibid., 17.

6. Ibid., 18.

7. Ibid., 36.

8. Ibid., 20.

9. Ibid., 241.

10. As cited in Van Riper, 36.

11. Leonard D. White, *The Jacksonians* (New York: Macmillan, 1954), 46.

12. Frederick C. Mosher, *Democracy and the Public Service*, 2d ed. (New York: Oxford University Press, 1982), 65.

13. Ari Hoogenboom, *Outlawing the Spoils: A History of the Civil Service Reform Movement, 1865–1883* (Urbana: University of Illinois Press, 1968), 1.

14. Leonard D. White, *The Republican Era, 1869–1901: A Study of Administrative History* (New York: Macmillan, 1958), 291.

15. Van Riper, 65–66. It is also important to underscore that according to Ari Hoogenboom, "The Jenckes bill received new and powerful support from George William Curtis," 33. So even in this early civil service reform legislation, Curtis was an important force on its behalf.

16. Van Riper, 62.

17. Curtis, 1: 247. Curtis's love of his own New England heritage is illustrated in these edited volumes of his orations and addresses by the several devoted to that topic such as "The Puritan Principle—Liberty Under Law," "Puritan Principle and Puritan Pluck," and "The Puritan Spirit."

18. As described by Edward Cary, *George William Curtis* (Boston: Houghton, Mifflin and Company, 1894), chapters 1 and 2 (especially pages 18–19).

19. Gordon Milne, *George William Curtis and the Genteel Tradition* (Bloomington: Indiana University Press, 1956), 10.

20. As cited in Milne, 10.

21. Odell Shepard, *Pedlar's Progress: The Life of Bronson Alcott* (Boston: Houghton Mifflin, 1937), 268.

22. Donald Kostner, *Transcendentalism in America* (Boston: Twayne Publishers, 1975), 3.

23. Octavius Frothingham, *Transcendentalism in New England* (New York: G. P. Putnam and Sons, 1876), 21.

24. Van Wyck Brooks, *The Flowering of New England* (New York: E. P. Dutton, 1936), 187.

25. Milne, 10.

26. Ibid., 12.

27. As cited in the introduction of Paul F. Boller, Jr., *American Transcendentalism, 1830–1860* (New York: G. P. Putnam, 1974), 15.

28. Hoogenboom, 33.

29. Milne, 18. Milne almost equates the sort of religious outlook that Curtis drew out of the Brook Farm experience to that of an Eastern religion with its emphasis on inward spirituality: "George Curtis shared this faith that man can glimpse the true light by looking within himself 'where the seed is sown.' "

30. Charles Eliot Norton to E. L. Godkin, February 1, 1867, unpublished letter, Godkin Papers, Harvard University Library.

31. *National Cyclopaedia of American Biography*, 97.

32. Though Curtis insisted he was not a politician, he certainly remained politically active throughout his life. As Gerald W. McFarland points out, "Public duty, Curtis insisted, required 'constant and active participation in the details of politics . . . on the part of the most intelligent citizens' to prevent public

affairs from falling 'under the control of selfish and ignorant or crafty and venal men,' " Gerald W. McFarland, *Mugwumps, Morals and Politics, 1884–1920* (Amherst: University of Massachusetts Press, 1975), 36. See also Curtis, vol. 2.

33. Curtis, vol. 2.

34. As cited in Lionel V. Murphy, "The First Federal Civil Service Commission: 1871–75," *Public Personnel Review* 3 (July 1942): 219.

35. *U.S. Statutes* 514 (1871).

36. Murphy, 322–23.

37. Ibid.

38. Richard E. Titlow, *Americans Import Merit: Origins of the United States Civil Service and the Influence of the British Model* (Lanham, Md.: University Press of America, 1979), 289.

39. Ibid.

40. As quoted in Cary, 298.

41. Stow Persons, *The Decline of American Gentility* (New York: Columbia University Press, 1973), 168–69.

42. As cited in Murphy, 318.

43. Dorman B. Eaton, *Civil Service in Great Britain* (New York: Harper and Brothers, 1880). The introduction by Curtis is especially well written and reflective of his enormous role in leading the civil service reform effort.

44. A. Bower Sageser, *The First Two Decades of the Pendleton Act: A Study of Civil Service Reform* (Lincoln: University of Nebraska Press, 1935), 35. For two recent accounts of the evolution of the merit concept, see Patricia Wallace Ingraham, *The Foundation of Merit: Public Service in American Democracy* (Baltimore: Johns Hopkins University Press, 1995), and Mark W. Huddleston and William W. Boyer, *The Higher Civil Service in the United States: Quest for Reform* (Pittsburgh: University of Pittsburgh Press, 1996).

45. Frank M. Stewart, *The National Civil Service Reform League: History, Activities, and Problems* (Austin: University of Texas Press, 1929), 32.

46. As told in Cary, 328.

47. Ibid.

3. Charles Francis Adams, Jr.: The Conscience of the Sunshine Commission

1. Thomas K. McCraw, *Prophets of Regulation* (Cambridge: Harvard University Press, 1984), 1.

2. Charles F. Adams, Jr., *Charles F. Adams, Jr., 1835–1915* (Boston: Houghton Mifflin Co., 1916), 10.

3. As quoted in Edward C. Kirkland, *Charles Francis Adams, Jr., 1835–1915: The Patrician at Bay* (Cambridge: Harvard University Press, 1965), 3.

4. As quoted in McGraw, 56.

5. As cited in Kirkland, 6.

6. Jack Shepherd, *The Adams Chronicles: Four Generations of Greatness* (Boston: Little, Brown and Co., 1975), 339–41.

7. Ibid., 344–45.

8. Adams, *Charles F. Adams, Jr.*, 3.

9. Shepherd, 366.

10. As cited in Kirkland, 23.

11. Adams, *Charles F. Adams, Jr.*, 130.

12. William G. McLoughlin, *Revivals, Awakenings, and Reform* (Chicago: University of Chicago Press, 1978), 140.

13. Shepherd, 379.

14. Kirkland, 36.

15. Alfred D. Chandler, Jr., *The Visible Hand: The Managerial Revolution in American Business* (Cambridge: Harvard University Press, 1977), 86.

16. Adams, *Charles F. Adams, Jr.*, 170.

17. Ibid.

18. Ibid., 171. For examples of his writings, see Charles F. Adams, Jr., "The Railroad System," *North American Review* 104 (April 1867); "Boston," *North American Review* 106 (January 1868); "Legislative Control Over Railway Charters," *American Law Review* 1 (April 1867); "Railroad Inflation," *North American Review* 108 (January 1869). For the best summary of his thinking, read Charles F. Adams, Jr., *Railroads: Their Origins and Problems* (New York: G. P. Putnam's Sons, 1878).

19. Adams, "The Railroad System," 479.

20. Ibid.

21. Ibid., 497–99.

22. Ibid.

23. Ibid.

24. Adams, *Railroads*, 141.

25. Ibid.

26. Adams, *Charles F. Adams. Jr.*, 172.

27. Charles F. Adams, Jr., "A Chapter of Erie," *North American Review* 109 (July 1869): 53.

28. As cited in Kirkland, 40.

29. Adams, *Charles F. Adams, Jr.*, 172.

30. *Massachusetts Acts and Resolves* (Boston, 1869), 699.

31. Adams, *Railroads*, 138.

32. William A. Craft, *State Railroad Commissions* (New York: The Railroad Gazette, 1883), 9.

33. Charles F. Adams, Jr., "Railway Problems in 1869," *North American Review* 110 (January 1870): 139.

34. Ibid., 143.

35. *Tenth Annual Report of the Railroad Commissioners, 1879* (n.p., n.d.), 54–55.

36. Adams, *Charles F. Adams, Jr.*, 174.

37. Ibid., 195.

38. Charles F. Adams, Jr., *Memorabilia, 1888–93* (n.p., n.d.), 18–20.

39. *Congressional Record*, 48th Cong., 2d sess., 1884, 329.

40. *U.S. Statutes*, vol. 24, secs. 18, 19, 23, 24 (1887).

41. I am well aware that regulatory bodies—at all levels of government—do far more today than what Adams originally conceived. Adams saw public regulation as achieved primarily through fact gathering, analysis, publicity, and public discussion. This was the means, he was certain, for getting business,

namely railroads, to clean up their acts or change their purely private-regarding behavior for the general good of the community, rather than have coercive power exercised directly over the private sector. Nonetheless, his approach marked the beginning of modern regulatory agencies. They fundamentally remain the institutional sources for how state power is exercised over industry today by combining two or three branches of governmental powers within one body, often independent of the other branches and staffed with highly expert professionals, who more often than not rely on voluntary compliance by the regulated industry. Adams's single-industry model for regulation remains dominant today, even though multiple industrial oversight began in the 1960s with the expansion of new regulatory units that pursued far wider social objectives; consider, for example, the Environmental Protection Agency, the Occupational Health and Safety Administration, and the Consumer Products Safety Commission.

4. Emory Upton: Prophet for Public Professionalism

1. As cited in Stephen E. Ambrose, *Upton and the Army* (Baton Rouge: Louisiana State University Press, 1964), 21–22.

2. Ibid., 4–5.

3. Ibid., 5.

4. As cited in Peter S. Michie, *The Life and Letters of Emory Upton* (New York: D. Appleton and Co., 1885), 476–77.

5. *Doctrines and Discipline of the Methodist Church* (New York: Methodist Publishing House, 1948), 32.

6. Ibid. For a recent work pointing out the increasing militancy of ministers during this era, see Christine Leigh Heyrman, *Southern Cross* (New York: Alfred A. Knopf, 1997).

7. As quoted in Winthrop S. Hudson, *Religion in America: A Historical Account of the Development of American Religious Life,* 2d ed. (New York: Scribner's, 1973), 122–23.

8. James H. Wilson, introduction to Michie, 11.

9. Michie, 12–13.

10. Ibid., 16.

11. Ambrose, 9.

12. Ibid., 11.

13. As cited in Michie, 53.

14. Ibid., 23.

15. Ibid.

16. As cited in Ambrose, 53.

17. Michie, 173.

18. As quoted in Russell F. Weigley, *Towards an American Army: Military Thought from Washington to Marshall* (New York: Columbia University Press, 1962), 103.

19. Ibid.

20. Emory Upton, *Military Policy of the United States* (Washington, D.C.: War Department, 1912), 428.

21. As cited in Ambrose, 64–65.

22. Upton's manuals went through several editions and were published by D. Appleton and Company: *Infantry Tactics* (1873), *Cavalry Tactics* (1874), and *Artillery Tactics* (1875).

23. Emory Upton, *The Armies of Asia and Europe* (New York: D. Appleton and Co., 1878), 319–20.

24. Ibid., 317.

25. Ibid.

26. Upton, *Military Policy*, 7.

27. Ibid.

28. As cited in Weigley, 111.

29. Ibid., 109.

30. Hudson, 123–24.

31. Samuel P. Huntington, *The Soldier and the State: The Theory and Politics of Civil-Military Relations* (Cambridge: Harvard University Press, 1957), 229.

32. Elihu Root, preface to Upton, *Military Policy*, 2.

33. Frederic Louis Huidekiper, *The Military Unpreparedness of the United States* (New York: Macmillan, 1916), 218.

34. For a brief comment on the influence of the professional military model on other civilian administrative units, read Frederick C. Mosher, ed., *Basic Documents of American Public Administration, 1776–1950* (New York: Holmes and Meier Publishers, 1976), 48–49. Nonetheless, the overall impact and significance of military ideas on American public administration remain to be analyzed.

35. No doubt his tragic suicide at a comparatively young age led to the romantic attachment to Uptonian ideas within the small, tightly knit military community of those days. As Walter Millis indicates, Upton was viewed by many as "the brilliant and tragic Emory Upton," which only increased the attraction and fame of his writings; see Walter Millis, *Arms and Men: A Study in American Military History* (New York: G. P. Putnam's Sons, 1956), 41.

5. Jane Addams: The Call from the Inner Light for Social Reform

1. Theda Skocpol, *Protecting Soldiers and Mothers: The Political Origins of Social Policy* (Cambridge: Harvard University Press, 1992); see especially chap. 9 and her conclusion (pp. 480–539), where she discusses this idea.

2. Jane Addams, *Twenty Years at Hull-House* (New York: Macmillan, 1910), 1.

3. Ibid., 9.

4. Ibid., 11.

5. Ibid., 7.

6. Ibid., 8.

7. James Weber Linn, *Jane Addams, A Biography* (New York: D. Appleton Century, 1935), 29.

8. As cited in Robert M. Crunden, *Ministers of Reform: The Progressive Achievement in American Civilization, 1889–1920* (New York: Basic Books, 1982), 19.

9. Allen F. Davis, *American Heroine: The Life and Legend of Jane Addams* (New York: Oxford University Press, 1973), 85.

10. Crunden, 18.

11. Addams, 2.

12. Ibid., 5.

13. Ibid., 15.

14. Linn, 81.

15. Ibid., 53.

16. As cited in Crunden, 20.

17. Addams, 64.

18. Ibid., 88.

19. It is striking how her autobiography reads almost like a biblical account of St. Paul being struck on the road to Damascus; after a revelation from God, "suddenly there shone round about him a light from heaven" (Acts 9:3). Compare that biblical text to Addams's own account from her autobiography, in which after watching a bullfight in Spain, "I felt myself tried and condemned, not only by this disgusting experience but by the entire moral situation which it revealed. It was suddenly made quite clear to me that I was lulling my conscience by a dreamer's scheme, that a mere paper reform had become a defense for continued idleness, and that I was making it a raison d'etre for going on indefinitely with study and travel. . . . Nothing less than the moral reaction following the experience at a bull-fight had been able to reveal to me that . . . I had been tied to the tail of the veriest ox-cart of self-seeking" (Addams, 86).

20. Linn, 48.

21. Ibid., 71.

22. Addams, 87.

23. Ibid., 127.

24. Ibid., 115–16.

25. Ibid., 123–24.

26. As cited in John M. Blum et al., *The National Experience: The History of the United States since 1865,* 4th ed. (New York: Harcourt Brace Jovanovich, 1977), 447.

27. Ibid., 447.

28. Unlike missionaries from various denominations who worked in urban areas at that time, the charter for Hull House clearly designates a far broader, more secular, and more experimental set of goals: "To provide a center for a higher civic and social life: to institute and maintain educational and philanthropic enterprises, and to investigate and improve the conditions in the industrial districts of Chicago" (as cited in Addams, 112). Particularly the social experimental and research goals of Hull House served to differentiate its innovative work from that of Toynbee Hall in the east end of London or the University Settlement House founded in New York City at roughly the same time. For details of these early settlement houses, read Herbert Stroup, *Social Welfare Pioneers* (Chicago: Nelson-Hall, 1986). For the source of the quotation cited in the text, see Addams, 125.

29. Linn, 421.

30. As cited in Crunden, 25.

31. Allen F. Davis, *Spearheads for Reform: The Social Settlements and the Progressive Movement, 1890–1914* (New York: Oxford University Press, 1967).

32. Addams, 96.

33. Crunden, 65.

34. Skocpol, 343–49.

35. Addams, 209–10.

36. Skocpol, 481.

37. Nancy P. Weiss, "Save the Children: A History of the Children's Bureau, 1903–1918" (Ph.D. diss., University of California, Los Angeles, 1974), 51, 53.

38. Skocpol, 522.

39. Ibid., 535.

40. According to John Farrell, "For Jane Addams, growing professionalization among social workers was a villain. Professionalization sapped the emotional drive of the early settlement movement. Social workers of a later generation were more scholarly, more detached and scientific in approach, and might be better social workers, she admitted. But the nonprofessional approach, she said frankly, had her sympathy. Specialization deflected an individual from his natural generous impulses and imposed a professional sense of duty on him which defogged and deadened human relationships. A specialized and limited sense of duty excludes the penetrating sense of the fundamental unity and interdependence of society," in John C. Farrell, *Beloved Lady: History of Jane Addams' Ideas on Reform and Peace* (Baltimore: Johns Hopkins University Press, 1967), 208.

41. As cited in Daniel Levine, *Jane Addams and the Liberal Tradition* (Westport, Conn.: Greenwood Press, 1980), 92. Hull House grew over the years from the original Hull mansion to thirteen buildings. Eleven of the facilities were demolished in the 1960s for the construction of the University of Illinois at Chicago. Today the first floor of the original Hull mansion has been restored, and the dining hall has been converted into a museum.

6. Frederick W. Taylor: Latter-Day Puritan as Scientific Manager

1. As cited in George F. Will, "A Faster Mousetrap," review of *The One Best Way: Frederick Winslow Taylor and the Enigma of Efficiency,* by Robert Kanigel, *New York Times Book Review,* June 15, 1997, 8–10.

2. Frank S. Copley, *Frederick W. Taylor: Father of Scientific Management* (New York: Harper and Brothers, 1923), 2: 228.

3. William Fannon, "Recollections" (unpublished manuscript in Taylor Library, Stevens Institute of Technology, Hoboken, New Jersey) as cited in Sudhir Kakir, *Frederick Taylor: A Study in Personality and Innovation* (Cambridge, Mass.: MIT Press, 1970), 86.

4. U.S. House Committee, *Hearings to Investigate the Taylor and Other Systems of Shop Management* (Washington, D.C.: U.S. Government Printing Office, 1912), 1: 339.

5. Ibid.

6. As quoted in Copley, 1: 12.

7. As cited in Kakir, 20.

8. As cited in George H. Sabine, *A History of Political Theory*, 3d ed. (New York: Holt, Rinehart and Winston, 1961), 316.

9. Copley, 1: 52.

10. Ibid., 53.

11. Copley, 1: 43.

12. Ibid., 67–68.

13. Frederick W. Taylor, "Why Manufacturers Dislike College Graduates," as cited in Samuel Haber, *Efficiency and Uplift* (Chicago: University of Chicago Press, 1964), 7.

14. Ibid.

15. Copley, 1: 5.

16. Ibid.

17. As cited in James Donnelly, *Fundamentals of Management*, 4th ed. (Plano, Tex.: Bass Publishers, 1983), 3. See also Charles D. Wrege and Ronald G. Greenwood, *Frederick W. Taylor: The Father of Scientific Management* (Homewood, Ill., Irwin, 1991), parts 4 and 5, for a good discussion of the development and spread of these ideas.

18. Daniel Nelson, *Frederick W. Taylor and the Rise of Scientific Management* (Madison: University of Wisconsin Press, 1980), 10. Nelson's essential point is that a new managerial elite was spawned by the revolutionary changes in technologies during this era, giving fertile soil to the birth, development, and spread of Taylorism.

19. Harlow Person, "The Origin and Nature of Scientific Management," in *Scientific Management in American Industry* (New York: Harper Brothers, 1929), 2. Person was a key Taylor disciple, and his perspective reflects the view of many of Taylor's supporters who believed that scientific management was a far more humane alternative to "rules of thumb" management that preceded Taylorism.

20. Frederick W. Taylor, "A Piece-Rate System Being a Step toward Partial Solution of the Labor Problem," *American Society of Mechanical Engineers Transactions* 16 (1895): 856. Note the emphasis on *reform* of the "labor problem" in the article's title. This theme is evident throughout Taylor's writings; see especially his book *The Principles of Scientific Management* (1911; reprint, New York: W. W. Norton, 1967).

21. Paul Van Riper, "Administrative Thought in the 1880s: State of the Art" (paper presented at the American Society for Public Administration, Indianapolis, Indiana, April 1986), 1.

22. Richard Hofstadter, *The Age of Reform: From Bryan to F.D.R.* (New York: Vintage, 1955), 15–16. The link between the moralism of the Progressives and their Protestant backgrounds is especially well discussed in Robert M. Crunden, *Ministers of Reform: The Progressives' Achievement in American Civilization, 1889–1920* (New York: Basic Books, 1982).

23. Sudhir Kakir in particular underscores this point (Kakir, 61–63), as do other interpreters of Taylor's life; see also Brian R. Fry, "Frederick W. Taylor," in *Mastering Public Administration: From Max Weber to Dwight Waldo* (Chatham, N.J.: Chatham House, 1989), 47–72.

24. Three books that deal with these are as follow: Kenneth Fox, *Better City Government: Innovation in American Urban Politics, 1950–1937* (Philadelphia: Temple University Press, 1977); Martin Schiesel, *The Politics of Efficiency: Municipal Administration and Reform in America, 1880–1920* (Berkeley: University of California Press, 1977); and Jon C. Teaford, *The Unheralded Triumph: City Government in America, 1870–1900* (Baltimore: Johns Hopkins University Press, 1984).

25. For a lengthy discussion of this topic, see Hugh Aitken, *Taylorism at the Watertown Arsenal* (Cambridge: Harvard University Press, 1960).

26. For an extended discussion of Cooke's role in bringing Taylorism into public administration, read Hindy Lauer Schachter, *Frederick Taylor and the Public Administration Community: A Reevaluation* (Albany: State University of New York Press, 1989), chapter 6. Though Schachter emphasizes Cooke's position linking Taylorism to public administration, as opposed to the New York bureau's, her work nonetheless represents an important reinterpretation of Taylor and his influence on the field. For the post–World War II interpretation of Taylor that Schachter argues against, read Dwight Waldo, *The Administrative State* (New York: Ronald Press, 1948), chapter 3.

27. Jane S. Dahlberg, *The New York Bureau of Municipal Research: Pioneer in Government Administration* (New York: New York University Press, 1966), 11. Clearly, Dahlberg's study remains the most thorough study of the bureau and its role in the development of public administration.

28. Ibid., 201–21.

29. Ibid., 13.

30. Schachter, 93.

31. Frederick C. Mosher, *Democracy and the Public Service*, 2d ed. (New York: Oxford University Press, 1982), 73.

32. As cited in Dahlberg, 187.

33. Ibid., 85.

34. Herbert Emmerich, *Federal Organization and Administrative Management* (Tuscaloosa: University of Alabama Press, 1971), 40–41.

35. As cited in Dahlberg, 190.

36. Ibid., 117.

37. For a thoughtful study of the origins of the Maxwell School and its links with the New York bureau and the broader "efficiency movement," read Peter J. Johnson, *The Progressive Movement, Municipal Reform and the Founding of the Maxwell School* (Syracuse, N.Y.: Maxwell School Publication, 1974).

38. James A. Smith, *The Idea Brokers: Think Tanks and the Rise of the New Policy Elite* (New York: Free Press, 1991), 226.

39. Ibid.

40. Ibid. For another recent excellent study of the role of think tanks in American governance, see David M. Ricci, *The Transformation of American Politics: The New Washington and the Rise of Think Tanks* (New Haven: Yale University Press, 1993).

41. Smith, 226.

42. Judith A. Merkle, *Management and Ideology: The Legacy of the International Scientific Management Movement* (Berkeley: University of California Press, 1980), 100. Another recent contribution to the immense literature on Taylor and his

subsequent impact on society is Robert Kanigel, *The One Best Way: Frederick Winslow Taylor and the Enigma of Efficiency* (New York: Viking, 1997).

43. It may seem incongruous here that Taylor combined such a massive faith in empirical, scientific research with professed normative beliefs that, by application of his methods of scientific management, peace, progress, prosperity, and human advancement could be achieved. Yet, it should be recalled that modern science developed in the sixteenth and seventeenth centuries, mainly among Protestant dissenters, such as Issac Newton, Francis Bacon, Thomas Hollis, Joseph Priestly, and their like, who had no problems reconciling their deeply held Protestant religious faith with the scientific search for discovering God's universal laws. See Don K. Price, *America's Unwritten Constitution* (Baton Rouge: Louisiana State University Press, 1982), chapters 1 and 2.

7. Richard S. Childs: Minister for the Council-Manager Plan

1. As cited in Richard J. Stillman II, *The Rise of the City Manager: A Public Professional in Local Government* (Albuquerque: University of New Mexico Press, 1974), 16.

2. Richard S. Childs, *Civic Victories: The Story of an Unfinished Revolution* (New York: Harper and Brothers, 1952), xvi.

3. Richard S. Childs, "William Hamlin Childs, 1857–1927," unpublished essay, 1957, p. 4. Manuscript in possession of author.

4. Richard S. Childs, "A Manchester Boy in the 1880s," unpublished essay, 1973, p. 22. Manuscript in possession of author.

5. Childs, "William Hamlin Childs," 4.

6. Ibid., 6–9.

7. Richard S. Childs, interview by author, October 18, 1977, National Municipal League, New York.

8. "Unfinished Political Reforms, 1976," an unpublished manuscript by Childs, is one example of his untiring devotion to this topic, even at age 95. Manuscript in possession of author.

9. Lent D. Upson, *The Growth of a City Government* (Detroit: Detroit Bureau of Governmental Research, 1931), 12.

10. Leonard D. White, *The City Manager* (1927; reprint, New York: Greenwood Press, 1968), 9.

11. Lincoln Steffens, *The Shame of the Cities* (1909; reprint, New York: Hill and Wang, 1917), 24–25.

12. Bernard Hirschhorn, *The Reformer Richard Spencer Childs: His Life, 1882–1978* (Ph.D. diss., Columbia University, 1982), 23–24. To the end of his life, Childs remained remarkably true to these Progressive reform beliefs, as evidenced in his last written but unpublished work, "Unfinished Political Reforms, 1976."

13. Richard S. Childs, "Woodrow Wilson's Legacy," *National Municipal Review* 47 (January 1957): 14.

14. This incident is the only time where Childs speaks poorly of his father. Possibly this event so deeply affected Richard that, given the close father-son relationship, it also became a major source motivating son Richard both to

prove himself to his father and to *improve* on his idealized image of his father that he seemed to internalize as his own self-proclaimed public image.

15. Childs, *Civic Victories*, 22–23. This tale is recounted in several versions throughout Childs's writings, which underscores its special meaning to shaping the central purposes and "mission" for his life. In one version he actually conceals his "chagrin" at his father's recommendation that he vote a straight party ticket, suggesting deep shame he may have felt and hid from the man he so much admired. Ultimately, it was that day that son Richard determined he wanted to become a reformer.

16. Ibid.

17. Richard S. Childs, *Short Ballot Principles* (New York: Houghton Mifflin, 1911).

18. Several commentators on Childs's work have remarked about his high energy level coupled with his intense focus on reform, even his willingness to carry on anonymously much of the financial burdens for his reform crusade. For example, see A. W. Stewart, "Richard Childs Created the Council-Manager Plan," *American City and County* 99 (Sept. 1984): 62. As Stewart remarks: "If municipal government in America is honeycombed with honesty, a major factor is the adoption of the council-manager plan . . . [which is due to] the initiative and unrelenting vigor of a single individual—Richard Childs."

19. Childs, "Woodrow Wilson's Legacy," 15–16.

20. As cited in *The Origin of the City Manager Plan in Staunton, Virginia* (Staunton: City of Staunton, 1954), 11.

21. Ibid., 9.

22. Ibid.

23. Ibid., 12.

24. Ibid., 34.

25. Ibid., 12.

26. Ibid., 17.

27. For a discussion of the pre-Staunton origins of the manager plan, read Stillman, 5–27.

28. Richard S. Childs, "Letter," *World's Work* 60 (May 1, 1931): 3.

29. As cited in Don K. Price, "The Promotion of the City Manager Plan," *Public Opinion Quarterly* 5 (Winter 1941): 564.

30. Ibid.

31. John Porter East, *Council-Manager Government: The Political Thought of Its Founder, Richard S. Childs* (Chapel Hill: University of North Carolina Press, 1965), 7.

32. Stillman, 18–19.

33. W. F. Willoughby, *The Government of Modern States* (New York: Macmillan, 1919), 528–29.

34. National Municipal League, "The Model City Charter," 7th ed. (Denver: National Civic League, 1989). For an interesting discussion of the evolution of this charter since the first edition was adopted in 1899, read the introduction to the booklet, pages 11–22.

35. There has been massive literature over the years on the plan, much of it

supportive and written by leading academics. For a "dragnet review" of this writing, see Stillman, 148–61.

36. Frederick C. Mosher, *Democracy and the Public Service*, 2d ed. (New York: Oxford University Press, 1982), 142.

37. J. Paul Williams, *What Americans Believe and How They Worship*, rev. ed. (New York: Harper and Row, 1962), 216–17.

38. "Wieldy constituency" was actually the term Childs liked to use to emphasize the importance of a compact community for effective government. It was one of his three basic principles for promoting good government; the other two were visible elective offices and well-integrated governments; see chapters 5, 6, and 7 in his *Civic Victories*. His intense preoccupation with local government reform and the neglect of federal or national-level reform throughout his life only underscores Childs's adherence to the fundamentals of self-governing Congregationalism that were transformed into civic reformism. For Congregationalists, the local self-governing church was the basic foundation to the advancement of the "reformed faith."

8. Louis Brownlow: Apostle of Administrative Management

1. Fred I. Greenstein, *The Hidden-Hand Presidency: Eisenhower As Leader* (New York: Basic Books, 1982).

2. Louis Brownlow, *A Passion for Politics: The Autobiography of Louis Brownlow—The First Half* (Chicago: University of Chicago Press, 1955), 27.

3. Ibid.

4. Ibid., 90.

5. Ibid.

6. Ibid.

7. Ibid., 53.

8. Ibid., 19.

9. Ibid., 80.

10. Ibid., 95. Brownlow reports that the strictness of the Protestant prohibitions included not only the "normal sins" of liquor and prostitution but also cards, dancing, and even reading novels—the latter of which he was fond of doing. For a good sense of the heavily Protestant environment of small midwest towns of this era, see the novel by Helen Hooven Santmyer, . . . *And Ladies of the Club* (Columbus: Ohio State University Press, 1982).

11. Brownlow, 95.

12. Ibid., 96.

13. Ibid., 113.

14. Ibid.

15. Ibid., 121.

16. Ibid., 503.

17. Barry Karl, *Executive Reorganization and Reform in the New Deal* (Chicago: University of Chicago Press, 1963), 83.

18. Brownlow, 424. It should be added that in this period he married Elizabeth Virginia Sims, whom he met in Nashville through family friends. This re-

lationship rates only two brief citations of less than a half-page out of the six-hundred-page first volume of his autobiography. The couple remained childless.

19. Frederic Haskin, *The American Government* (New York: J. J. Little & Ives Co., 1911).

20. Brownlow, 583.

21. Ibid., 593.

22. Louis Brownlow, *A Passion for Anonymity: The Autobiography of Louis Brownlow—The Second Half* (Chicago: University of Chicago Press, 1958), 7. Of note, however, his facility with words or "as a note taker" set him apart as being far superior to the average public administrators of that era, most of whom tended to come from engineering backgrounds. As a result of his superb capacity as a wordsmith, Brownlow stood out as a leader in a field that was not noted for its language skills.

23. Karl, 103.

24. Brownlow, *Passion for Anonymity*, 102.

25. Ibid.

26. As cited in Richard J. Stillman II, *The Rise of the City Manager: A Public Professional in Local Government* (Albuquerque: University of New Mexico Press, 1974), 28.

27. The photo can be seen in Brownlow, *Passion for Anonymity*, 134–35.

28. For an excellent discussion of the development and roles of public official associations, read David S. Arnold and Jeremy F. Plant, *Public Official Associations and State and Local Government: A Bridge Across One Hundred Years* (Fairfax, Va.: George Mason University Press, 1994).

29. Brownlow, *Passion for Anonymity*, 23.

30. Ibid., 22.

31. Considerable disagreement exists in the literature regarding who invented the term "administrative management." Was it Brownlow or Charles Merriam? The two worked so closely together that it most likely emerged out of their lengthy, intense discussions and thus was a product of joint authorship. Although we can never be certain who actually invented the term, for Brownlow and many who worked on the committee, the term meant "overall management," especially "top management," which Brownlow had experienced and idealized in the council-manager plan and which was later embodied in the recommendations of the Brownlow report. For a discussion of this as well as the background of the report, see Herbert Emmerich, *Essays on Federal Reorganization* (Tuscaloosa: University of Alabama Press, 1950), especially pages 80–82.

32. As cited in Arnold and Plant, 75.

33. For an extensive background discussion of governmental reorganization, see Karl and Emmerich; also see Richard Polenberg, *Reorganizing Roosevelt's Government* (Cambridge: Harvard University Press, 1963).

34. Brownlow, *Passion for Anonymity*, 371.

35. Ibid., chapters 28 and 30; both provide excellent summaries of the report and Brownlow's involvement in its development.

36. For the summary of the committee report, read Frederick C. Mosher, ed., *Basic Documents of American Public Administration, 1776–1950* (New York: Hol-

mes & Meier, 1976), 110–38. Mosher offers an excellent introduction to the report, which also should be read in addition to the enabling legislation that put the report into practice. The story of the report's piecemeal implementation is long and complex and is especially well told in Polenberg.

37. For an overview of the opposition to Brownlow, see Karl and Polenberg.

38. James W. Fesler, "The Brownlow Committee Fifty Years Later," in Frederick C. Mosher, ed., *The President Needs Help* (Lanham, Md.: University Press of America, 1988), 18. Better than most retrospectives, the essays in this book reflect the profound importance of the Brownlow Committee's recommendation on the American presidency by those who witnessed the transformation firsthand throughout their lifetimes.

39. Mosher, ed., *Basic Documents*, 138.

40. President's Committee on Administrative Management, *Report of the Committee* (Washington, D.C.: U.S. Government Printing Office, 1937), chap. 6.

41. See Arthur M. Schlesinger, Jr., *The Imperial Presidency* (Boston: Houghton Mifflin, 1973).

42. Jonathan Edwards, "Thoughts on the Revival in New England," 1740; for more on Edwards, see S. E. Dwight, ed., *The Works of Jonathan Edwards* (Carlisle, Penn.: Banner of Truth Trust, 1974) and Perry Miller, *Jonathan Edwards* (New York: Sloane, 1949).

9. Conclusion: American State Creation as Moral Transformation

1. Herman Finer, "The Hoover Commission Reports," *Political Science Quarterly* 64 (September 1949): 412.

2. Clinton Rossiter, *The American Presidency*, rev. ed. (New York: Harcourt, Brace and World, 1960), 130.

3. Richard Hofstadter, *The Age of Reform: From Bryan to F.D.R.* (New York: Vintage Books, 1955), 233–34.

4. Alexis de Tocqueville, *Democracy in America* (New York: Vintage Books, 1954), 1: 314.

5. As quoted in Max Berger, *The British Traveller in America, 1836–1860* (New York: Columbia University Press, 1943), 133–34.

6. Robert Baird, *Religion in America* (New York: Harper and Brothers, 1844), 188.

7. Philip Schaff, *America: A Sketch of the Political, Social and Religious Character of the United States of North America* (New York: Scribner, 1855), 72.

8. André Siegfried, *America Comes of Age* (New York: Harcourt, Brace and World, 1927), 33.

9. H. K. Carroll, *The Religious Forces in the United States* (New York: Christian Literature Co., 1893), 35.

10. G. K. Chesterton, *What I Saw in America* (New York: Dodd, Mead, 1923), 11–12.

11. *New York Times*, January 12, 1975, 1.

12. See Richard Hofstadter, *The Progressive Historians* (New York: Alfred A. Knopf, 1968), especially chapters 4 and 6.

13. Robert P. Swierenga, "Ethnoreligious Political Behavior in the Mid-Nineteenth Century: Voting, Values, Cultures," in *Religion and American Politics: From the Colonial Period to the 1980s,* ed. Mark A. Noll (New York: Oxford University Press, 1990), 146.

14. Richard J. Jensen, *The Winning of the Midwest: Social and Political Conflict, 1888–1896* (Chicago: University of Chicago Press, 1971), 62.

15. Paul Kleppner, *The Cross of Culture: A Social Analysis of Midwestern Politics, 1850–1900* (New York: Free Press, 1970), 37.

16. Samuel P. Huntington, *American Politics: The Promise of Disharmony* (Cambridge: Harvard University Press, 1981), 15.

17. Max Weber, "The Protestant Sects and the Spirit of Capitalism," in *From Max Weber: Essays in Sociology,* ed. H. H. Gerth and C. Wright Mills (New York: Oxford University Press, 1946), 302–22; R. H. Tawney, *Religion and the Rise of Capitalism* (New York: Harcourt, Brace and World, 1926); and for an extensive overview of the current debate regarding Weber's thesis, see: Hartmut Lehmann and Guenther Roth, eds., *Weber's Protestant Ethic: Origins, Evidence, Contexts* (Cambridge: Cambridge University Press, 1987).

18. Michael Walzer, *The Revolution of the Saints* (Cambridge: Harvard University Press, 1965), 1.

19. H. Richard Niebuhr, "The Protestant Movement and Democracy in the United States," in *The Shaping of American Religion,* ed. James Ward Smith and A. Leland Jamison (Princeton: Princeton University Press, 1961), 24.

20. Charles Goodsell, *The Case for Bureaucracy* (Chatham, N.J.: Chatham House, 1983), 2.

21. For an extensive discussion of the "myths" about American bureaucracy, however, see Richard J. Stillman II, *The American Bureaucracy,* 2d ed. (Chicago: Nelson-Hall, 1996), chap. 1.

22. Woodrow Wilson, "The Study of Administration," *Political Science Quarterly* 2 (June 1887): 197.

23. Dwight Waldo, *The Enterprise of Public Administration* (Navato, Calif.: Chandler and Sharp, 1980), 189.

24. If Americans are continually confused by the meaning of "state" as well as its place in their constitutional order, they might note that the French only refer to "Estat" in capital letters.

25. Wallace Sayre, "Bureaucracies: Some Contrasts in Systems," *Indian Journal of Public Administration* 10 (1964): 228.

26. Wilson, 197–222.

27. Francis Fukuyama, "The End of History," *National Interest* 2 (Summer 1989): 3–18; and Samuel P. Huntington, "The Clash of Civilizations," *Foreign Affairs* 72 (Summer 1993): 22–49.

28. Richard Rosecrance, "The Virtual State," *Foreign Affairs* 75 (July/August 1996): 45–61. For an interesting study of where the idea of "American exceptionalism" is today, especially in the global context, read Seymour Martin Lipset, *American Exceptionalism: A Double-Edged Sword* (New York: Norton, 1995).

29. For speculations about the impacts of globalization on the administrative state, read Andrés Pérez Baltodano, "The Study of Public Administration

in Times of Global Interpenetration: A Historical Rationale for a Theoretical Model," *Journal of Public Administration Research and Theory* 4 (1997): 615–36.

30. For two recent books underscoring the profound importance of reformism on American government as a whole, refer to Paul C. Light, *The Tides of Reform: Making Government Work, 1945–1995* (New Haven: Yale University Press, 1997) and G. Calvin Mackenzie, *The Irony of Reform: The Roots of American Political Disenchantment* (Boulder: Westview Press, 1996).

Bibliographic Essay

ONE OF THE MOST STRIKING DEVELOPMENTS in the social sciences during the last two decades has been the influence of so-called return-to-state literature, or the frank recognition that state institutions matter in the governing processes. Perhaps these institutions are the only factors that matter and even hold the keys to unlocking our understanding of critical issues concerning modern governance. These scholars argue that at least by including "state" in our analysis, we can arrive at far more realistic and balanced perspectives on contemporary politics and government. Yet, ironically, while the institutionalists emphasize—or rather reemphasize—the role of "state" in governing society, they almost entirely stress sociopolitical, military, and economic factors as the chief causal variables for the state's origins and growth while they neglect broader cultural, moral, and religious values. Scanning the indexes of important recent additions to the American state literature, one fails to see any mention of morals or religion. See, for example, Stephen Skowronek, *Building a New American State: The Expansion of National Administrative Capacities, 1877–1920* (Cambridge: Cambridge University Press, 1982); Richard Franklin Bensel, *Yankee Leviathan: The Origins of Central State Authority, 1859–1877* (Cambridge: Cambridge University Press, 1990); Bartholomew Sparrow, *From the Outside In: World War II and the American State* (Princeton: Princeton University Press, 1996); and G. John Ikenberry, *Reasons of State: Oil Politics and the Capacities of American Government* (Ithaca: Cornell University Press, 1988). Religious and moral factors are missing as well in contemporary collections of state theorists; see, for example, James A. Caporaso, ed., *The Elusive State: International and Comparative Perspectives* (Newbury Park, Calif.: Sage, 1989) or Edward S. Greenberg and Thomas F. Mayer, eds., *Changes in the State: Causes and Consequences* (Newbury Park, Calif.: Sage, 1990).

Remarkably, even in recent significant historical studies of public administration the religious and moral factors are neglected entirely, such as John A. Rohr, *To Run a Constitution: The Legitimacy of the Administrative*

State (Lawrence: University Press of Kansas, 1986); James A. Stever, *The End of Public Administration: Problems of the Profession in the Post-Progressive Era* (Dobbs Ferry, N.Y.: Transnational Publishers, 1988); Patricia Wallace Ingraham, *The Foundation of Merit: Public Service in American Democracy* (Baltimore: Johns Hopkins University Press, 1995); and Michael W. Spicer, *The Founders, the Constitution and Public Administration* (Washington, D.C.: Georgetown University Press, 1995). Also, new texts on growth and change in bureaucracy omit mention of these influences entirely and solely stress sociopolitical and economic factors, as in James Q. Wilson, *Bureaucracy: What Government Agencies Do and Why They Do It* (New York: Free Press, 1989) or B. Dan Wood and Richard W. Waterman, *Bureaucratic Dynamics: The Role of Bureaucracy in a Democracy* (Boulder: Westview Press, 1994).

By contrast, the significance of religion, particularly Protestantism, in the rise of modern capitalism is well documented in R. H. Tawney, *Religion and the Rise of Capitalism* (New York: Harcourt, Brace and Co., 1926) and in Max Weber, *The Protestant Ethic and the Spirit of Capitalism*, translated by Talcott Parsons (1904 [in German]; reprint, New York: Scribners, 1930). The Weberian thesis certainly has been subjected to intensive scholarly debate as reflected in Hartmut Lehmann and Guenther Roth, eds., *Weber's Protestant Ethic: Origins, Evidence, Contexts* (Cambridge: Cambridge University Press, 1987), yet religion, especially Protestantism, still remains, on balance, a decisive factor in explaining the sources of modern capitalism.

A few classics in public administration mention, at least briefly, the importance of Protestant values for the development of the field. See, for example, Dwight Waldo, *The Administrative State: A Study of the Political Theory of American Public Administration* (New York: Ronald Press Co., 1948), 17; Frederick C. Mosher, *Democracy and the Public Service* (New York: Oxford University Press, 1968), 68; and Don K. Price, *America's Unwritten Constitution: Science, Religion and Political Responsibility* (Baton Rouge: Louisiana State University Press, 1983). Also, some works in the social sciences that focus on American exceptionalism underscore the importance of the religious factors in shaping America: Samuel P. Huntington, *American Politics: The Promise of Disharmony* (Cambridge: Harvard University Press, 1981); Seymour Martin Lipset, *The First New Nation: The United States in Historical and Comparative Perspective*, rev. ed. (New York: W. W. Norton, 1979); and Richard Hofstadter, *The American Political Tradition and the Men Who Made It* (New

York: Alfred A. Knopf, 1948) or his *The Age of Reform: From Bryan to F.D.R.* (New York: Vintage, 1955).

To be sure, books written about life in the nineteenth century point out the critical role of the church in small towns; see, for example, the popular novel by Helen Hooven Santmyer, . . . *And the Ladies of the Club* (New York: Berkley Books, 1984); popular "how-to" books of that era, such as Freeman Hunt, *Worth and Wealth: Maxims for Men of Business* (New York: Stringer and Townsend, 1856); travelogues of the period, such as Philip Schaff, *America: A Sketch of the Political, Social and Religious Character of the United States of North America* (New York: C. Scribner, 1855); or historical and political studies such as James Bryce, *The American Commonwealth*, 2 vols. (London: Macmillan, 1891). Until recently, for analyses of the nineteenth century, however, primarily theologians stressed religious factors in shaping the context of American civilization.

Contemporary American historians during the last decade or so have done the most to revive the "religious factor" as central to the explanation of events and life during the nineteenth century. See William G. McLoughlin, *Revivals, Awakenings and Reform: An Essay on Religion and Social Change in America* (Chicago: University of Chicago Press, 1978); Robert M. Crunden, *Ministers of Reform: The Progressives' Achievement in American Civilization, 1889–1920* (New York: Basic Books, 1982); Henry F. May, *The Divided Heart: Essays on Protestantism and the Enlightenment in America* (New York: Oxford, 1991); Jon Butler, *Awash in a Sea of Faith: Christianizing the American People* (Cambridge: Harvard University Press, 1990); and Robert H. Abzug, *Cosmos Crumbling: American Reform and the Religious Imagination* (New York: Oxford, 1994). For a useful general collection of essays by modern historians pertaining to this topic, read Mark A. Noll, ed., *Religion and American Politics: From the Colonial Period to the 1980s* (New York: Oxford, 1990).

As the central thesis of this book underscores, the best methodology for tracing the influence of religion on the development of America's administrative state can be understood by looking, in some detail, at the lives of key state creators. As the endnotes indicate, this book draws from several sources in linking the creators' personal religious values with the specific administrative reforms they prescribed. First and foremost were the primary sources of original letters, speeches, and personal writings. Fortunately, all of these individuals were prolific writers, and collections of their works are not only plentiful but also reveal much about their moral attitudes. See, for example, the three volumes titled *Orations and Addresses of George William Curtis,* edited by Charles Elliot Norton (New York: Harper and Brothers, 1894) or Peter S. Michie, *The Life and Letters of Emory Upton* (New York: D. Appleton and Co., 1885). Several were not shy in writing extensively about themselves, and their contributions can be seen in autobiographies; see, for example, Louis Brownlow's excellent two-volume autobiography, *A Passion for Politics* (Chicago: University of Chicago Press, 1955) and *A Passion for Anonymity* (Chicago: University of Chicago Press, 1958) and Jane Addams, *Twenty Years at Hull-House* (New York: Macmillan, 1910) and her sequel, *The Second Twenty Years at Hull-House* (New York: Macmillan, 1930). Sometimes the autobiography is disguised as a reform polemic but nonetheless is quite revealing, as in the case of Richard S. Childs, *Civic Victories: The Story of an Unfinished Revolution* (New York: Harper and Brothers, 1952).

Second, official and semi-official documents were vital to demonstrating how the values of these administrative reformers came to reflect government policy. Connecting personal beliefs with their translation into public action can be discovered by carefully reading such seminal administrative state founding documents as the Civil Service Act (Pendleton Act of 1883), the Act to Regulate Commerce (1887), the Act Creating the General Staff (1903), the Report of (Taft) Commission on Economy and Efficiency (1912), the Model City Charter of the National Municipal League (1916), the Budget and Accounting Act (1921), and the Report of the President's Committee on Administrative Management (the Brownlow Committee, 1937). Many are found in Frederick C. Mosher, *Basic Documents of American Public Administration, 1776–1950* (New York: Holmes and Meier, 1976). Some of these studies can be highly technical, but they are nonetheless significant for uncovering the assumptions and ideas of their authors; see, for example, Charles Francis Adams, Jr., *Railroads: Their Origins and Problems* (New York: G. P. Putnam's Sons, 1878) or Emory Upton, *Military Policy of the United States* (Washington, D.C.: War Department, 1912). Frequently, "disciples" wrote important studies supported by their mentors; see Dorman Eaton, *Report Concerning the Civil Service in Great Britain* (New York: Harper and Brothers, 1880) (see especially its introduction by George William Curtis). Frederick Taylor's books were certainly *not* official government documents, but to many of his ardent followers they were the gospels of scientific management. See *The Principles of*

Scientific Management (1911; reprint, New York: Harper and Brothers, 1947) and *Shop Management* (1903; reprint, New York: Harper and Brothers, 1947).

Third, secondary sources offer several impressive contributions but need to be read selectively. For example, some authors were probably too close to the various individuals to provide balanced accounts of their ideas; see, for example, Frank S. Copley, *Frederick W. Taylor: Father of Scientific Management*, 2 vols. (New York: Harper and Brothers, 1923), which is thorough yet was the authorized biography by Taylor's widow. Those scholars who were more distant and critical of their subject provided more useful interpretations; in the case of Taylor, see, for example, Daniel Nelson, *Frederick W. Taylor and the Rise of Scientific Management* (Madison: University of Wisconsin Press, 1980); Judith A. Merkle, *Management and Ideology: The Legacy of the International Scientific Management Movement* (Berkeley: University of California Press, 1980), and Hindy Lauer Schachter, *Frederick Taylor and the Public Administration Community* (Albany: SUNY Press, 1989). Some of these secondary sources do not have any founder's name in their title but are highly important for piecing together a particular individual's impact on the institutional development of the American administrative state. See especially Jane S. Dahlberg, *The New York Bureau of Municipal Research: Pioneer in Government Administration* (New York: New York University Press, 1966); Barry S. Karl, *Executive Reorganization and Reform in the New Deal* (Chicago: University of Chicago Press, 1963); and Thomas K. McCraw, *Prophets of Regulation* (Cambridge: Harvard University Press, 1984).

Fourth, in tracing the general impact of individual values on institutional development in the United States, I relied on books that discussed general aspects of American administrative history, such as Paul P. Van Riper, *History of the United States Civil Service* (Evanston, Ill.: Row, Peterson and Co., 1958); Alfred D. Chandler, Jr., *The Visible Hand: The Managerial Revolution in American Business* (Cambridge: Harvard University Press, 1977); and Russell F. Weigley, *Towards an American Army: Military Thought from Washington to Marshall* (New York: Columbia University Press, 1962). Numerous interpretative scholarly essays were also immensely helpful, such as Lionel V. Murphy, "The First Federal Civil Service Commission: 1871–75," *Public Personnel Review* 3 (July 1942). In most cases, however, these scholarly treatments missed the explicit connection between religious ideas and institutional creation.

Institutional formation was frequently viewed independently of the Protestantism so influential in shaping the lives of the various state creators.

Finally, I was influenced by recent scholarship from various fields that stress how much morality shapes the conduct of daily affairs; see, for example, Amitai Etzioni, *The Moral Dimension: Towards a New Economics* (New York: Free Press, 1988); John W. Gardner, *On Leadership* (New York: Free Press, 1990); and Philip Selznick, *The Moral Commonwealth: Social Theory and the Promise of Community* (Berkeley: University of California Press, 1992). Recent books in political science also underscore reformism as critical to the operations of modern American government (though miss the connection with its religious roots), particularly Paul C. Light, *The Tides of Reform: Making Government Work, 1945–1995* (New Haven: Yale University Press, 1997) and G. Calvin Mackenzie, *The Irony of Reform: The Roots of American Political Disenchantment* (Boulder: Westview Press, 1996). Certainly throughout his scholarly career, Dwight Waldo, much like Max Weber, stressed the "value problem" as centrally important for the study of our field. See Dwight Waldo, *The Study of Public Administration* (New York: Random House, 1955), especially chapter 6. It must be added, however, as I mentioned at the beginning in the preface, that it was my own interest in answering the nagging question, what were the sources for "chinking-in" the American administrative state at the dawn of the twentieth century, that led to my efforts to find a reasonable explanation. Economics, politics, and warfare ultimately seemed less convincing explanatory causations than religion, morality, and broader cultural factors, as this book attempts to argue. In the end, though, it must be left up to the reader to conclude whether I made a convincing case.

Index

About the Author

RICHARD J. STILLMAN II IS A PROFESSOR OF PUBLIC ADMINISTRATION in the Graduate School of Public Affairs, University of Colorado at Denver. He has taught on the faculties of George Mason University and California State University-Bakersfield and is the author or editor of several books: *The Integration of the Negro in the U.S. Armed Forces, The Rise of the City Manager, A Search for Public Administration* (with Brack Brown), *Professions in Government* (with Frederick C. Mosher), *Results-Oriented Budgeting, The American Bureaucracy, The American Constitution and the Administrative State, The Effective Local Government Manager* (with Wayne Anderson and Chester Newland), *Preface to Public Administration*, and *Basic Documents of American Public Administration Since 1950*. His textbook, *Public Administration: Concepts and Cases*, 6th edition, is used at more than three hundred universities and colleges. Stillman has served on the editorial boards of the *American Review of Public Administration, Administrative Theory and Praxis*, and *Public Administration Review*. His article "The City Managers: Professional Helping Hand or Political Hired Hand?" was selected as a *PAR* Classic Article, and he has been awarded the John W. Dobenmeier as well as the William E. and Frederick C. Mosher prize for his scholarship in the field. He was graduated from Harvard University (with honors) and received his master's degree and doctorate in public administration from the Maxwell School, Syracuse University. He has been a NASA university fellow; public administration fellow; research fellow at the Institute of Governmental Studies, University of California, Berkeley; and the Robinson Fellow at George Mason University. In 1991 he was the visiting professor of public administration at Leiden University (Netherlands) and in 1993 was the John Marshall Professor at Budapest University of Economic Sciences (Hungary). He has lectured at Erasmus University (Netherlands), Germany's Postgraduate School of Administrative Sciences (Speyer, Germany), the National School of Public Administration (Beijing, The People's Republic of China), and CIDE (Mexico City). His books have been translated into Chinese, Korean, and Hungarian.